Thanks for being such great friends.

Basat

Execution
of the Penalty

Execution of the Penalty

A Letter to James Dean

Brent C. Flynn & Linda D. Flynn

PUBLISHER
BLADE MANAGEMENT, LLC

Web site: http://www.classicbookpublishers.com

Cover Designs by Linda D. Flynn

Library of Congress Cataloging-in-Publication Data

      Execution of the Penalty: A Letter to James Dean / by Brent C. Flynn
    and Linda D. Flynn. -- 1st ed.
          p. cm.
    Includes bibliographical references and index.
    LCCN 2009900819
    ISBN 978-0-615-27443-0 (pbk.)
      1. Mormon Church—History—19th century.
      2. Church of Jesus Christ of Latter-day Saints—Doctrines.
      3. Book of Mormon—Evidences, authority, etc.
      4. Book of Mormon—Criticism, interpretations, etc. I Title.

BX8678.B43A3 2005
289.3'3—dc21

To our children Julie, Jason, Jessica and James Dean

and all who are caught in the middle.

CONTENTS

*How can you answer a man who tells you
that he would rather obey God than men,
and who is therefore sure to deserve heaven
in cutting your throat?*

Voltaire
(1694-1778)

Prologue

A nurse caught up to us in the hallway. Linda and I turned to her as she announced, "Oh and we think your son is also deaf." I looked at her calmly and replied, "Is there anything else?"

As a young couple, Linda and I faced a large unknown. Our eldest son, Jason, was born with too many red blood cells. At four days old, his body struggled to eliminate them. The result produced jaundice, a yellowing of the skin. We immediately took him back to the hospital where he lay in observation just long enough to experience significant brain damage. After the doctors decided they could not handle the worsening symptoms, they placed him on a life-flight helicopter, and flew him 50 miles north to the neonatal regional hospital in Omaha, Nebraska. There he received a blood transfusion and his life threatening symptoms abated.

Less than one week after his birth, we sat pensively waiting in a room beyond the entrance of the neonatal center. Jason lay in a plastic box on the other side of the door. A doctor arranged this meeting to inform us Jason indeed suffered brain damage. Various tests revealed tiny scars throughout his brain. His prognosis appeared dismal. The doctor told us he would be severely mentally retarded, have cerebral palsy, and suffer from epilepsy (seizure disorder). In addition, Jason would not be able to recognize a ball, and if by chance he did, physically he would not be able to respond to it.

His tiny brain bounced in and out of seizures even as the

doctor spoke. He then gave us some good news. We would be allowed to take our baby home in just a few days.

We left the doctor's office in a state of confusion. We tried to take this news as though we knew what to do with it. We told ourselves that we would do our best with whatever the future held for us. We could only absorb a limited amount of this traumatic information. Some innate protective mechanism quickly arose in our brains shielding us from the full impact of this devastating news. However, simple processes like breathing became painful. Jason's early struggles represented the first great shock of our lives. The experience left us dumbfounded and heartbroken. Our worst nightmare had come true.

On the night we took him home the temperature dipped well below zero. We bundled his tiny body in layers of blue blankets. The nurse stopped us as the automatic glass doors slid open; a bitter gust portended the message rehearsed upon her lips. She informed us that in addition to the brain damage, Jason was profoundly deaf. Without expression, we paused just long enough to ask what else we might need to know about our bundle of joy. The nurse said nothing more, but gave us a concerned look, before she turned away.

Raising Jason forever changed our perspectives and altered the course of our lives. Not knowing how he would develop presented a fear we had to endure, yet eventually accepted.

That being said, this book is about the "second" time in our lives when we were dumbfounded with shocking news that would forever alter our lives. It is about an event not unlike that which we faced with the birth of Jason. It became a challenge of facing hard facts; soul searching, accepting another reality and learning to live in a world we did not know existed.

Who claims moral authority over your life? Who holds the rights to the legacy you wish to leave behind? For the first forty-seven years of my life I believed such authority rested in the hands of my beloved prophet. I was born and raised in a devout Mormon family. I followed all the rules, laws and ordinances required to enter heaven. I recited the sacred temple covenants so that I would be permitted to pass by the angels, on my way toward Godhood. I diligently instructed my children to follow God's true prophet. I felt blessed to be born into "the one and only true church on the face of the earth."

Within the pages of this book I will share with you the seemingly benign discovery that caused my initial doubt. I will also share the personal angst I felt as my religious heroes began to fall. As the true history of my heroes became known unto me, the current authoritative claims by my living prophet began to ring hollow.

This realization set me on a path of discovery requiring a deep-seated struggle to reestablish my identity outside of Mormonism. Unfortunately, a cacophony of cultic-inspired events swirled around my family even as we awakened to a new reality.

Our epiphany, along with the stance we took, set off a chain reaction of dramatic events affecting our lives and the lives of our extended family. My wife Linda and I will also share our previously held worldview, and the profound way it changed when we chose to leave Mormonism.

In the first three chapters I briefly recount the historical elements, which led my ancestors in and out of the religions of their day, and their consequences. Chapters 4 through 12 contain our personal family history dealing with the religion we inherited. Chapter 13 sums up the affects of my ancestors' journeys upon us. Chapter 14 is written to my youngest son, James Dean. Chapter 15 is an entirely separate account, written by Linda, covering her perspective of our second life challenge.

CHAPTER 1

For God, Queen and Country

A baby is born a baby, not a religion.

John grit his teeth and charged down the hill. He fired his musket and kept his bayonet aimed directly ahead. A moment later his leg exploded and he crumpled to the ground in a cloud of gun smoke.

The flick of another man's finger rippled the pond of John's young life. The flick came from a Russian peasant armed with a flintlock musket of the Napoleonic period. Tsar Nicholas I conscripted this peasant-turned-soldier to defend the honor and authority of the Russian Greek Orthodox Church. John fell on a cold spot of grass on a northern peninsula in the Black Sea, a peninsula called "Crimea."

Trouble brewed on a wind-swept patch of land east of the Russian port city of Sevastopol, also known as "The Inkerman." On this Sunday, The Inkerman awoke to a dense morning fog clinging to the bluffs, ravines and gullies. Grassy shawls with muddy undertow peaked through the fog, revealing slumbering soldiers already in battle with the cold. The piercing echo of frenzied church bells snapped the soldiers to life. The church bells of Sevastopol broke into full bloom as a new day dawned. They rang to encourage Russian solidarity rather than to call the faithful to worship.

Forty-two thousand Russian troops, with 134 cannons, amassed between Sevastopol and The Inkerman. The sound of men screaming and bayonets clashing grew louder from all sides through the dense fog. The deadly Russian advance had begun in earnest. Scattered across the clouded bluffs and hidden in the ravines of The Inkerman were eight thousand five hundred British troops with 38 cannons, and 7,500 French troops with 18 cannons. Sullen faces anxiously awaited the order to charge.

John Flynn enlisted as a foot soldier at age 20 with the 49th regiment in the British Army. He served at the pleasure of Queen Victoria. That same year, 1845, Ireland suffered a disastrous famine resulting from the failure of the potato crop. A large number of his countrymen fled the famine and immigrated to America. Another large portion died of starvation. John escaped poverty just as his father had before by enlisting in the Army.

John entered the world joining an austere household in the county of Tipperary, Ireland in February 1825. With no formal education, he painted houses before enlisting. His 5' 9" frame grew sleek, accented by his fair hair, complexion and steel grey eyes. The Roman Catholic Parish of Cahir baptized him shortly after birth, then registered him with the Diocese of Lismore. The die of his life was cast before he spoke his first word. Nine years after enlisting, John Flynn, now a Corporal, stood in line with musket in hand, overlooking the fog on the bluffs of the Crimea. The distant roar of the Black Sea surf lessened as men took to boots and columned in a prelude to battle. Indeed, John stood a long, long way from his impoverished, yet bucolic upbringing in Tipperary.

A flurry of diplomatic activity filled with bellicose rhetoric failed to resolve which Catholic Church would control Christians living on the Crimean peninsula. Tsar Nicholas I believed the Russian Greek Orthodox Church deserved such privilege while the French and British knew unequivocally that only governance by the Church of England, with its uncomfortable alliance with the Holy Roman Catholic Church, merited God's acceptance.

Corporal Flynn stood blinded by the morning fog, and what lay before him. Ultimate church authority disappeared with the stars at dawn on that Sunday morning. Yet, John clearly knew if his side did not prevail, he would be killed. He fought just two months prior in the battle of Alma, which recorded 2,002 British casualties. Fifteen of his close friends in the 49th Regiment died in the battle.

John made ready for the charge dressed in knee-high boots, dark pants and his smart bright red and white jacket with long sleeves and tail. He proudly wore a tall black hat topped off by a round tuft of white feathers. The bright gold corporal emblem across the front of his hat advertised his rank. With sword at his side, he raised his musket with attached bayonet into firing position. He stood shoulder to shoulder with the rest of his regiment and the bulk of the British armies on a location they called "Home Ridge."

The Russian infantry assiduously advanced through the drifting fog in dense columns. They met small pickets of British soldiers hidden in the ravines around the base of Home Ridge. These valiant skirmishes quickly folded under the overwhelming mass of the approaching Russian army. But what the British lacked in number, they made up for in strategic location and arms.

The British minié-rifled muskets gave quicker, longer ranged, and more accurate fire than the Russian flintlock muskets. The cap firing mechanism also proved infinitely more reliable in wet conditions. In addition, the bottleneck formation of the terrain prevented the Russians from making their final approach toward Home Ridge on a broad front.

The first Russian column to attack emerged from the constricted ground and advanced to the left. John and his 49th Regiment fired a volley into the column and charged with bayonets. They drove the Russians down the slope and across the valley. Other British regiments joined the fray, attacking the column directly at the bottleneck. John, along with other members of the 49th, flanked the column from the left side. A pitched hand-to-hand bayonet battle ensued. The ebb and flow of the bloody conflict pitted will-verses-strength as the ear-shattering clash of steel played against the cries of men facing death.

Both sides relied upon the hand of God to win the day. But it was not the hand of God, rather the finger of the peasant-turned-Russian conscript, who squeezed the trigger rippling the pond of young John Flynn's life forever. With the flick of his finger a baby-stamped "Greek Orthodox" launched a whistling ball from his musket that found its mark on the inside of a baby-stamped "Holy Roman's" right thigh. When the smoke cleared and the fog lifted over The Battle of The Inkerman, the British lost 2,357 men; the French reported 929 casualties, and the Russians suffered a staggering loss of 12,000. John lay wounded on the field of battle with blood pulsating from his right leg. The Crimean War would eke out another few years of its dismal existence, but for John Flynn, one of the countless wounded that day, his "Charge of the Light Brigade" ended.

History paints the Charge of the Light Brigade in the glow of heroic terms. Its hapless cavalry charge, led by Lord Cardigan during yet another battle in the Crimean, ended in disaster. The grim reality of this war simply pits two equally certain beliefs in God against one another. Time, ignorance and certainty mix to repeat the process. John Flynn entered a boiling pot of violence where the true root of humanity is revealed in the age-old animalistic maxim: it is better to eat than be eaten. Such prosaic brutality lay thinly veiled behind the mask of religion and is vehemently justified in the name of God, Queen and Country.

Florence Nightingale arrived in Scutari with 38 nurses.1 Scutari laid on the outskirts of Istanbul. This small port managed the brisk business of receiving the dying and wounded from the nightmare journey aboard overcrowded transport ships crossing the Black Sea. The dry brown streets lay in sharp contrast to the stark white walls surrounding the barracks-turned army hospital of Scutari. Nightingale arrived just in time to provide comfort to the suffering soldiers wounded on the fields of The Inkerman. Perhaps the greatest miracle of John's life was that he survived the filthy conditions presented by this gruesome makeshift hospital.

It is a travesty of justice to allow the sterility of thought to pass over the human suffering at Scutari. Ten times more soldiers died from typhus, typhoid, cholera and dysentery than from battle wounds. Conditions in the barracks-turned-hospital grew so unsanitary for the patients that a British General visiting the hospital wrote: "they might as well be killed there (referring to the battlefield) as die of cholera here."

A stagnant sewer system, poor ventilation, overcrowding, lack of medicine and rotting food greeted the wounded of the Crimean. The barracks bore only a few small windows. Even in the daytime, the surgeons had to work by candlelight. Such conditions gave birth to Nightingale's nickname "the Lady with the Lamp."

Wards and hallways became awash with the sound of impending death. Patients covered the floors, sometimes on layers of straw, with their agonies made worse by rat infestations. Men often lay side by side with the dead. The stench of decomposing bodies permeated the air. Germs were not understood and modern antibiotics had yet to be discovered.[2] The indelible mark of war and its aftermath would follow John to the grave.

After two agonizing months at Scutari, John left, crippled for life. The army labeled him an "invalid," and then shipped him back to England to make the most of the rest of his life. He survived the battlefield, his time at Scutari, and now lay in an English hospital for weeks as clots of blood formed in and around the sizable wound. His doctors reported his leg to be in a "varicose state of the varix" with "scars from boils on the hip." There he pondered the merits of God, Queen and Country.

Long hours in a hospital bed turned into months. He wondered why England dragged him into a war on the Crimea. He realized he fought in nothing less than a "Christian Crusade," only instead of fighting the usual suspects, Muslims, heretics and witches; he actually fought against other Christians. It seemed to him that Christians were not above killing one another where national pride and land grabs were at stake. John surrendered a leg and endured a world of hurt to learn this lesson.

Did it really matter which branch of the Catholic Church, Greek or Roman, ruled over the Christians on the Crimean peninsula? Would he have fought just as valiantly had he been stamped at birth with the baptism of the Greek Orthodox Church? John languished for another 3 years under the confines of army dictates. Yet during those years of ineffectual army duty a beautiful ray of hope illuminated his life. She appeared from around the curtain separating John's bed from injured comrades. Her slender figure supported a narrow face with a broad smile and high cheekbones Hair pins held back most of her long flowing black hair with a few fallen lockets dangling freely in front of her ears. Her name was Catherine Foley and she too had been wounded. Her darkened eyes eloquently expressed the emotional pain of the loss of her young husband to the same war. Catherine's delicate hands help mend John's persistent wounds while at the same time mending the hole left in her heart. Their relationship grew despite a growing storm determined to divide them.

Catherine bore the stamp of a Quaker. She grew under the watchful eyes of her conservative Quaker parents. They longed for an egalitarian society under Christ. Catherine longed for love. John and Catherine quietly married and the consequences immediately thundered down upon them.

Religions "execute a penalty" toward members who break their rules, or choose to leave the fold. Catherine's Christ-loving Quaker community quickly condemned her to hell for having married outside their faith. A letter, of the time, spelled out Quaker judgment toward Catherine:

*"UNTO YOU WHO ONCE KNEW THE TRUTH, BUT BEING
TURNED FROM IT INTO THE UNCLEAN WORLD, IT IS NOW
YOUR CONDEMNATION;*

*Did you once know the truth, and are you now like the dog
turned to the vomit, and the sow that was washed, to the
wallowing in the mire.*

*Oh! How doth my soul mourn and lament for you in secret, at
the consideration of your state... as you yielded obedience to that
which manifested evil and gone back again into Egypt's
darkness, amongst the flesh-pots, which causeth you to have an
ill savor?*

*Oh foolish and unwise people, forever will be your
condemnation, that you will become two-fold more the Children
of hell, than you were before.*

*Oh! Your state is sad, and your condition lamentable, who
turned from the light, into darkness, to be tempted and led away
of the devil. Your state is miserable!*

*Oh! Because of you, offences come, it were better that a mill-
stone were hanged about their necks, and they cast into the depth
of the sea, for God will not be mocked...*

*Oh! Let none hearken to that, for that is the seed of the evil
one, the devil... In which day the wolf is seeking to worry you,
and the ravenous beasts to make a prey of you; Praise and
magnify the God of your salvation, by walking in obedience to
what he requires of you."*

In tender love,

John Banks [Quaker Minister in Ireland]."3

The Quaker's hot displeasure toward Catherine did not
match the power wielded by the Catholic Church to mount a
greater execution of the penalty upon John. When the Roman
Catholic Church discovered John married outside their faith,
they promptly excommunicated him. The civil law at the time
stated the punishment of excommunication was limited to:

*"Separation of a Christian, leading a disorderly life, disgracing his profession, from the Christian Congregation, and a banishment of such person from the Church."*4

However, early 19th century Catholic excommunication, in Ireland, amounted to more than just banishment from the Church. Bishop of St. Asaph declared:

*"Excommunication from the Catholic Church is, in Ireland, not simply a separation from the Body of the faithful, but, to all intents and purposes, an Interdiction: ab aqua et igni; that no Catholic dares to administer a cup of cold water, or a crust of dry bread, or any other necessary sustenance to an excommunicated person."*5

Fortunately, for the young couple, the growing secular Irish government saved them from being put to the stake. Nevertheless, Catholic and Quaker communities exiled John and Catherine. John's reservoir of religious belief drained to a trickle. What little standing he held as a disabled soldier in the community evaporated.

Officials released John from active duty after giving 12 years and 8 days of service, and his right leg. Medical officers declared him "totally unfit for service" in the British Army. He received a badge of good conduct and a pension of 6 pennies a day, the equivalent of just under $2.00 US dollars.

John managed to ambulate with a limp and a cane. Due to his lack of education, sullied reputation in the community and physical disabilities, at age 37, he signed up to become a pensioner guard for the ever-growing British penal colonies in Australia. John and Catherine gave birth to a girl and a boy while still living in Tipperary, Ireland.

The couple, along with their children, boarded the convict ship "Norwood" and left Ireland in 1862. Catherine gave birth to their third child while at sea. Whooping cough, seasickness and untenable living conditions plagued the passengers on the voyage to Australia.

Upon their arrival, the British government provided a small wooden cottage on government property where John labored as a prison guard for the next 7 years. Eventually John's right leg was amputated to the hip, which relegated him to a wheelchair. Yet during those years, John and Catherine welcomed three more sons. The youngest they named Michael.

After 7 years of service in the Enrolled Pensioner Force, John received title to an acre of land at "Pensioners Village" just outside Perth, Australia. At 59, John Flynn died of consumption. His tenacious widow, Catherine, survived him by 30 years. She kept the family going with a small dairy herd, which grazed on commonly held ground. She eventually built five brick homes on the site, living at one and renting out the others.

Catherine did not raise her children in any organized religious tradition. She long since distanced herself from Ireland. She endured the hardening life experiences with the loss of her first husband to war, and her difficult life with her war-diminished second husband. Stung by the excommunication of John, she also remained unaccepted by the Quakers of her up bringing. Oral family tradition has it that her husband's brother, who moved to America, became a priest. Upon his death, he willed some money to Catherine, but she turned down the money because it was "Catholic money."

Michael, her youngest son, inherited her home and became a farmer raising cows and goats. He also grew fruit trees, vegetables and grapes for wine. He became a skilled bricklayer, and began to raise a family of his own.

Michael grew up under the influence of a mother who suffered the full brunt of a life stunted by religious certainty. Although he allowed the christening of his children at birth into the local Protestant Church of England, he treated religious dogma with disdain. He remained skeptical and did not attend. He would not raise his children under the umbrella of a singular faith-based life. Michael did, however, make one critical error, once again rippling the pond in another young man's life.

CHAPTER 2

A Land Down Under

Of Claims, Pioneers and Legacy

Several men gathered in front of the old post office on Main Street. They stood like sheep at a watering hole with mouths agape. Two young men with foreign accents, dressed in white shirts and ties, captured their attention. Armed with certainty, they boldly handed out pamphlets and spoke of a message coming directly from heaven.

Reuben Flynn, Michael's son, dropped out of school at age 14. He viewed school as a concentration camp run by the military. This disappointed his mother who had a law degree in mind for him. By 19, Reuben became an accomplished journeyman bricklayer like his father. He lived a normal and happy childhood with his two sisters.

Muriel, his older sister, fell victim to a horse cart accident at a young age. She remained an invalid for the better part of her 74 years. His younger sister, Valerie, cast a delicate shadow and spoke in whispered tones. Reuben also had a younger brother who lived only 6 months and died of bronchitis when Reuben turned four.

Reuben's boyish confidence extended through his strong wiry frame. Michael kept Reuben's hair shaved above his ears, which slightly protruded. His strong work ethic easily matched his serious demeanor. He grew up a second-generation Aussie, grandchild of John, whose scars stretched from the Crimean to the Land Down Under.

On a dry dusty Friday in 1922, in Perth, Australia, Reuben wandered into town after a long day of bricklaying. He happened to walk by the post office where he spied the group of men gathered around the young Americans. He stood behind the others who stopped to hear the white-shirted Yanks. What he heard amazed him.

The strangers traveled all the way to Australia to deliver a special message. These 19-year-old boys were Mormon missionaries, and they made many claims. They declared themselves to be messengers of Jesus Christ.

The young missionaries spoke with purpose and certainty. As the rest of the group trailed off, Reuben lingered and listened intently. They invited him to church to hear more. They instructed him to come early to ensure a seat. He obediently arrived early Sunday morning at the rented hall to find himself alone with the two missionaries. That evening Reuben shared with his parents the exciting events of the day. Their initial reaction rang quite negative. They informed Reuben the Mormon Church was nothing more than "*a lowly cult, even lower in standing than other churches.*"

Undaunted by his parent's feelings, Reuben met secretly with the missionaries and listened to their stories. Through a series of well-orchestrated lessons, he heard the missionaries make the following claims.

They said a modern-day Prophet sent them to Australia. They asserted that in 1820, God, the Father and Jesus Christ, appeared to a young boy named Joseph Smith. They argued Joseph Smith discovered God and Jesus had physical and tangible bodies of flesh and bones. Smith maintained he went into the woods to ask God which of all the churches was true. He alleged God introduced Jesus to him in the woods, and Jesus instructed him to join none of the churches. According to Smith, Jesus advised him: (referring to all religions)

"they were all wrong; and the Personage who addressed me said that all their creeds were an abomination in his sight..."[1]

Smith further stated Jesus Christ would restore his "true" church on earth through Joseph Smith. The young Mormon missionaries proclaimed that Joseph Smith received a great many revelations from God to help restore Jesus' true church on earth, which is the Mormon Church.

According to Smith, angels directed him to an ancient book made out of "gold plates" buried in the ground. Smith allegedly translated the plates by the "power of God," and they contained the history of God's dealings with the ancient inhabitants of America. The missionaries argued that this "translated" book contained the fullness of Jesus' Gospel. The translation is called the "Book of Mormon." Smith declared;

"...the Book of Mormon was the most correct of any book on earth, and the keystone of our religion, and a man would get nearer to God by abiding by its precepts, than by any other book."[2]

The missionaries further professed God and Jesus are two separate individuals and God was once a man like us. They stated if men obey and do what the Mormon Church requires; they too will become Gods of their own universe.

Young Reuben then made a decision that would forever alter the legacy of his life. Enticed by what he heard, he started to read the Book of Mormon. Its pages reveal heroic tales about good people who followed ancient American prophets of God. It also recounts their constant wars against disobedient people of America. The Book of Mormon alleges that modern day Native Americans are descendents of the "disobedient people" and they received their darkened skin as a direct curse from God, on account of their wicked behavior. The book further teaches that American Indians came "principally" from Jerusalem and are Jewish by decent.

Reuben knew about the aborigines of Australia. They were looked down upon by all self-respecting English gentry of 19th century British colonization. In retrospect, it is easy to see how such racism did not preclude Reuben's acceptance of the overt racism against Native Americans infused throughout the disjointed narrative in the Book of Mormon. He requested permission for baptism into the Mormon Church. He needed permission, as he had not yet reached the age of consent. His parents, Michael and Ella May, turned him down. In Reuben's words: *"My parents were not pleased with this decision and tried in every way to discourage me, but I was more determined than ever to be baptized."* So, through obfuscation, he asked them if he could be baptized into the Church of Christ, a somewhat respectable church in the eyes of his parents. The Church of Christ stood in a fine new building down the street. His parents agreed to the baptism into the Church of Christ, not knowing Reuben really meant the Mormon Church, which cites "Christ" in its official moniker. Despite his parent's attempts to keep him out of Mormonism, he found a way in.

Shortly after his baptism, he worked with the missionaries to help construct a Mormon chapel in Sidney. His talent for bricklaying, and the Mormon's desire to build, cemented a life long relationship. Within a few years, he laid enough bricks to pave his own path from Australia to America. At 21, he purchased a one-way ticket and boarded a large and beautiful ship bound for San Francisco.

Sixty-seven years after Reuben's grandfather, John, stepped his "good" foot on the soil of the Land Down Under, Reuben planted both his feet, and new life, on the grounds of Zion, Salt Lake City, Utah. Reuben became a pioneer. He no longer broke bread with the family he knew in Australia. He left his parents, his invalid older sister and fun-loving younger sister, aunts, uncles and cousins. Distance and diverging beliefs separated Reuben from his family. While attending an Australian missionary reunion in Salt Lake City, Reuben met and married a girl who hailed from Brisbane, Australia. Her name was Ethel, and she became my grandmother. Ethel and Reuben bore three sons. The oldest is my father.

Reuben spent the rest of his life trying to live up to Mormon theology and dogma. He served two missions for the Mormon Church during the great depression. He returned with his young family back to Australia, where he labored with brick and mortar to construct yet another chapel. He then left his wife and three young boys at home, back in Utah, and journeyed to Tonga to build again. He faithfully attended all church meetings. He married in the Mormon temple, where they promised to make him a king of his own heaven, so long as he remained faithful to the Church until the day he died.

He raised his three sons in the faith and sent all three on missions when each turned 19. He did all this with no financial help from the Church. He supported his family while he served the Church during the great depression. With little formal education he worked with his hands and back. Along the way, he paid 10% of his income to the Church, with other required monthly fees. He served in church callings and assignments. The Church became his life. All his activities revolved around it. Its goals became his goals. Adherence to Mormonism became his legacy. It is the legacy he promoted and impressed into the consciousness of his children.

Publicly, the Mormon Church presents three main goals: 1. Perfect its members, 2. Convert the world, and 3. Save the dead. (Mormons collect information about people who died outside the Church. They then do proxy baptisms, and other ordinances, so the dead can go to heaven to become Gods as well.)

These goals are presented to new members and are often repeated from the pulpit. What is not made clear to new converts are the secret oaths and covenants they will be required to take behind the guarded doors of Mormon temples. According to

Mormonism, these secret oaths and covenants are required in order to gain entrance into heaven. Members pay a considerable amount of money, in the form of tithing, before they are considered "worthy" to enter temples.

These three openly declared goals quickly vanish when Church interests are threatened. The Church's self-preservation, as an institution, trumps all. The secret temple narrative dictates:

"You and each of you covenant and promise before God, angels, and these witnesses at this altar, that you do accept the Law of Consecration as contained in this, the Book of Doctrine and Covenants, in ***that you do consecrate yourselves, your time, talents, and everything with which the Lord has blessed you, or with which he may bless you, to the Church of Jesus Christ of Latter-day Saints [Mormon Church]...*** *"* 3

This "secret promise" to preserve, support and protect the Mormon Church, at all costs, was taken as an oath under the threat of a bloody honor killing in the form of self-sacrifice. They are known as "blood oaths." They mimic cutting open one's throat, chest and guts. To reveal any of these secrets outside the Mormon temple requires "The Execution of the Penalty," as demonstrated to all who entered the temple:

"The Execution of the Penalty *is represented by placing the thumb under the left ear, the palm of the hand down, and by drawing the thumb quickly across the throat to the right ear, and dropping the hand to the side."*

"The Execution of the Penalty *is represented by placing the right hand on the left breast, drawing the hand quickly across the body, and dropping the hands to the sides."*

"The Execution of the Penalty *is represented by drawing the thumb quickly across the body, and dropping the hands to the sides."* 4

The truculent phrase "Execution of the Penalty" was repeated in the temple narrative no less than 13 times. Reuben practiced the execution of the penalty by drawing his thumb quickly across his throat, across his chest, and across his bowels every time he attended the temple. The Church quietly removed these blood oaths in 1990, well after Reuben's death. For all members who entered a Mormon temple prior to 1990, including myself, the execution of the penalty struck a stark warning and submission into all who received it. Today, Mormon leaders call temple oaths sacred not secret even though the word "secrecy" is still peppered throughout the temple narrative. (for more complete temple excerpts see: "Reference Notes" under Chapter Two).5 It is only clever sophistry to call these secrets, sacred.

Joseph Smith's legacy became the legacy of my grandfather. With absolute conviction, Reuben believed Smith's tales and complied with his blood oaths and mandate to save the world. In cult-like fashion, Reuben quickly lost his own sense of empowerment, identity and personal family history. He accepted his limited understanding of Mormon history and made it his own. He learned and utilized internal Mormon lexicon, and bought into the Mormon doctrine that blind obedience is a virtue, rather than a vice, and he obeyed whatever the Church required.

His newfound beliefs remained unjustified in the mind of his parents. Reuben, young and impressionable, took a leap of faith into the illusionary world of Mormonism, a world full of angels, visions, golden books, magic stones, mysterious writings found with mummies and secrets oaths. He believed the fantastical Book of Mormon tales, about early "Christian Jews" colonizing America, and God's curse of dark skin placed upon evildoers.

What more could Michael and Ella May have done to inoculate an unsuspecting Reuben against the fabulous claims presented with certainty by Mormon missionaries? This would become a paramount question revisited upon Reuben's own offspring, in just two short generations to come.

CHAPTER 3

Detroit Meets Hope

*Every object in a state of uniform motion tends to remain in
that state unless an external force is applied to it.*
Newton's first law of motion

A knock shook the door at 7:00 p.m. sharp. Inside, three
anxious girls stopped their chatter and locked eyes on one
another. Colleen, the most excited of the three, sported shoulder-
length dark hair, brown eyes and a narrow turned-up nose. The
girls gathered in her home. Her parents sat patiently on the couch
exchanging pleasantries when the knock interrupted. Colleen's
father, Chester Christensen, known to all as "Chet," arose from
the couch at the sound. Chet, a confident man in both speech and
demeanor, had done this before. He knew the drill. Colleen's two
young girlfriends straightened their shoulders as Chet reached
for the door.

Ann Marie, the first of the two friends, appeared slender
and blond with pale blue eyes. She hailed from a Swedish
Lutheran tradition and carried a general air of seriousness about
her. Ann Marie's friend, Sylvia, completed the last of the trio.
Sylvia possessed natural beauty, with lovely brown eyes, and her
hair pulled back in a tight ponytail. Her slender figure and fair
complexion were highlighted by a beauty mark at the corner of
her mouth.

Sylvia grew up loosely affiliated in a Methodist tradition. She tried to avoid this meeting altogether. She invited Ann Marie to join her at Colleen's house that night. She did not want to go alone.

Sylvia worked in downtown Detroit. She had the good fortune of getting a ride to work with Colleen and her father, Chet. Chet drove the car, and the conversation. Chet served as the Branch President for the local Mormon Church. A successful businessman, Chet engaged in something Sylvia thought odd, a penchant for religious discussions. Chet constantly invited Sylvia over to his house to share "church" information. Sylvia politely declined on several occasions, but to appease him, she finally agreed to the meeting. Little did she know this meeting would alter the course of her life.

Sylvia Ellison grew up in a broken home. Born and raised in Montréal, Canada, she was the last of 8 children. She spent much of the time with her older sister. For all Sylvia knew, she could have been brought into this world through an immaculate conception. She knew no natural father until age six.

On Monday, May 1, 1939, excitement filled the Ellison's flat. Sylvia's brother Tom prepared for marriage. An older visitor, dressed in an army uniform, attended the occasion. Everyone, except Sylvia, knew him. Most referred to him as "Uncle Bob." A few of her siblings called him "Pop." This confused young Sylvia's inquiring mind. She wanted to know Uncle Bob's real name.

After a few days, Uncle Bob sat next to Sylvia and told her that he was her father. His name was Robert Ellison. Sylvia remained unimpressed with this revelation, but she nevertheless began calling him "Pop" during his infrequent visits. Robert left Sylvia's mother, Dorothy, four years prior to Sylvia's birth. From time to time, he visited her mother, and on one such occasion conception occurred.

Dorothy did not want Sylvia to become attached to Bob. She believed he would not be a stable influence in her life. Indeed, Bob was prone to long separations from Dorothy. He enlisted with the Canadian Army in both the First and Second World Wars. Bob took a bullet in the hand while fighting in France during the First World War. But Bob's absence from Dorothy kept secrets alive. Even on furloughs and after the wars he wandered. He enjoyed a good drink of ale with cohorts, displayed a happy-go-lucky personality, and remained completely irresponsible regarding his family.

Sylvia's mother swung the pendulum the other way. Dorothy worked two jobs to provide for her large fatherless family. They felt lucky to be renting a flat during the depression and the war. The incompatible match between Bob and Dorothy fizzled to a strained but amicable friendship, as Dorothy helped Bob financially from time to time.

World War Two took a toll on the Ellison family. Sylvia's brother "John Ernest" joined the Merchant Marines. He was torpedoed on three different ships, found floating in the water twice, and never came home. Brothers, Cam and Tom joined the Army. Her brother-in-law, Joe, joined the Navy. Three of Sylvia's older sisters died young, through a series of unfortunate events; Marjorie from bronchitis; Elsie from pneumonia and Audrey from a freak accident in a wagon. Sylvia bounced between her mother's flat and Cam's flat. The war, family finances, and domestic instability dominated her young life.

Mr. John Ernest Clarke smoked incessantly and possessed a full head of white hair. He bore the same first and middle name as Sylvia's older brother who had been lost at sea. Mr. Clarke, known as "Ernie," worked hard and became a successful supervisor in the Cadillac Motor Company in Detroit, Michigan. His bushy brows hid behind thick lenses, as his eyes constantly scoured the latest best seller. He knew Sylvia's mother for over 40 years when they decided to marry.

At age nine, Sylvia's mother left Montreal and headed for Reno, Nevada. She left Sylvia behind. Dorothy took up residence in Nevada to effectuate the quickest divorce from Uncle Bob allowed by law, 12 months. During that time, Sylvia moved into a flat with her brother and sister. With the divorce finally granted, Dorothy headed to Detroit where she quickly married the yellow-fingered autoworker. They then summoned Sylvia at age 11. She moved to Detroit to start a new life. Eight years later, she sat uncomfortably on the edge of the couch in the living room of Colleen's home, as Chet opened the door.

Outside the door stood two Mormon missionaries. At 20 years of age, the pair struck a dapper pose. They donned full suit jackets, pressed pants, white shirts and well-placed ties. Both wore well-groomed hair and enthusiasm. The taller missionary sported broad shoulders, a friendly smile and a happy disposition. His nametag read "Elder Flynn."

Elder Flynn, or Richard Flynn, was born in Salt Lake City in 1931. He was the eldest child of Reuben and Ethel Flynn. Raised in the Mormon Church, he sipped in all its doctrine from the tip of a spoon. He kept chickens and rabbits for food, helped out around the house and orchard, and sold eggs to raise much needed money. Richard's family constantly struggled financially as the depression raged on. His father left home for years at a time, serving the Church on foreign missions. During these hard times, pigeon racing became Richard's outlet. By necessity, he accepted responsibility and did his best to help raise his two younger brothers. For a time he served as the man of the house.

Richard's mind beamed bright and retentive. His proclivity toward academics came naturally. He possessed gravitas. His studious habits made him destined for higher education. In the mold of all good Mormon kids, at age 19, he faithfully served a two-year mission for the Church. At 7:00 sharp, Richard knocked on the door of the tightly packed row of homes under the shadow of over-grown elms lining Detroit's suburbs. Chet met him with a smile and a handshake.

At first, Sylvia feared what the missionaries might say. But she felt obliged to be attentive as Chet, for so many days, gave her rides to work. She listened intently to the miraculous Joseph Smith stories. The missionaries repeated the same Mormon mantras Reuben Flynn heard in Australia some 21 years earlier. The well-rehearsed and sharpened polemic hit its target. Within a short time, both Ann Marie and Sylvia began to believe the representations made by Joseph Smith through the missionaries. Richard Flynn baptized Sylvia and confirmed Ann Marie only a few months after that first encounter at Colleen's home. Chet's persistence paid off.

Sylvia turned 18 shortly before her conversion to Mormonism. Her mother received the news with discontent but did not interfere. Her older brother Cam reassured Dorothy, "it's just a phase Sylvia will pass through." He also added, "Mormons are just a cult and her infatuation won't last."

While still living in Michigan, Sylvia turned down numerous wedding proposals. At age 19, she left Detroit to attend Brigham Young University, commonly known as BYU. BYU is a private university, owned and operated by the Mormon Church. It lies at the foot of Mount Timpanogos, a mostly snow covered mountain which towers over Provo, Utah.

One blustery Sunday morning, Sylvia drove 50 miles north to Salt Lake City with a group of friends. They arrived just in time to attend a reunion of Detroit-area members who gathered for a church conference. Once there, she became reacquainted with Richard Flynn, the tall broad-shouldered missionary who baptized her just one year and four months earlier. Richard now stood as an eligible bachelor who already began matriculation at the University of Utah, studying medicine. Richard immediately asked her out for the following weekend. By the end of their first date Richard stopped referring to Sylvia as "Sister Ellison," and Sylvia no longer called him "Elder Flynn." They began to fall in love.

Sylvia returned home to Detroit for summer break after her first year in college. During that summer, a second-hand Desoto with worn out tires came to a stop in front of her small brick home. Rueben and Ethel Flynn stretched as they climbed out the front seats. Richard bolted out of the back.

Richard arranged the trip. Ostensibly, the purpose represented a religious pilgrimage back to the beginnings of

Mormonism. They endured the long drive from Salt Lake to Palmyra, New York to attend the annual re-enactment of the miraculous stories Joseph Smith told to the locals. This annual re-enactment included an outdoor play performed on the side of a hill where Smith claimed to have met an angel who directed him to a buried treasure, a golden book of ancient scriptures. Reuben first heard this story as a young man in Australia. He enthusiastically drove the entire distance under the speed limit, his eagerness tempered only by his lack of money for gas. Ethel, born into the Mormon Church, remained quietly excited for the experience. Richard looked forward to a different experience and treasure altogether. He required no angel to show him the way.

Richard invited Sylvia to join them. She packed a few things, and sat next to Richard in the back seat as the old Desoto belched black smoke all the way to New York. They rented two hotel rooms in Palmyra, a small rural farm town in Upstate New York. Ethel and Sylvia shared one room with Reuben and Richard in the other. Inclement weather plagued the outdoor play. A final deluge of cold showers scattered disappointed pilgrims, running for cover. But all of heaven's fury could not stop the plans of a certain young man, now on a mission of his own.

A rain-soaked and muddy set of parents remained at the hotel that night. Richard received permission to borrow the old car and off he sped to take Sylvia for a ride that would not stop for the rest of her life. Heavy droplets pelted the old car as it came to a rest overlooking the grove of trees where Smith alleged to have seen Jesus. Within the dry confines of the jalopy, and through the clatter on the roof, my father, Richard Flynn, professed his love for my mother, Sylvia, and proposed. She said "yes," followed by a romantic kiss.

Sylvia would never again live in Detroit. She would only visit Canada on special occasions. She moved to Salt Lake City where her mother stood outside the Mormon temple while her baby girl married Richard inside. In the temple, Sylvia bowed her head and said, "yes" as she committed herself to the Mormon

Church and then to Richard.

Mormon rules do not allow non-Mormons, no matter how righteous they may be, inside their temples. Even Mormon children are not allowed to witness weddings of their siblings. Only adult members who qualify may enter the temple. To qualify, members must pay a full tithe, 10% of their income, for at least one year prior to the marriage. Members must also agree not to "affiliate" or have "sympathy with" any "group or individual" that has "opposing views" to Mormonism. In addition, two separate Church officials interview members to insure they are worthy to enter the temple. Interviewees are presented with 14 carefully crafted questions, and must answer them all correctly. Question number 6 reads:

"Do you affiliate with any group or individual whose teachings or practices are contrary to or oppose those accepted by The Church of Jesus Christ of Latter-day Saints, [the Mormons] *or do you sympathize with the precepts of any such group or individual?"*[1]

This temple qualification, still in place today, stood as a barrier between Dorothy and her daughter.

After they married, Richard and Sylvia moved from Salt Lake to Baltimore; then on to San Francisco; and to New York; all to finish up Richard's medical training. My brothers and sisters arrived along the way. I was the San Francisco baby. After Dad's schooling, our family moved back to Utah where Dad accepted a job in a small pediatric clinic. We settled into a little slice of rural Mormon heaven, a town called Bountiful, Utah where I spent my childhood years.

Forty years later, I serendipitously experienced the second greatest challenge of my life. It would become a life changing event no less difficult then the birth of my disabled son, Jason. Like Newton's first law of motion, an external force would be required to stop the continuing movement of a rough stone rolling over our lives.

CHAPTER 4

I Hope They Call Me on a Mission

Ignorance and certainty make an excellent preacher.
Voltaire

The stench of unwashed human bodies permeated the air of the crowded bus. I clasped the top of my bag with one hand while the other firmly gripped the slippery bar overhead. A peasant woman with dark skin and long black braids stood uncomfortably close. The warmth of her robust body pressing into mine heightened the unpleasant smell. Mental distance and a happy primary song carried me away from my discomfort. I always wanted to be the last on the bus. I couldn't stand being wedged body-to-body with smelly alpaca sweaters perfumed with body odor. This circumstance became particularly disconcerting because, as a missionary, I sought out the salt of the earth among the desperately poor and odorous souls of Peru.

Grandpa Reuben accepted the pitch in Australia. It is easy to see how his uneducated demographic falls prey to polished stories of Mormonism. The idea we Mormons are right, while the rest of the world is wrong may be stupendously arrogant, but it reassures its adherents and dangles like a bright lure on a line in a pond already filled with nets. Born into the Mormon assembly line Richard, my father, dutifully replicated the Mormon identity upon all who listened. Thankfully for me, my mother took the bait.

The fix was in for me before the puny sperm rammed the colossal egg. A new hatchling duck will immediately imprint upon the first thing it sees and follow. In like manner, Mormon toddlers are paraded up to the pulpit from the moment they are able to bear their own weight. Led by brothers, sisters, primary teachers, Sunday school teachers and parents, they mimic the words whispered in their ears, "I know the Church is true, I know the Book of Mormon is the word of God, I know that Joseph Smith was a true Prophet, and I love my Mom and Dad." This mental branding occurs well before they can read. It begins shortly after mumbling becomes coherent. It teaches children to directly link natural love for their parents to love for Joseph Smith.

A more calculated indoctrination may not exist. Adult products of this same system heap positive feedback to children on tiptoes whose delicate lips reach upward toward the microphone. The cycle is completed and justified with the words "out of the mouth of babes."

My father endured this spoon-feeding from birth, as did I. My destiny may as well have been written in the stars. An astrology not born in the twinkle of my mother's eye, but out of stale-aired discourses delivered ad nauseam from an endless list of meetings. With warm moisture, its whisper filled my ear, and like the hatchling, I imprinted and followed.

Mormon boys require additional mandates, including preparation for a mission. Parents save money and proudly watch their boys sing glorious missionary songs in church. They ring out in pride and strength. There does not exist a Mormon boy who has not heard and sung the catchy lyrics:

> *"I hope they call me on a mission,*
> *When I have grown a foot or two,*
> *I hope by then I will be ready.*
> *To teach and preach and work*
> *as missionaries do."* 1

At 19, I fulfilled my destiny. I wore a white shirt and tie. I guarded the scriptures in the satchel at my side. My nametag, considered part of my uniform, read "Elder Flynn." It hung on my pocket. A banner of certainty hung in my head. I knew without a doubt, I served the Lord. Like my great-great grandfather, John Flynn, who followed his father's foot steps into the British Army, I followed my father's footsteps into God's Army. I unabashedly proclaimed to all who would listen the same Joseph Smith stories delivered to my mother, from my father, and to my grandfather, Reuben, from yet another viral pair of missionaries.

The regimented life of a Mormon missionary is controlled almost down to the minute. Any variation from the standard invites discipline from a strict authoritative hierarchy. Missionaries never travel alone. Companionship changes are designed to maximize the effectiveness of the harvest while minimizing any doubt about the urgency of the entire affair. Each companion is assigned to write the mission president a weekly letter detailing the activities and relationships of the companionship. This "Companion Inventory Work Sheet" contains numerical goals carefully plotted and reported. They include the weekly number of street contacts, lessons given, baptismal challenges extended, visits with member families, meetings attended, etc. Its business model and dedication would put any door-to-door sales company to shame. The accountability to superiors is unmatched. All goals served only one purpose, convert baptisms. Missionaries who baptize quickly move up in status among the internal hierarchy. They are advanced to become senior companions, then district leaders, followed by zone leaders. I proudly oversaw a zone of missionaries nine months after I arrived in Peru.

On yet another crisp sunny day, we found ourselves smothered between unwashed peasants bouncing along in a bus headed toward the post office on the top of the hill. The impoverish barrio assigned to me carried the name "Francisco Pizarro." History records Pizarro as a heroic Spanish conquistador. He helped subdue the heathens of the once great Incan Empire under the Catholic sword. The desperately impoverished nature of the inhabitants of Francisco Pizarro bares a forgotten legacy of another religious imperative, the Holy Spanish-Catholic inquisition.

The bitter fruits of that brutal history are seen throughout Peru in the myriad ornate Catholic cathedrals that adorn the town squares of virtually every city. They stand as impressive rock edifices that will tower for another thousand years. Their corner stones and arches were hewn from quarries by the blood and sweat of countless peasants forced into labor by the pious hands of a cloaked priesthood. Extracted indulgences, mixed with ritualistic acts of faith, paid to free loved ones from purgatory (A paradigm copied today in Mormons' third openly declared goal: "to save the dead."). Nonbelievers endured systematic torture, then hung to death from large and spacious buildings. At the tip of Spanish steel, hundreds of thousands of brown-skinned natives slaved lives away to improve the Catholic kingdom of God on earth. South American gold weighted ships sailing for the holy soil of Spain and Rome.

The dust cloud following the bus proclaimed the telltale legacy of poverty brought on by 500 years of Catholic rule. A brown city of mud walls, tin roofs and half naked skinny children with bloated bellies completed the dismal existence of its inevitable outcome. Barrios like Francisco Pizarro blanket the Peruvian landscape with shameful poverty.

My companions and I made no attempt to remove the sting of hunger or disease. Instead, we confidently promised the poor a future world with riches beyond all comprehension, a heaven costing only 10% of their already negligible income. In addition, it required a lifetime of dedication to believe and share Joseph Smith stories with all friends, family and acquaintances.

I sang praises to Smith for two years while proselytizing his gospel in Peru. I worked to gain people's trust. I helped save dozens of people's souls from hell. Did I break up families and family traditions along the way? Yes, but that did not matter. I knew the gospel of Jesus Christ, as revealed by Joseph Smith. I recognized if people did not accept and participate in Mormon ordinances and rituals, either in this life or the life to come, they would be denied entrance into heaven. I felt guilty when I came across people uninterested in my memorized discussions. I carried my "elect" status with pride. All primary children learn they are the elect of God, chosen to serve him even prior to their birth. I was special. I carried the gospel and Peruvians did not.

New adherents are taught to show their newfound faith by leaving behind family members who refuse to join. As missionaries, we walked fast, keyed in on perspective converts and wasted little time. Our mission leaders reminded us the end drew near, and wasting even a moment constituted a sin. I became expert in following the 167 strict dictates of the "Little White Bible," a missionary rulebook all missionaries are required to carry.2

I looked at the people of Peru as my church-inspired upbringing taught me. Peruvians inherited the curse of a once righteous people. I believed what the Book of Mormon states, namely, all American Indians, including South Americans, bore God's curse of dark skin, as a punishment for their ancestors wickedness. I also believed, as the Book of Mormon prophesied, if they accepted the gospel of Mormonism, they would become a white and delightsome people, like me. Specifically the Book of Mormon states:

"And he [God] had <u>caused the cursing to come upon them</u>, yea, even a sore cursing, because of their iniquity. For behold, they had hardened their hearts against him, and they had become like unto a flint; wherefore, as <u>they were white, and exceedingly fair</u> and delightsome, that they might not be enticing unto my people the Lord <u>God did cause a skin of blackness to come upon them</u>."3

My first seven companions wore the "skin of blackness" curse. I sat in on countless discussions in which my Peruvian companions argued with their fellow countryman that if they accepted the gospel, and recognized themselves as the cursed offspring of a once white and delightsome people, then they too would have the curse lifted. Being white and delightsome myself, I just smiled and nodded. In retrospect, I never really pondered why none of my Peruvian companions ever turned white. Nor did I consider myself a racist at the time. I exemplified the typical conceited white Mormon missionary who exhibited humility and hubris at the same time. I had a snappy answer for everything. I don't know if I could have been more ignorant.

The Mormon Prophet, Spencer W. Kimball led the Church during the time I served as a missionary in Peru. He openly taught that American Indians, who accepted the gospel, were indeed turning white. According to Kimball:

*"I saw a striking contrast in the progress of the Indian people today.... The day of the Lamanites is nigh. For years they have been growing delightsome, and they are <u>now becoming white</u> and delightsome, as they were promised. In this picture of the twenty Lamanite missionaries, <u>fifteen of the twenty were as light as Anglos,</u> five were darker but equally delightsome. <u>The children in the home placement program in Utah are often lighter than their brothers and sisters</u> in the hogans on the reservation. At one meeting a father and mother and their sixteen-year-old daughter were present, the little member girl-- sixteen--sitting between the dark father and mother, and it was evident <u>she was several shades lighter than her parents</u>--on the same reservation, in the same hogan, subject to the same sun and wind and weather....<u>These young members of the Church are changing to whiteness and to delightsomeness.</u>"*4

A few years after my mission, 1984, the Church quietly replaced the word "white" with the word "pure" in the Book of Mormon. As it turns out, no Native American has ever turned "white" as a result of accepting the Mormon Gospel, despite the prophesies in Smith's Book of Mormon.

Prophet Kimball also taught that "all" Native Americans are Lamanites, a Book of Mormon term. Kimball taught:

*"The term "Lamanite" includes all Indians and Indian mixtures, such as the Polynesians, the Guatemalans, the Peruvians, as well as the Sioux, the Apache, the Mohawk, the Navajo, and others. It is a large group of great people."*5

Apostle Boyd K. Packer, like all Church leaders, proclaimed Native Americans are literally a remnant of Jews who came to America, as is stated in the Book of Mormon. According to Apostle Packer:

*"Today thousands of Lamanites are coming into the Church. More than one hundred Lamanite branches have been organized among the stakes and within the missions. In many of these branches the leadership is provided by the Lamanite members.. In some cases whole Indian communities are being affected."*6

Sadly for the Church, Prophet Kimball, Apostle Packer and Joseph Smith, the Book of Mormon would be proven wrong again, this time by DNA evidence. Thousands of DNA samplings of Native Americans, from all over North and South America, have genetically linked Native Americans to their ancestors in Siberia and North Asia.7-26 As it turns out, there is no such thing as a Lamanite (a Jewish bloodline in Native Americans).

In 2007, the Mormon Church quietly changed the Book of Mormon, again. This time they changed the introduction, which incidentally was written, in 1981, by Apostle Bruce R. McConkie, Mormon Prophet Thomas S. Monson and Apostle Boyd K. Packer. The introduction originally stated:

*"After thousands of years, all were destroyed except the Lamanites, and they are **the principal ancestors** of the American Indians."*

Now it states:

*"After thousands of years, all were destroyed except the Lamanites, and they are **among the ancestors** of the American Indians."* 27

These Book of Mormon changes occurred years after my mission. As a missionary, I argued with conviction that our Mormon promises of heaven differed from Catholic promises. Most Peruvians receive the Roman-Catholic stamp at birth. I testified our gospel came directly from God to Joseph Smith. I basked in the triumph of all partakers who converted to our version of heaven. I proudly shared holy experiences with other missionaries, the mission president and, of course, with my parents back home.

Joseph Smith proclaimed the Catholic Church is the "whore of the earth," just as it is stated in his Book of Mormon. He further taught that all other Christian churches are harlots of the great whore. I happily knew and preached the Mormon Church was the only true Kingdom of God on earth.

Ironically, most of the money collected by the Mormon Church funnels directly into construction of more church buildings, which follows the same paradigm as the previous Catholic imperative.

In retrospect, it is a wonder I helped convert any Latinos. I told the peasants they belonged to a church, which is the whore of the earth. I also pointed out that God cursed them with brown skin due to the wickedness of their ancestors, who murdered millions of righteous "white and delightsome people," like me.

In The Decline and Fall of the Roman Empire, Edward Gibbon wrote: *"So urgent on the vulgar is the necessity of believing, that the fall of any system of mythology will most probably be succeeded by in the introduction of some other mode of superstition."* With persistence and certainty, I facilitated the destruction of Catholic mythology and replaced it with Mormon superstition.

Nevertheless, news of a new convert baptism received accolades at home and congratulatory letters followed. All Mormon mothers are asked to write weekly to support the testimony (beliefs) of their missionary sons and daughters. My mother, a convert herself, wrote me every week. Of all the letters she wrote over the two-year period, I only remember one. Although I read it over 30 years ago, July 27, 1979, I still picture right where I stood as my eyes rolled over the first line… "Your grandfather Reuben passed away today." My red nose sniffed and the world paused for a moment.

I was not a handsome child. My fair complexion and freckled face burned with regularity in the light of day. After one particularly hurtful verbal drubbing from a couple of fence-sitting "hick" neighbors, I resolved to ameliorate the ugly injustice poured out so abundantly across my face. I took an SOS pad and scrubbed the freckles off the end of my nose. When the puss finally abated, there remained a large scab across my sniffer. I wore a band-aid over it for a month. It happily hid my freckles. I was one year dumber then the hicks were stupid. To my great surprise, when I removed the covering, some weeks later, most of the freckles disappeared. My skin remained damaged, pink and tender and would never be the same. I smiled.

As I grew up, I viewed my grandfather Reuben through the eyes of a child who could barely see past the end of his nose. My six siblings and I cut a wide path of mischief wherever we went. Grandpa, being elderly and only having raised 3 boys of his own, occasionally lost patience for our obstreperous behavior. He often quipped, "cut it, cut it," which is better understood in its Americanized vernacular "knock it off."

Grandpa never parted with his Australian accent, a novelty we sometimes mimicked. His overly thick fingers and unusually strong brick-laying hands trapped skinny wrists like a vise grip. To be grabbed by Grandpa meant a sure struggle for survival. But to his credit, he maintained a cheery disposition around us grandkids, and he endured a lot with each impetuous invasion. He always carried with him a well-worn handkerchief as he suffered from the daily barrage of Salt Lake City pollen.

Grandpa suffered from all the typical Mormon fears with their accompanying names, signs and tokens. The world he perceived engendered an almost constant fear of the future, and all things "not" Mormon. He stored extra gallons of gasoline in the bottom of his empty swimming pool, a pool he dug himself. He built a coal-burning furnace in the middle of his house, in preparation for the end of the world. He tried to become as self sufficient as possible. He drilled a well in his backyard. He dug a large fireproof vault, the size of an oil drum, under his front porch. It protected his valuable genealogy papers required by the Church to save his kindred dead. He often spoke of governmental conspiracies. His basement contained multiple copies of a book entitled "None Dare Call it Conspiracy." He never developed a worldview beyond those espoused by Mormon leaders.

When I knew him, he was elderly. He had long since retired from work. His home stood tidy and austere. Reuben, no doubt, remained deeply affected by the great depression. He mixed water with milk and diluted his soda pop to make it last twice as long. He owned two and half acres of fruit trees in the backyard and kept chickens. He added a stiff layer of plastic over the bench seats in his 1964 Ford Falcon. He embodied frugality.

We often took trips from Bountiful to Salt Lake to visit Grandma and Grandpa. Their small red brick home held a musty odor. Whenever I passed Grandma's old wooden dresser my great-grandfather James Dean gazed down at me through a dusty glass frame. I snooped in Grandpa's basement meat locker and shuttered, traumatized at the sight of rabbits still dressed in fur. I could never believe Grandpa capable of such things.

My fondest memories of Grandpa involve the hours he spent philosophizing with Dad at family reunions. I often listened and found pride when Dad made just a bit more sense than Grandpa. I never saw him be unkind to Grandma, who mostly fluttered around the kitchen and doted upon her garden.

She worked with her hands, and over time developed bent and twisted knobs at the ends of her fingers. She amicably welcomed all with a slight crack in her voice and, more importantly, she kept the cookies in the breadbox. Her cookies were thick, like a thumb, and slightly stale, but sweet enough to be prized by our scruffy lot.

In the five personal histories Grandpa left, he never said why he doggedly pursued missionary work. He never mentioned a spiritual experience of his own. He just wanted everyone to believe. He fell under the spell of the Book of Mormon and tales from Joseph Smith. Smith declared he translated it by the power and gift of God from golden plates. Smith proclaimed the Book of Mormon to be the "keystone" of his religion, and the "most correct of any book on earth." Grandpa believed. He quoted contemporary Church leaders as if they were God. He spent his life trying to measure up to a standard and morality he thought originated in the Mormon Church. He enjoyed reading, and collected a small library, which he later sold off during the great depression. But his conviction to the stories told by Joseph Smith dominated his life's narrative. He filtered all of his important life choices through the dictates of Church leaders. To my knowledge, he neither had access too, nor researched the actual history of the man whose stories mandated the legacy he felt compelled to follow.

Grandpa never returned to school. He found the one true gospel of God on earth. To his mind, all information paled in comparison. When he learned he was dying of cancer, he elected not to have it treated. He gave his adult life to Mormonism. It was as if he looked forward to the afterlife. He died 30 days after his diagnoses of colon cancer.

Two weeks after his death, a letter arrived in the small box labeled "Mormon Missionaries" in a one-room post office, atop a dusty hill, in the impoverished barrio of Francisco Pizarro. "Your grandfather Reuben passed away today.".... A painful lump developed in the back of my throat. The knowledge that I engaged in a legacy he desperately sought, made me proud. But it did not lessen the hurt welling up in my neck. I stood on a brown mountain, in a foreign country, gripping a flip chart full of pictures glorifying the life and times of Joseph Smith. I carefully replaced the letter in the envelope, slid it in my pocket and turned to look for anyone who might be walking into town after a long day of bricklaying. I would make my grandfather proud. I would find the next Reuben Flynn to unleash upon the world.

CHAPTER 5

Life in the Fast Lane

*Everyone has a story, if you don't write it yourself,
someone else will write it for you.*

I arrived home from Peru in the fall of 1981. I returned to the
heartland of Mormonism, Salt Lake City. My younger sister took
over my old bedroom in my absence. My parents recommended I
sleep in the office. I pointed out the office lacked a bed and a
dresser. The room had a small closet, but it bulged with office
paraphernalia. Dad solved the predicament by unfolding a
rollaway bed in between the desk and the bookcase. Somewhat
disappointed, I opened my suitcase on the desk. I got the
message loud and clear. My life lay outside that home. I spoke in
sacrament meeting my first week back. This speaking
engagement awaits missionaries who return home honorably. I
reported on the wonderful successes experienced in Peru and
dutifully recommended all young men prepare themselves to go
on missions.

In my second week home, I enrolled in the "Lord's
University," BYU. While at BYU I dated, then married a
wonderful southern California girl named Linda. We wed in the
Los Angeles Mormon temple. To contemplate marriage outside a
Mormon temple is considered sinful for two faithful Mormons. I
graduated from BYU, University of Nebraska and finally from

Indiana University. Linda and I conceived four children along the way.

Our first daughter, Julie, entered the world the summer we left Provo, Utah, for Lincoln, Nebraska. Her curly locks and infectious laughter melted all hearts. She possessed a squeaky voice that exuded pure fun. Our first son, Jason, arrived two and a half years later, during my junior year in dental school.

Bleak and colorless skies constantly delivered ice crystals to the windshields across the wind swept plains of Nebraska. The same two inches of snow that fell in November still clung to the grass in February. The shortening winter days portended another darkening to come. The flurries of this barren tundra provided a fitting backdrop for Jason's arrival. His birth brought pain, grief and fear, not to mention lots of work. As I alluded to the circumstances of his birth in the prologue, his early brain damage led to a multiplicity of handicaps. His condition necessitated constant attention. As his parents, we felt a good deal of guilt in shifting nearly all of our attention away from Julie to meet Jason's needs.

The third year of dental school, junior year, qualifies as the most difficult year of my life. All juniors need to fulfill the bulk of their clinical requirements, pass the national dental boards, and in my case, apply for postgraduate work. I also studied feverously to remain ranked at the top of my class. Jason arrived in the middle of my junior year, during the heart of one of the coldest Nebraska winters on record. I not only felt the stress of all my schoolwork and Jason's birth, but also felt I needed to be strong for Linda who was physically and emotionally exhausted. When my classmates inquired about our newborn, I could not bear to tell them what we were going through. The pain of it all was just too great to acknowledge. I felt a deep physical pain in my chest. No matter which direction I turned, pain stared me in the face. It sat on my forehead and I couldn't shake it off. I could not understand how others around me laughed and told meaningless jokes. The words "if only" I had done this, or that, than perhaps Jason may not have suffered the brain injury. This recurrent thought resonated in my mind and wore heavily upon my shoulders for nine months. All the "if onlys" eventually morphed into the phrase "life goes on." I quietly worked my way through the stages of grief, while at the same time trying to be strong and encouraging toward Linda, who bore the brunt of the Jason's endless medical needs. I dared not cry, afraid if I started, I would never stop. Perhaps the greatest fear of all was the unknown. What would become of Jason? Would the doctor's predictions come true? Would Jason become a mental vegetable? We had to accept that we did not know the answer. We tried to find happiness despite our lack of certainty and foreknowledge.

Of course, we served ever faithful and did not miss our church meetings. While all of our personal travails ensued, our bishop abruptly kicked us out of our ward. We showed up one Sunday and during the sacrament meeting the Bishop announced that three families had been chosen to permanently travel across town and attend a different ward, to help out their fledgling membership. The Bishop explained that in the early pioneer days of Utah, Brigham Young placed letters in the Salt Lake City post box marked "Box B." These letters assigned faithful Mormon families to leave the Salt Lake Valley and colonize new cities somewhere out west. Our Nebraska bishop told us, in the spirit of Box B, he assigned us to a different ward. He gave us no choice in the matter. The first we heard of it occurred during the sacrament meeting in which he blurted out our names. The Bishop literally told the congregation to look at the three families, whom he had chosen, for the last time. He declared us no longer welcome in his ward. Only years later, I discovered that Brigham Young used the Box B method to get rid of members who threatened his authority in Salt Lake City.

As members learned about Jason's medical condition they constantly said nonsensical and sometimes offensive things. The most common comment we heard was, "God thought you somehow extra special to be blessed with a handicapped child." We figured people just don't know what to say, so they say stupid things. By the way, the correct thing to say is "I'm sorry to hear about your son's struggles, is there anything I can do to help." It seems like such an obvious thing to say, yet it surprised us how few ward members could figure it out. Unlike the usual platitudes we heard from our "ward family," Linda's parents flew out from California to help shoulder the load, as did my parents, who flew out from Salt Lake City. My mother in particular spent many days and long hours assisting us. Linda and I put the brakes on expanding our family for a few years, as we struggled to raise Jason.

Jason endured constant physical and occupational therapy. He wore ankle braces, sat in wheelchairs and gripped walkers. We carried, walked and pushed him to hearing and speech therapists. He attended special schools and visited a cadre of medical professionals.

Jason's brain damage could have been prevented. He was born normal, according to our pediatrician, who checked him out of the hospital the day after his birth. We took him back to the hospital when we noticed his skin began to yellow. At four days old, our pediatricians agreed he looked jaundiced, and immediately put him under bright lights to break down the harmful elements building up in his blood stream. He laid under the lights for the next 12 hours while his bilirubin count (a measure of broken-down red blood cells) continued to grow higher and higher. Our pediatrician informed us that too much bilirubin in the blood of a newborn could cross the blood-brain barrier and cause damage. The lights failed to bring the dangerous levels down and our two pediatricians, a partnership, sat on their hands until Jason began to exhibit posturing, an odd arching in his back. They told me it signaled brain damage had begun.

At this point, I became exasperated. I begged the doctors to do something. The doctors finally admitted they did not know what to do, so they called a neonatologist 50 miles to the north, in Omaha. He instructed them to do a blood transfusion. My doctors did not want to perform the transfusion. I desperately asked them why they would not do it? They stated the neonatologist was better equipped to deal with transfusions. So they sent Jason, by helicopter, up to Omaha, where he finally, several hours later, received the blood transfusion that saved his life. Unfortunately, the damage was done. The neonatologist told us it all could have been prevented had our pediatricians acted sooner.

We sued Jason's pediatricians. When we tried to get a copy of their hospital notes, the hospital refused to give them to us. They told us the doctors needed to finish writing in them before they could be released to us. The case went to trial. Our pediatricians dressed smartly and sat flanked by their lovely wives.

On the witness stand, the head pediatrician testified that I ordered him "not" to give Jason a blood transfusion, which is why he sent Jason to Omaha. I was in shock! My jaw hit the floor. I leaned over and asked my attorney how the doctor could openly lie in a court of law? My attorney looked at me and whispered, "What, did you think he was going to tell the truth?" Yes, actually I did.

In all the depositions taken, none of the doctors' courtroom lies were recorded. No doctor notes stated that I wanted someone else, someone I never heard of no less, to do Jason's blood transfusion. I had never heard of the neonatal center in Omaha. My pediatricians concocted this big lie to weasel out of their mistake. The attorneys representing the doctors called a witness who was not on any witness list, and the judge allowed her testimony. She testified that she overheard a conversation between the pediatricians and myself. She testified I told them not to do the transfusion, and to let someone else do it. "Stunned" only begins to describe how I felt. Why would this nurse dramatically appear through the court doors, unannounced to us, support the doctor's lie with another lie, and then leave the court just as quickly as she had entered? I noticed as she scurried out of court, she neither looked at me, nor toward the doctors.

I remained completely dumbfounded. All the evidence

clearly showed these doctors simply made a mistake in not administering a blood transfusion. Yet after all the doctor notes, all the medical articles and all the expert witnesses, we lost the case. My faith in those pediatricians had already crumbled, and now my faith in the legal system shattered.

Afterwards, our attorneys interviewed several of the jurists to inquire the reasoning behind their judgment. They rendered a verdict rather quickly. They universally believed the testimony of the "good" doctor, that I stopped him from doing his job. They believed this based upon his testimony and the supporting testimony of the nurse.

We lived in a small town. We knew the cards were stacked against us from the get-go. Several of the jurists took their children to see these same pediatricians. One even attended his church. This we discovered when our attorneys interviewed the potential jurists. The judge would only allow us to remove a few of them, but several others remained seated. I knew the doctor lied to save his reputation, and money, when he blamed me for Jason's brain damage. But what motivated the nurse to lie? This perplexed me for a number of years. The answer came in the form of a phone call I received years later. Another nurse, who worked in the same nursery the night we took Jason back to the hospital, called. She informed us that the nurse, who testified against us, had been sleeping with the good doctor, which is why she lied on his behalf. She said all the nurses knew this, but fear of retribution precluded them from saying anything against such a powerful figure. The nurse who called us no longer worked for the hospital and had moved to another state.

The permanent damage done to Jason pierced us to the core. We, Jason, Linda and I, live with it. Fortunately for Jason, not all of the doctors' predictions came true. Jason is very intelligent. He excels in math and plays chess at a high level. He drives a car, and attends college. He is becoming an excellent writer. He loves to laugh, and exhibits a wild imagination. He does suffer from cerebral palsy (a condition that affects muscle control), and he is hard of hearing. He signs, reads lips and speaks, albeit somewhat labored. The simple mistakes the doctors made are unfortunate, but forgivable. We are all human. We all make mistakes. The fact they blamed me, as a way out of accepting responsibility for their error, was hard to accept. Other than the nurse, who eventually shared with us the reason for one of the lies, neither of the two pediatricians has ever apologized.

Shortly after we lost the case, the medical partnership of the two pediatricians ended. We learned through our attorneys that the pediatrician, who remained silent, left their partnership. Presumably he could no longer work with his dishonest partner. The "silent" pediatrician had pushed for an out-of-court settlement. The dominant, senior partner let pride and ego stand in the way of truth, and he won in court.

Linda and I knew the truth. Documentation corroborated what we witnessed first hand. Yet, 12 jurors became convinced of a false history simply based upon the testimonies of two liars. Why? It is true the pediatricians appeared much older, distinguished and more authoritative than me. Perhaps the jurors did not want to consider what they did not "want to believe," that their "good" pediatricians not only make mistakes, but also lie to cover them up. To reach such a conclusion would have shattered their faith. So they quickly looked past obvious contradictions and retain their belief in these doctors.

What would have allowed the jurors to reach a decision, which reflected actual history? How could they so easily accept a false and self-serving history made up by the doctor? The answer requires them to look beyond their positive bias toward the doctors and freely examine evidence, which they apparently glossed over. I do not fault the jury because they were not dealing with full information. At the last minute, our star witness, the neonatologist from Omaha, could not make it to the trial. In addition, they were not made aware of the adulterous situation between the nurse, who testified against us, and the doctor who lied. Although it does explain why she left the courtroom without looking over at the doctor, seated next to his lovely wife.

The jury made a judgment based upon their bias and their limited view of the evidence. They all agreed with one another. They felt confident in their judgment. They were wrong.

Almost nothing good came out of this trial. It wasted much of our time, energy and money. It exposed us to the disreputable character of a pediatrician who, due to his lie, is still held in high regard in his community. It made me less trusting of doctors. I now know justice is not always served in a court of law. I did learn a valuable lesson. People who base their beliefs upon testimonies of others, without examining available evidence, may very well be wrong. But would I apply this lesson to my own life?

During our 10 years of college, we lived off scholarships, guaranteed student loans, my evening employment as an orthodontic laboratory technician, and occasional monies sent from our parents. We lived in government housing for a time. We also added an additional $40,000+ debt, charged to us by our attorneys for Jason's trial.

After school our family set up shop in Mesa, Arizona, where I practiced as an orthodontist. Our practice grew and I finally earned enough money to support our family. Linda bore two more children, completing our family. We named our third child Jessica. She seemed destined for stardom. Then came our fourth and last child, James Dean. James Dean, known to us as JD, is 9 years younger than Jason. JD, like Jason, entered the world normal and healthy. I stand in awe with JD's athleticism and agility. When compared to all the work involved in raising Jason, JD practically raised himself.

Mormon philosophy governed my thought processes as we settled into life in Mesa. Weekly meetings and assignments reinforced my thinking and left me with little spare time and energy for family. I faithfully paid tithing and fast offerings to the Church so I would be considered a worthy member. Mormonism teaches if one pays tithing, one will not be burned to death when Christ comes back to earth.1 They also require tithing be paid as a prerequisite to attend the temple. Members considered unworthy to attend, are unworthy for heaven. After all we endured, we definitely wanted to remain worthy for heaven. We even paid tithing while we paid off our school debts. The Church encourages members to pay tithing using credit card debt, if necessary. Like most life-long Mormons, I can list a very long and impressive number of voluntary church assignments, or "callings" I fulfilled.

All seemed to finally be working in our favor when fate came knocking in the form of bad luck. Twelve years after we arrived in Mesa all the planets seemed to be aligned. I earned a good living. We lived in a respectable neighborhood. We actively raised our kids in Mormonism. All of our friends and thoughts reflected our belief. We moved to a street where Mormons filled every home. We whispered in the ears of our children the good news that God picked Joseph Smith to be the first of a procession of latter-day prophets. We belonged to the only true church on the face of the earth. We taught our children to only date Mormons so they would be able to marry in the temple. Our boys learned to look forward to fulfilling Mormon missions for the honor of our family, and for their own salvation. However, one planet slipped out of alignment, appearing daily in the form of serious reoccurring back pain.

After 6 years in a busy orthodontic practice the pain finally overcame me. My first back surgery required 6 months of convalescence before I managed to go back to work. I worked for another 5 years before a second major surgery ended my career. It seemed God once again blessed me with another challenge, that of ending my lucrative orthodontic practice due to persistent and debilitating back pain. The diagnosis read "degenerative disc disease coupled with severe arthritis."

CHAPTER 6

An Awakening

"If a faith will not bear to be investigated; if its preachers
and professors are afraid to have it examinated,
their foundation must be very weak."
Mormon Prophet George A. Smith 1

Two thousand five marked a banner year for the Mormon world. While the earth counted another rotation around the sun, Mormons celebrated the 200th year anniversary of the birth of Joseph Smith. A cacophony of accolades filled meetings alongside fervent testimonies expressing gratitude to the man who gave birth to our shared beliefs. Mormons believe approval is required from Jesus Christ and from Joseph Smith to enter heaven. Hymnbooks still contain a song entitled "Praise to the Man," a song dedicated to Joseph Smith, which echoed through the corridors of every Mormon meeting hall around the world.

In December of 2005, I finally jumped on the bandwagon and decided to honor Joseph Smith. After all the church-wide celebrations extolling the honor and virtues of his life, I felt the need to rededicate myself to his legacy. I began to study the life and times of Joseph Smith. Serendipity happened.

Nature, or God, depending on whom you want to blame or give credit to, dealt me a weak back for my chosen profession. I remained sidelined from work after a couple of back surgeries and enjoyed ample time to read. With no more excuses, I delved into the life of our beloved prophet, Joseph. Little did I know a window was about to open in my life. I literally opened up Windows, on my PC, and googled the name "Joseph Smith."

I found a great many websites in favor of Smith as well as an equal number negative toward him. I was not surprised to see anti-Smith literature as I had been taught Satan's prime directive aimed squarely at destroying Smith's reputation and hence the legacy of God's only true church. So, I decided to start my study of his life on what I thought to be solid footing. I studied his marriage to Emma.

It somewhat disarmed me to learn the names of Smith's other wives. I also learned the dates of those marriages. This surprised me because, as an active church-going Mormon, I never heard the name of any of his wives, except that of Emma, his first wife. This fact intrigued me. I wondered why if temple marriage is the key that opens heaven's door, are none of his other wives ever acknowledged. This did not make sense to me.

I immediately drove down to the Church's bookstore, Deseret Book, and purchased the official seven-volume History of the Church.2 I also went to the official Mormon website "familysearch.org," and looked up the names of the wives of Joseph Smith listed there. I then cross-referenced each and every marital date of Smith's marriages to the actual date recorded in the seven-volume history of the Church. I discovered that not one single wedding was recorded in official Mormon Church history. Yet on each day a wedding occurred, Smith did record other mundane events. Again, I was confused. How could one aspect of the Church, the Genealogical Department, not be supported by another aspect, its "Official History?" This mystery intrigued me. What was the history of Smith's polygamy, anyway? As a devout Mormon intent on honoring the legacy of his birth, did I not have the right to know the man in whom I dedicated so much of my life's time, talents and money? At this point I did two things Mormon leaders view as evil. I took upon myself the authority to study, and did not belittle the power of reason.

At first, massive confusion poured through my mind as an avalanche of undeniable evidence of abuse fell in my lap. I could not believe what I read. Could Joseph Smith really have been a con man instead of the holy man I revered from birth? Suddenly, a light turned on in my head. Joseph Smith may not have been a true prophet! A sense of fright and excitement gripped me at once; frightened Satan was trying to lure me away from truth, and excited that a life altering epiphany had just happened. My excitement outweighed my fear, and nothing would stop me from getting to the bottom of the widening gap between what I read and what I had been taught in church.

I sought original source documentation to confirm or reject any derogatory history of Smith. The deeper I dug, the more I began to see reoccurring patterns that soon became so obvious they became predictable. What the Church calls "anti-Mormon" literature is simply an accurate reflection of the documented historicity of Joseph Smith. In fact, the Church brands its own early Mormon documents anti-Mormon. Another obvious pattern emerged. Church-sponsored apologists engaged in rationalization, minimization, misdirection and a plethora of other obfuscation techniques to dissuade members from reading original Church material. They consistently undermined the accuracy of the very history upon which the Church makes its divine claims. At the same time, they make Mormon history sound like a mysterious and complicated thing, when in reality it is clearly documented. I later found the Church employs groups of apologists, BYU F.A.R.M.S., among others. Church leaders themselves do not address the giant discrepancies between the Church-sanitized version of the life of Smith, and their own documented history of Smith. Rather, they define anything distasteful, abusive or fraudulent as "anti-Mormon."

Sadly, all the pieces of the puzzle of Smith's life, including confirmatory evidence written by his own hand, opened my eyes to the only conclusion that made sense. Joseph Smith was not a prophet. But I wanted him to be God's true prophet. Yet, his documented history is undeniable. Joseph

Smith committed rampant frauds, lies and schemes. Equally devastating to me was my modern-day prophets either purposely lied to me, or they were so oblivious to Mormon history they in no way could be considered "inspired." As a member, am I supposed to know more about the history of the Church than my living prophet, a prophet whose very authority depends upon that same history?

Smith's history reveals one fraud after another. He not only married some 33 women including girls as young as 14, but he married and committed adultery with at least 11 women who were already married.3 Official Church history and original source documentation record that Smith lied about these clandestine marital relationships to his wife, other husbands, the Church and the world at large via the press. His proclivity toward other men's wives and young girls represents only the proverbial tip of the iceberg of a well-documented life filled with cons, lies and sexual liaisons.

I hoped somehow the Church could still be true. At times I slipped into denial. I even tried to rationalize Smith's actions by repeating well-worn church clichés, such as *"God's understanding is higher than man's,"* or *"A prophet will never lead you astray,"* or *"When a prophet speaks, the debate is over."*4 But I could not deny the authenticity of the sources of the most damning information. I came to the conclusion it would be a sin against myself not to follow truth, wherever it led me. If I believe in a God of truth, then I must follow truth.

Smith's motives became obvious; money, sex, power. At one point he founded a bank, The Kirtland Safety Society, and printed money even though the State of Ohio turned him down for a banking charter.5 According to Smith's cashier, Warren Parrish, and later-to-be Prophet Wilford Woodruff, Smith prophesied:

"I have listened to him [i.e. Smith] with feelings of no ordinary kind, when he declared that the AUDIBLE VOICE OF GOD, INSTRUCTED HIM TO ESTABLISH A BANKING-ANTI

*BANKING INSTITUTION, who like Aaron's rod <u>SHALL SWALLOW UP ALL OTHER BANK[s] and grow and flourish and spread from the rivers to the ends of the earth, and survive when all others should be laid in ruins.</u>"*6

History also records his bank failed in less than a month, and he escaped like a thief in the night to avoid prosecution and numerous lawsuits filed against him.7 He fled to another town to begin preaching anew. Of course, I had always been taught he fled Ohio because Satan wanted to destroy him and the "only" true church. Later I came to realize that Satan is a great friend to the Mormon Church. Satan is the justification to any responsibility Mormon leaders refuse to accept.

I did not want to believe any of this. It contradicted the benign historical account of Smith's life fed to me from birth. Yet, every original source document I could get my fingers on, including original first-edition early-Mormon books, confirmed the tawdry tale. Even the revelations Smith used to build his church constantly underwent revisions by Church leaders in an obvious attempt to make them fit the changing social climate.8

At this point, I am not going to go into the labyrinth of lies and obfuscations currently propagated by the Mormon Church concerning Joseph Smith. A more detailed explanation of his history can be found in my wife's account, Chapter 15.

Sadly, I realized, I would have to lie to myself if I were to accept the history of Smith as taught by the Mormon Church today. The Australian missionaries lied to my grandfather. My father unknowingly propagated these same falsehoods to my mother while serving his mission. As a missionary, I unknowingly lied to thousands of people in Peru. I raised my children under a false religious illusion. All of my Mormon friends, family and neighbors promoted a false history of Smith. It all amounted to one lie after another, and the trail of lies lead directly back to Joseph Smith. The lies predictably changed with time to serve the needs of the Church. Through the years, Mormon leaders have so raped the truth of their own history, it remains elusive to its adherents. As one current Mormon apostle put it, when referring to early Mormon Church history:

*"Some things that are true are not very useful."*9

    Simple honest history destroys Mormon faith. Smith first named the Church: "Church of Christ." He then changed it to: "Church of Latter Day Saints." He then changed it for a third time to: "The Church of Jesus Christ of Latter-day Saints." I learned virtually none of Smith's prophetic revelations came true. Smith and other Church leaders altered his revelations "post facto" to make them sound credible. Today, Mormon leaders teach that Jesus selected the name of the Church and gave it to Smith through revelation. If this is true, it only took Jesus three times to get it right.10 Prophet Gordon B. Hinckley proclaimed:

*"Each of us has to face the matter, either the Church is true, or it is a fraud. There is no middle ground. It is the Church and kingdom of God, or it is nothing."*11

Hinckley also stated:

*"On this occasion <u>I am not going to talk about the good or bad</u> of Prohibition but rather of<u> uncompromising loyalty to the Church</u>."*11

    The realization of the truth in my findings, from original source documentation, became nothing short of a life altering epiphany for me. The real cathartic moment, or my true Cartesian moment, cogito ergo sum12, came when I admitted to myself the only thing I really knew was, that <u>truth is not a lie</u>. And it certainly is not the web of lies currently propagated by Mormon Church leaders.

    "The Mormon Church is not what it claims to be." To adherents of other faiths and philosophies this sentence appears in the form of 10 words. For a dyed-in-the-wool believer like me to reach this conclusion required grappling with the Mount Everest of personal honesty. It demanded a thorough examination of my personal identity. It quickly passed me from the comfort and security of certainty, into a world of uncertainty. It forced me to make the decision between finding certainty in a lie, or to forsake the lie and forge my own path in life. A great many sleepless nights followed until one night I had a dream so vivid, years later I still remember it.

I played basketball with friends. I could jump and float to the basket. Everyone had a good time. Off in the distance I heard the bellowing of a ship's horn. Everyone began to race back toward the ship. As I followed along, I realized I had been on an island filled with people all having fun in parks and other beautiful places. As I reached the shoreline, I saw a beautiful ocean liner with many ropes dangling over the side. People struggled to climb up the ropes to board the ship as it pulled away from the island. I managed to climb a rope and slipped onto the deck. The ship heaved forward and began to sail away dragging people who dangled from the ropes.

People began falling into the ship's wake. This infuriated me. I yelled at the captain demanding he stop and help the people board. The captain ignored me and blew the horn. As I turned back, I noticed the entire hull of the ship appeared corroded, as if it had been on the bottom of the ocean for many years. I could see into all the rooms and hallways of the ship. All chambers darkened with mud and rust, yet passengers seemed to ignore the filth around them as they made their way around the ship. I returned to my room. It faced aft. The room was not as I had remembered it. Where beautiful furniture once adorned the cabin, now laid rust and debris. I looked out the window and saw people drowning in the wake. The water churned with blood. I peered through the depths and saw piles of human bones littering the ocean floor.

In distress, I returned to the deck and again yelled at the captain to stop. I shouted, "people are dying," and "the sea floor is littered with their bones," and if they would stop I would prove it. The captain again ignored me and the ship moved forward until it came to the next small island. This island was made up of many small docks all bound together. I climbed down a rope and dove into the water and swam beneath the ship. I saw piles of human bones lining the path we had taken. I surfaced with evidence. I returned to the docks and shouted up to the captain. People again clamored toward the ropes. My shouts were lost in the crowd trying to board. I turned and saw some people simply ignoring the ship. They continued to play, as they had been, waterskiing and riding jet skis. I saw my wife climb on a small boat. She wore a swimsuit, lifejacket and headed away from the ship. She waved to me wearing black gloves. The large ship moved on. I could see people dangling from its ropes like flies in a spider's web. Some fell off while others clung for dear life. I stood on the dock confused. I no longer wanted to board the ship I knew to be full of filth. But I wasn't sure what to do on the dock. I also could not figure out why my wife wore black gloves and waved to me with friendly enthusiasm. Then I woke up.

At the time, Linda and I celebrated 24 years of marriage. We always shared our thinking with one another. We privately discussed all our new findings. What would these discoveries mean for us? We simply could not get past living or promoting a lie to our children under a philosophy that the ends justify the means. When we started studying church history, Linda served as the Relief Society President. She served 118 women under the close scrutiny of the Bishop. I worked as Ward Membership Clerk. Both of us faithfully fulfilled these church callings for over 2 years.

I quietly asked the Bishop to release me without giving any explanation as to why. A short time later I stopped attending church. Both of us worthily held temple recommends (a temple recommend is a card signed by two Church authorities authorizing "worthy" members entrance into a temple). We both rehearsed the blood oaths of secrecy in the temple. We knew the execution of the penalty.

Having been raised in the Church, we knew other members would see our lack of church attendance in a very negative light. Ironically, as the Ward Membership Clerk it had been my job to keep track of all members who missed meetings. I collected attendance rolls and reported the names of absent members to the Bishop and Stake President. I also submitted actual names of ward members not considered temple worthy or who did not possess a current temple recommend. I knew if we did not attend at least one priesthood meeting or one relief society meeting each month, our names would land on the list of "less active" and receive special attention in the leadership planning meetings. We also knew members would begin to believe there was something sinfully wrong with us.

Mormons are taught the only reasons people leave the Church are due to personal unworthiness, or that a local leader or ward member has offended them.13 The general consensus would be that we had a problem, not the Church. The Church does not tell members the real reason most people leave, which is, they no longer believe Mormon Church claims.

Linda and I did not expect to have our blood spilt as recommended in the temple by the execution of the penalty. We did learn, however, that many members who left the Church during the days of Joseph Smith and Brigham Young were "used up," as they called it, murdered at the hands of Mormon assassins. The "Danites," and the "Destroying Angels" within the Danites, carried out this horrific task. Today, the execution of the penalty involving murder is prohibited under U.S. law. The Church now employs social destruction, labeling, excommunicating and shunning as their execution of the penalty. This is not unlike the treatment dealt out upon the heads of John and Catherine in early 19th century Ireland by the Quakers and Catholics. The motives, language and justifications are identical.

We spoke to no one in our ward regarding our findings. We knew to do so would only invite the full fury of condemnation and excommunication upon us. We worried for our children. We did not want them ostracized by Mormon friends and neighbors. Unfortunately, we lived in a fishbowl. Every family on our gated street belonged to the Church. Inevitably, members showed up on our doorstep, usually on Sundays. They tried to find out our problem. Some of these encounters were quite comical, others less so.

On one Sunday afternoon, the president of the priesthood quorum showed up on my doorstep. He visited our home at the request of the Bishop. I met him with a smile and asked him what I could do for him. He replied it was not what I could do for him, but what he wanted to do for me. He invited me back to church and told me how much he personally missed me. He said he liked me as a friend. I smiled back at him and said, "thank you." An awkward silence followed. He expected me to confide in him "why" I elected not to attend church. I knew whatever I said would immediately be reported back to the Bishop and used against me. I said nothing. He then repeated all he had said before and I followed it by thanking him for having concern for me. Again, silence. He repeated himself a third time, delivering the same rehearsed words, only with more feeling and he added he loved me. I again thanked him. Frustrated that I would not give him information to report back to his superior, he shook my hand and left. His purported love for me apparently ended as he walked out the door. I knew his visit came by way of assignment from the Bishop, and his figure never darkened my doorway again.

The same type of visit followed a few Sundays later, only this time the Bishop stopped by our home. He eerily repeated the same platitudes the previous quorum leader recited and offered the same love and friendship. In keeping with our commitment not to give our Mormon neighbors enough rope, or information in this case, to hang ourselves, I simply thanked him for his concern and told him we were doing just fine. Both of these leaders expressed a sense of entitlement to know the reason why we stopped attending church. Both left frustrated and unable to condemn us with our own words. They met the minimal level of commitment required by their superiors to fulfill their assignments by visiting us. They failed, however, to acquire their primary goal, to find out "our" problem.

Some of our closer acquaintances within the Church were summoned to the Bishop's office and grilled for information concerning us. We know this because these friends later told us of their experiences.

Many do-gooders within our congregation began to send their children over to our home to save our kids from the impending hell they expected us to endure. Envelopes with messages of concern, addressed to our children, slipped under our doors. One even slipped through the window of our son's room. JD passed the envelope to me. Its writer pleaded with our son, encouraging him to escape from our home and come back to church. Organized ambush prayer meetings greeted our daughter in members' homes. Ward members did not know what was going on with us, but that did not matter. Mormons are not taught proper boundaries. They are, in fact, taught personal boundaries represent an expression of sinful pride. This thinking clearly resounded in all the grossly inappropriate actions of entitlement expressed toward our children.

On yet another Sunday, the church primary president showed up on our doorstep. I answered the door and politely greeted her. She immediately asked to speak with JD. I asked what it regarded. She replied, "it doesn't involve you, I just want to speak with him." I kindly, but firmly informed her any business she had with my son, who is a minor, does indeed involve me. She persisted saying, "No, I just want to speak with him, alone." I had been the home teacher to this kind lady's family for nearly three years. As her home teacher, I delivered the Prophet's monthly message in her home. Home teachers are supposed to report back to the bishop if anything seems amiss in the families they visit. Now here she stood in my doorway presuming her rights, as a primary president, superseded my rights as a father. The entire concept of boundaries eluded her.

Eventually we placed a sign on our front door, which read, "Please do not disturb." We placed this sign on the door every Sunday; the day when members felt obligated to relieve the guilt they acquired attending church earlier in the day, by bothering us. They left us alone the rest of the days of the week. This sign did not deter some members who literally walked around the side of our home and knocked on a different door. We greeted all people amicably, but told no one the reasons we no longer attended.

When we attended our annual Home Owners Association meeting, the group offered a prayer with a blessing specifically singling out Linda and myself. We found out later they discussed how best to do missionary work on us. We began to feel trapped on our own street and in our neighborhood. We received phone calls from members who frankly could not take the gossip and wanted to know directly from us, our problem. The institutionalized arrogance of such inquiries only reinforced our growing resentment toward the Church and its upside down sense of entitlement. Never mind Joseph Smith chronically lied and secretly married under-aged girls and other men's wives, the Church now acted like a cult.

We decided the only way to disentangle ourselves from this awkward position required relocation. If you are a non-Mormon in a predominately Mormon neighborhood, the Mormons will ignore you only after they fail to convert you. If you are perceived to be remotely interested, they will hound you until they know whether you are with them or against them. Our actions presented a problem of uncertainty for Mormon members. We presented the picture of a perfect Mormon family, but without warning, we entirely stopped attending. We said nothing negative toward the Church, so the members were uncertain if they should openly condemn us. Uncertainty kills Mormonism. The growing wall of speculation by local members began to spread throughout the greater Mormon community. Old friends, who had not spoken to us in years, called us up to find out what was going on. Gossip, with its forked tongue, slithered through the wards in Mesa. We lived this way for a year before we finally moved out of Arizona.

When our neighbors found out we were moving to California it set off yet another round of hearsay. Members told us directly that California is an evil place and the people there are wicked. They advised us it would be the biggest mistake of our lives. As a Mormon, I lived with certainty, fear, and lacked boundaries. This mentality reflected perfectly back on us as members projected their fears of the unknown combined with the certainty of hell upon our children.

When the Bishop heard about our plans he again showed up at our door. He came unannounced. Unfortunately, JD answered the door. I joined him at the door, but the Bishop had already entered. The Bishop expressed his concern about our decision to move to California. He then looked JD right in the eyes and declared that if he, the Bishop, decided to move to California his son would never forgive him. Needless to say we came to expect meaningful, but ignorant church members to spew openly offensive things without the slightest recognition they completely overstepped our personal boundaries. They simply followed the pattern set by Joseph Smith when he requested some church members to give up their young daughters to him in secret polygamist wedding ceremonies.

With my newly acquired and personally troubling knowledge, I approached one of my best friends. He served in a bishopric in an adjacent town. I relayed my dream to him and he interpreted it. He kept it simple.

According to him, the big ship represented the Church, and the islands, the world. He explained, "When you recognized the Church is not what it claims to be, you saw the ship for what it is, and chose not to board. It distressed you that others did not recognize this. They either clung to the dangling ropes for dear life, or fell away from the Church only to be churned to death by the ships propellers." He further explained that when Linda waved to me wearing black gloves, it represented my uncertainty as to how she would react to all this new information.

To my surprise he already knew my big Mormon secret. He said he had wrestled with doubt some 32 years prior. He majored in Philosophy and concluded the Church contained false teachings shortly after arriving home from his mission. We had been very close friends and I demanded to know why he did not tell me some 17 years sooner. He responded saying that I rebuffed his hints, and was not ready to hear it. He said, on occasion, he "shot salvos across the bow of my ship," but like the captain in my dreams I simply ignored it and sailed forward, gripping the ropes of full belief in the Mormon ship.

But the question remained, with or without his input, how could I have been duped for so many years? I knew how to study. I earned three college degrees. I graduated Summa Cum Laude. I applied those skills in my studies of Mormon history. I get it now; the Mormon Church is not what it claims to be. The greater question is how so much of my life passed me by without recognizing the illusion? According to Freud, the secret of the strength of an illusion lies in the strength of those wishing it to be true. This may be accurate, because, even as the illusion began to break, I kept wishing that the Church could still be true. I had to be willing to entertain new thoughts and desire further education. It required acceptance of information even when it contradicted my previously held beliefs. When I decided to be honest with myself first, my journey toward understanding began.

I read church books, psychology books, cult awareness literature, and historical books. I studied the granddaddy of them all, philosophy. In short, I pursued a long overdue education in the liberal arts. At 47, the eyes of my understanding finally began to open. I left the dark covers of "belief" and awakened to the full light of reality. I could no longer live a lie, nor did I want to. I certainly don't have to be ashamed to state what now is quite obvious to me; the Church was never "true." It doesn't require faith or some mysterious knowledge from God to discover this simple truth. It only requires personal honesty and study of the history of the Church as it flowed from the pen of Joseph Smith himself. It also requires a stronger desire to know, rather than to simply believe without investigation.

This friend and I have since shared philosophies and worldviews heretofore banned from the Mormon mind. He remains a practicing Mormon despite his awareness of its false claims. He is operating under what we jointly call the "usefulness argument." His argument states that all roads in life lead to the same place, so why not pick one, which causes the least disruption in your life and is more useful for yourself...a philosophy eerily similar to Nietzsche, Heidegger and Hitler.

He believes most people follow their birth traditions because it is most useful to them. He argues if you are born a Muslim and find yourself in a Muslim culture, you should follow it because it is useful and you will have fewer conflicts with the culture at large.

I fully understand his argument. I also appreciate his valid fear that if he were to reveal his unbelief, he would face the wrath of the Church. He would be excommunicated and labeled a heretic and an apostate. He may even lose his wife in divorce. The Church teaches the only way she can go to the highest level of heaven is to be escorted by a "temple-worthy" Mormon husband. He would lose esteem and love from his children and grandchildren.

All Mormons are taught that those who leave the Church are slated for the deepest recesses of hell. The appellation they picked for such a place is "outer darkness."14 Such draconian ideology mixed with secret temple promises, along with the execution of the penalty, effectively keeps the faithful away from the light of reality and breeds divisiveness when pitted against family members. I understand his argument and his dilemma. I lament his predicament. I personally lived many of the consequences he fears. Fortunately, I have not been subjected to them all.

The beauty of Linda's physical appearance is only surpassed by her perceptive mind and honest heart. To her absolute credit she rose above the fray and continues to amaze me with her clear perceptions and personal honesty. Her story is perhaps more compelling than my own, and her own words are presented in Chapter 15 entitled: "A Crack in the Sky."

Cognitive dissonance theory15 is a psychological term, which describes a very real human trait. It states one's beliefs; behavior, emotions and even attire must be in sync, otherwise an internal mental conflict arises, "cognitive dissonance." When we learned the Church was not true it literally sickened us to attend weekly church meetings. The rampant denial and self-deception spewed from the pulpit, all drowning in interminable ignorance, became unbearable. The Church cannot survive in its present form unless a very false historical portrayal of Joseph Smith is believed. It is that simple.

A young man preparing to leave on his mission instructed the last priesthood meeting I attended. His eyes welled up as he described the tarring and feathering of Joseph Smith who, preach forgiveness the next day. Another brother commented that no man could have a friend as devoted and dear as Brother Joseph. Upon hearing this, I could no longer restrain myself. I raised my hand and queried, "Why did they tar and feather him?" After an awkward and uncomfortable pause, the priesthood leader in charge of the meeting turned around in his seat, looked me in the eye, shook his head and said: "Because Satan wanted to kill him." Others joined in condemning me for asking such a stupid question. I said no more. I knew I stood outside of their shared illusion; an illusion immersed in waters of ignorance and certainty.

For the record, Smith and his wife stayed at the farm home of John Johnson for seven months. Luke Johnson, John's elder son, organized and led the men who tarred and feathered Smith. Smith was rumored to have made inappropriate advances toward Miranda Johnson, the 15-year-old daughter who also lived in the home. Luke Johnson took the extraordinary step to invite Dr. Dennison to castrate Smith. Luke himself records that at the last minute the doctor's "heart failed him and he refused to operate." History also records Luke was right to have defended his sister's honor. Miranda Johnson became Joseph Smith's 10th wife just 4 years later. He married her in secret after she moved out of the Johnson home. He also married her without the knowledge of his own wife, Emma.16 Had I mentioned any of this history during my last priesthood meeting, I likely would have been tarred and feathered in the strongest condemnation allowed under U.S. law. Such is the strength of the Mormon illusion.

The usefulness argument is very appealing on several levels. But in my mind it carries a price I cannot bear. While it may have been easier to follow the path of my birth religion, something fundamental changed in me, which completely destroyed the usefulness argument. I knew better, and I felt betrayed due to the Church's purposeful withholding of information. I cannot consign my children to a life of illusion when I know better. If everyone is allowed to know better, then the usefulness argument may be justified. But where a person or institution precludes the opportunity for individual choice, I strongly disagree with the usefulness argument.

I jumped off the cloud of illusion and allowed my feet to feel the pebbled texture of reality between my toes. I set onto a path, leaving lies at my back and smiled at the possibilities ahead. This is a journey my children will be allowed to take.

I do not condemn my grandfather who joined the Mormon Church as a young uneducated Australian bricklayer. Nor do I condemn the actions and motives of my mother, who joined the Church and married the man who baptized her. They followed their hearts and understanding, as they knew it. Unfortunately, neither of them had information available to make an informed decision regarding the true life of Joseph Smith. They were denied informed consent and full disclosure. They, like myself, were only given an extremely sanitized and naive version of his life.

Since I left the church, I have met dozens of happy people who have recognized similar religious illusions in their own lives at a much younger age. What took me so long?

CHAPTER 7

A Bountiful Harvest

The power to question is the basis of all human progress.
Indira Gandhi

The echoing chaos of prepubescent 7th graders man-handled by upperclassmen struck fear in the hearts of the incoming innocent. Hard linoleum floors stretched from locker to locker down the darkened corridors of the old armory-turned-junior high school. Rows of young boys lined the floor with their noses engaged in intense penny-pushing races down the halls. Upperclassmen provided the necessary motivation with swift kicks to the rear. These and other degrading experiences marked my first days of junior high school in the tough and rural 1970's town of Bountiful, Utah.

Bountiful lies 15 miles north of Salt Lake City. The obligatory mark of small town anywhere, a big cement "B", clings to the mountainside overlooking the mostly Mormon enclave. Short chain-linked fences separated the orchards and thick green grass of my childhood. But such borders only marked the end of where one boy mowed and another began. My young friends and I knew no such boundaries in our roaming games and play. We crossed fences and climbed trees. We ate cherries, apricots and pears at will. All youth exercised this entitlement in my "Mayberry." The only barrier we did not cross was one we did not know existed, an invisible wall of silence.

Mr. Johansen was a short, portly teacher with a receding hairline and wrinkly white skin. An uglier man I have never seen, though his true ugliness had little to do with his unkind physical features. At age 14, I demonstrated the audacity to show up to his class unprepared for an oral presentation. An educator of his caliber would not tolerate such indolence. The next hour of my life lasted for many years. As if waiting for the precise moment to commit murder, Mr. Johansen seized the opportunity to masterfully destroy my personal esteem and social standing. In a tour de force, my Utah history teacher inflicted deep psychological humiliation on an ever-shrinking boy seated in the front row. His next moves portended a dark episode my memory would hold in chains forever. It held me and I held it.

Mr. Johansen's normal pedantic manner gave way, and his face reddened with rage, as he flared into a verbal rant. Unfortunately for me, the attack was not limited to a review of my class performance, but included gross and demeaning speculation on my past and future. The attack ended only after I sheepishly grabbed my ankles in front of the class and received the "board of education," which I bore with relief knowing the bell would soon sound. Abuse doled out by upperclassmen appeared microscopic when compared to the much larger and widely held practice among the erudite of our small piece of Zion.

Only time, distance, and technology loosened the 35-year-old chains empowering those sordid memories. I made my peace with Mr. Johansen. As he has long since died, this reconciliation only occurred in my mind. Something happened in my life that caused my long-held spite for Mr. Johansen to melt away into a feeling of sorrow for the poor man's predicament. I finally studied Utah history and suddenly it all made sense.

One can only imagine the acidic frustration etched upon the psyche of a teacher hired to illuminate a subject that he was not allowed to teach. Utah history, as it was presented in Mr.

Johansen's class, had little to do with the actual history of Utah. His purview over the subject matter precluded him from presenting any information considered to breach the wall of silence imposed upon all who dwelt in the richness of Bountiful. The prevailing enforcers of social and cultural norms masterfully erected this wall of silence. Bountiful, a Mormon town, sat comfortably nestled in the palm of the Church. A prominent Mormon leader Apostle Boyd K. Packer perhaps best sums up the construction of this wall. When speaking to educators in the history department at BYU he said:

*"there is no such thing as an accurate or objective history of the Church" "The Lord made it very clear that some things are to be taught selectively and some things are to be given only to those who are worthy... It may be read by those not mature enough for "advanced history"... You do not do well to see that it is disseminated." "Some things that are true are not very useful."*1

And

*"Church history can be so interesting and so inspiring as to be a very powerful tool indeed for building faith. If not properly written or properly taught, it may be a faith destroyer."... "In the Church we are not neutral. We are one-sided. There is a war going on, and we are engaged in it. We are therefore obliged to give preference to and protect all that is represented in the gospel of Jesus Christ, and we have made covenants to do it."*1

The covenants to which he refers are made behind the secretive doors of Mormon temples. This self-serving stance on history comes into direct conflict when one endeavors to study Utah history, since Utah history and Mormon history are inseparably connected. According to Mormon leaders, Mr. Johansen, likely a Mormon himself, made a covenant only to teach parts of Utah history that are "faith promoting" to the Mormon Church. The vast majority of the residents of Bountiful were Mormons. Had Mr. Johansen taught actual Utah history, his disobedience to the covenant, the wall of silence, would have quickly been met with ecclesiastic reprisals.

Lest one think this attitude unique to Apostle Packer, consider the words of another Mormon Apostle and former President of BYU, Dallin H. Oaks, when he said in referring to events from Utah's history:

*"It's wrong to criticize leaders of the church, even if the criticism is true."*2

Can history be portrayed void of any "criticism [that] is true?" Yet members are lead to believe that only those influenced by Satan begin to think for themselves and criticize Mormon leaders.

*"He (Satan) wins a great victory when he can get members of the Church to speak against their Leaders and to do their own thinking."*3

Surely this dilemma faced not only Mr. Johansen, but also all faithful Mormons in the heart of Utah. For Mormons who don't feel obligated to follow the words of mere Apostles, consider a Utah history teacher's dilemma when he hears the words of the modern day Mormon Prophet Gordon B. Hinckley. When commenting on the murderous atrocities perpetrated by Mormons on the Fancher wagon train at the Mountain Meadows in Utah, Hinckley proclaimed:

"No one can explain what happened in these meadows 142 years ago. We may speculate, but we do not know. We do not understand it. We cannot comprehend it. We can only say the past is long since gone. It cannot be recalled. It cannot be changed. It is time to leave the entire matter in the hands of God, who deals justly in all things. His is a wisdom far beyond our own."... *"Let the book of the past be closed!"*4

Given the Mormon Church mandate to avoid Church criticism, even if it is true, Prophet Hinckley's desire to "close the book of the past" is understandable. This book of the past reeks of self-serving obfuscation, particularly when a mountain of evidence, or perhaps in this case, a meadow of evidence remains. Mormon bulldozers accidentally unearthed bullet ridden skulls when they attempted to place a monument at the site of the massacre. A monument not meant as an apology for a known history, but rather as Hinckley stated: "*It cannot be recalled.*"

Volumes of documents, journals, letters and diaries lend valuable insight into the events of that fateful day, September 11, 1859. On that black day in Utah history, local Mormon leaders arranged for and participated in the slaughter of over 120 innocent non-Mormon pioneers on their way to California when they stopped in Utah. The Mormon leader, and strangely enough, the only individual found guilty of the crime, John D. Lee, wrote a death-bed biography and confessional of the entire affair, including his own involvement. The fact Prophet Hinckley's official proclamation denies that this history can be known underscores a callous disregard and reflects an institutionalized arrogance in the most pejorative sense.

To construct a wall of silence in the face of such overwhelming evidence, Prophet Hinckley clearly spoke out of both sides of his mouth. In the same speech he declared:

"*No one can explain what happened in these meadows 142 years ago, We may speculate, but we do not know. We do not understand it. We cannot comprehend it. We can only say the past is long since gone. It cannot be recalled…*"

Hinckley completely contradicted himself, declaring, there is a history of this event, he studied it, and he concluded Brigham Young was not involved. The exact quote reads as follows:

*"I sit in the chair that Brigham Young occupied President of the Church at the time of the tragedy. I have read very much of the history of what occurred here. There is no question in my mind that he was opposed to what happened."*4

If this history cannot be known, then how could Hinckley draw such a favorable conclusion toward Brigham Young? Mormon history only exists when it favors current Church position. If it does not, a new history is taught, or alternatively, silence is invoked.

Mike Wallace interviewed Prophet Hinckley on the television program "60 Minutes." The following exchange took place:

Wallace: *"From 1830 to 1978 Blacks could not become Priests in the Mormon Church, Right?"*
Hinckley: *"That's correct."*
Wallace: *"Why?"*
Hinckley: *"Because, the leader of the church, at that time, interpreted that doctrine that way."*
Wallace: *"Church policy had it that Blacks had the mark of Cain. Brigham Young said, Cain slew his brother and the Lord put a mark upon him which is the flat nose and black skin."*
Hinckley: *"It's behind us, look, that's behind us. Don't worry about those little flicks of history."*5

To refer to 148 years of ugly discrimination perpetrated against an entire race of people by Mormon leaders as "little flicks of history" is unconscionable. But perhaps even worse is to further justify it by claiming God started it in the first place as a form of punishment.

Indeed, the unbreakable wall of silence remains as prominent and poignant to Utah's history today. That may have been the dilemma inciting Mr. Johansen's rage. A substantial, colorful and meaningful amount of Utah history did not fit into the limited scope of the Mormon definition of history. This became Mr. Johansen's problem. He labored under a holy mandate to conceal it.

Under Mr. Johansen's tutelage, we memorized the counties of Utah, the state flower, state bird, state emblem and we sang the State song entitled "Utah We Love Thee." We memorized all the governors of the state. We learned about the states natural resources, its geographic size in comparison to other states. We did not, however, learn anything about its rich prehistoric/dinosaur history dating back millions of years, a slight oversight which incidentally contradicts Mormon founder Joseph Smith's teaching that the earth is less than 7,000 years old. Nor did we learn about Utah's more recent history regarding the large displacement of Native American populations by Mormon emigrants beginning in 1845.

He said nothing regarding Brigham Young's polygamist mandates:

"Now, if any of you will deny the plurality of wives, and continue to do so, I promise that you will be damned!"[6]

Nothing was said about the Edmond Tucker Act of Congress of 1877, which mandated the abolishment of polygamy in the territory of Utah as not only a condition for Statehood, but with the threat of US troops invading and confiscating Mormon Church assets. Johansen said nothing about the next Mormon Prophet, John Taylor, and his defiance of United States laws. Taylor proclaimed he received a revelation from God declaring polygamy God's will, and that it would not be abolished: *"Under the banner of Heaven."* John Taylor died while in hiding, still living the polygamous lifestyle.

Teacher Johansen neglected to tell us the next Mormon Prophet, Wilford Woodruff, recanted John Taylor's revelation from God and reissued a new manifesto from heaven. Woodruff publicly rescinded polygamy to appease pressures from the US doctrine of Manifest Destiny, which appeared to be a greater manifestation of God's will, than the local prophet's polygamy prophesies.

Mr. Johansen, bound by silence, dared not broach the unsavory subject of the bloody Utah Reformation, which occurred between 1855-1859. During this time, Mormon Prophet Brigham Young taught, condoned and practiced honor killings; under a doctrine he called "Blood Atonement." Church leaders followed his lead and murdered member "sinners," including those who tried to leave the Church. According to blood thirsty Brigham Young and his counselors, this murderous doctrine benefited members:

*"I say, that there are men and women that I would advise to go to the President immediately and ask him to appoint a committee to attend to their case; and then let a place be selected, and let that committee shed their blood."*7

*"I have known a great many men who have left this Church for whom there is not chance whatever for exaltation, but if their blood had been spilled, it would have been better for them."*8

*"I know, when you hear my brethren telling about cutting people off from the earth, that you consider it is strong doctrine; but it is to save them, not to destroy them."*9

*"If they are covenant breakers, we need a place designated, where we can shed their blood...They are a perfect nuisance, and I want them cut off, and the sooner it is done the better."*10

*"I know that here are transgressors, who, if they knew themselves, and the only condition upon which they can obtain forgiveness, would beg of their brethren to shed their blood, that the smoke thereof might ascend to God as an offering to appease the wrath that is kindled against them, and that the law might have its course. I will say further; I have had men come to me and offer their lives to atone for their sins."*11

"This is loving our neighbor as ourselves; if he needs help, help

*him; and if he wants salvation and it is necessary to spill his blood on the earth in order that he may be saved, spill it. Any of you who understand the principles of eternity, if you have sinned a sin requiring the shedding of blood, except the sin unto death, would not be satisfied nor rest until your blood should be spilled, that you might gain that salvation you desire. That is the way to love mankind."*12

When Linda and I repeated similar blood oaths in the temple, we in essence, gave the Church permission to extend the execution of the penalty upon us. The oaths repeated the threat of revealing temple names, signs and penalties with the words: "Rather than do so, I would suffer my life to be taken." These same phrases justified Brigham Young's reign of terror over isolated members in the Utah Territory. His proclamations invoked the imminent wrath of his vengeful God. Rumors of his atrocities finally leaked out of the territory and into the ears of the post Civil War Congress. It took the fortitude and courage of one of the 56+ wives of Brigham Young to shine the light of hope on those who suffered under his reign.

It may not have been important to know that 19 of Brigham's wives preceded him in death, 10 divorced him, 23 survived him and 4 are unaccounted for, or to know they were often fed and clothed out of the coffers of the Church. Yet, to know one of the women who left his authoritative dominion, Eliza Ann Young, is to know the genesis of Utah as a State. This information should have been taught front and center in our "Utah State History" class.

Some women are endowed with an extraordinary ability to reject abuse from the hands of men. Eliza Ann exemplified this trait. In her autobiography, *Wife No.19*, Eliza Ann left Brigham, fled to the east and unabashedly exposed horrific abuses, which are normal part and parcel to the practice of polygamy. She exposed this male dominated culture targeting prepubescent girls, presumably in accordance with God's holy plan. Crusty lips of old men sanctified themselves through obedience to unquestionable revelations, manifested in the holy marital rape of young girls.

Eliza Ann Young escaped Utah and encouraged Congress to enact the Edmond Act of 1877, and the subsequent Edmond Tucker Act of 1878, which finally forced Prophet Woodruff to acquiesce and publicly denounce polygamy, which in turn, paved the way for Utah Statehood.

How important is polygamy to Utah history? In 1890 the Prophet of the Church publicly condemned the practice, yet condoned it in private for at least another 10 years. The main body of the Mormon Church secretly maintained the practice behind temple doors. The practice continued with unbridled vigor throughout Utah, the Western States and Canada. The Mormons established colonies in Mexico as a safe haven for their polygamy. In fact, Presidential candidate and politician Mitt Romney is a product of that secretive polygamy system. The wall of silence even applies to Romney, who will never, as long as he remains an active Mormon, speak openly about the nefarious escapades of the instigator of Mormon polygamy, Joseph Smith. If Romney remains silent, he becomes part of the wall of silence. He has taken upon himself the same oath and covenant of silence in the Mormon temple just as I did.

Male attitudes toward early Mormon women may best be reflected in the words of then Apostle Heber C. Kimball:

*"I think no more of taking another wife then I do of buying a cow."*13

Speaking to a group of departing missionaries Apostle Kimball complained:

*"The brother missionaries have been in the habit of picking out the prettiest women for themselves before they get here, and bringing on the ugly ones for us; hereafter you have to bring them all here before taking any of them, and let us all have a fair shake."*14

This attitude of male superiority still slips through lips of current Mormon leaders. Prophet Hinckley gaffed:

*"Men, treasure your wives, they are your most valuable possession."*15

To this day, Mormon women are not allowed to hold priesthood power, and require the approval of a man for any important Church decision.

In a similar modern-day nightmare, the testimony of a survivor of an equivalent abusive system, a system that still persists to this day in Utah, Arizona and Texas, came forward and testified to the same behavior by the FLDS Mormon Prophet, Warren Jeffs. Jeffs currently is serving a sentence of two, 5-year terms in prison for facilitating the marriage of a minor girl to her first cousin against her wishes. Jeffs' behavior pales in comparison to the abuses perpetrated against women by Mormon Prophets Joseph Smith and Brigham Young.

When I read this history, after my lifetime in Mormonism, I wonder how I ever accepted Brigham Young as a true Prophet of God. His evil behavior and bloody reformation far outweighs those acts of Warren Jeffs. I clearly comprehend Jeffs is no more than a control freak who uses religion as a cover to gain power, money and sex. Why then should I search to justify Brigham Young's overtly immoral behavior? Today I purposefully avoid telling people I graduated from BYU. I don't want its stigma attached to me. I instead talk about the other two universities outside of Utah from which I graduated. I find nothing honorable about Young's life, and I'm embarrassed to be associated with a University that actively suppresses information from its students and stifles the flow of knowledge from its professors.

To graduate from "Brigham Young" University seems oxymoronic. Brigham Young scorned formal education. He took pride in his ability to use his own common sense. He was an ardent Methodist before he fell under Smith's spell. Smith easily manipulated him into following. When Young began to "speak in tongues," a practice he acquired as a religious seeker, Smith quickly praised him and declared it a gift of God. Young became one of Smith's top leaders. Smith constantly created new organizations within his church to allow many men to feel empowered as top leaders. Joseph Smith talked Brigham Young into polygamy. After Smith's death, Young declared himself the new Prophet and persuaded the greater part of the Church members to follow him across the plains to settle the Utah territory.

Emma Smith stayed behind with a lesser number of members. The members who stayed in Nauvoo did not practice polygamy and were not run out of their homes. Emma Smith stayed in the mansion Joseph built for her with Church funds. Emma outlived Brigham Young.16

Once Young geographically isolated his followers he began to reveal his lack of education. He brutally proclaimed bizarre doctrines, such as "Personal Blood Atonement" and the "Adam-is-God theory."17 Young, in his crudely prosaic fashion, declared:

*"So it is with regard to the inhabitants of the sun. Do you think it is inhabited? I rather think it is. Do you think there is any life there? No question of it; it was not made in vain. It was made to give light to those who dwell upon it, and to other planets; and so will this earth when it is celestialized."*18

In the name of God, he consolidated his power; built Utah's first whiskey distillery;19 married scores of women and girls; sent internal threats abroad to colonized lands far from home; and released the "Danites" to kill those who openly opposed him. The Danites, also known as the Daughters of Zion, a euphemism to disguise the fact they were all men, took a secret oath of allegiance to Joseph Smith. Smith organized these ruffians in Missouri. Danite's sworn allegiance required them to do whatever the Prophet commanded, regardless of whether it was right or wrong. The secret oath they took read as follows:

"In the name of Jesus Christ, the Son of God, I do solemnly obligate myself ever to regard the Prophet, and the First Presidency of the Church of Jesus Christ of Latter Day Saints, as the Supreme Heads of the Church on Earth, and to obey them in all things the same as the Supreme God; that I will stand by my brethren in danger or difficulty, and will uphold the Presidency, right or wrong: and that I will ever conceal, and never reveal, the secret purposes of this society, called the Daughters of Zion. Should I ever do the same, I hold my life as the forfeiture, in a caldron of boiling oil."[20]

After taking this oath, Smith then anointed them with oil and blessed them:

"...and set you apart, for the holy calling, that you may consecrate the riches of the Gentiles to the House of Israel, bring swift destruction upon apostate sinners, and execute the decrees of Heaven without fear of what man can do unto you. So mote [shall] it be. Amen."[20]

Given Smith's mandate, the Danites threatened and used up (murder) dissenters who challenged his authority. They plundered homes and farms of "Gentiles," non-Mormons in Missouri, until Missourians finally retaliated and drove them from their state. Brigham Young maintained this secret organization of dragoons in Utah. John D. Lee, the only Mormon prosecuted for the Mountain Meadow Massacre, confessed he too swore this same oath. William Hickman made the same confession near the end of his life in his book entitled, "Brigham's Destroying Angel: Bill Hickman, the Danite Chief of Utah."[21]

Additionally, "The Law of Vengeance" remained a secret temple oath until 1927. It required members to: *"avenge the blood of the prophets upon this nation."*[22]

Even today, secret oaths of loyalty are taken in Mormon temples. I took similar oaths when I attended the temple prior to my mission. All missionaries are required to attend the temple prior to their missions. Before I knew what was happening, I took the following oath:

"Each of you bring your right arm to the square. You and each of you covenant... that you do <u>consecrate yourselves, your time, talents, and everything with which the Lord has blessed you, or with which he may bless you, to the Church of Jesus Christ of Latter-day Saints</u>, for the building up of the Kingdom of God on the earth and for the establishment of Zion".... *"Each of you bow your head and say "yes.""*22

I further promised to never reveal temple secrets or: *"Rather than do so, I would suffer my life to be taken."* I took upon myself the same blood oaths my father and grandfather were obliged to take. I received them under the secret Mormon edict, which described in gruesome detail slitting my throat, cutting open my chest, and disemboweling my belly. As missionaries we never revealed these blood oaths to our investigators. After all, who would join the Church if they knew what lay at its heart?

The graphic, suicide-like, blood oaths were finally removed in 1990 due to decreased temple attendance, but the same oaths of loyalty to the Mormon Church remain today.23

This ugly, but true history explains the remarks of Apostle Russell M Nelson, who, when referring to Mormon history said:

*"Indeed, in some instances, the merciful companion to truth is silence; some truths are best left unsaid."*24

As the Mormon "wall of silence" began to crumble around me, I understood the evil acts of the early prophets and the reason they started secret covenants. I became ashamed of true Mormon history. No wonder it required a good scrubbing to be presentable to children and investigators.

When I recited those secret blood oaths of loyalty, I had no idea they involved the complicit cover up of a history kept hidden from my eyes. I rescind any and all oaths I have taken without informed consent and full disclosure. The Mormon religion requires too many secrets to be kept, both past and present. They are as sick as their secrets.

Only when I allowed myself to seek and see information did I learn that in every state Joseph Smith practiced polygamy, it was not only illegal, but also cut against the social mores of his day. Smith justified his affairs in the name of religion, and hid his nefarious rendezvous behind oaths of secrecy. Safely behind the Wasatch Mountains, isolated in the Utah Territory, Brigham Young, in his words *"Let the cat out of the bag,"* and preached men could not attain heaven unless they too practiced polygamy.[25]

Utah history is still being written. Currently Mormons are taught polygamy is indeed the very order of heaven. Mormon men are, to this day, sealed to multiple heavenly wives in Mormon temples. When Apostle Dallin Oaks' first wife died, he remarried and was "sealed" to his second wife in heaven. According to Mormon scripture, he will become a polygamist God.[26] (Section 132 of the Doctrine and Covenants is still Mormon scripture. It openly declares polygamy is still God's law for men. It is also interesting to note women cannot be sealed to more than one man.) Only prevailing sentiments and laws of the United States holds overt Mormon systematic abuse of women at bay.

Mormonism continues to be a male dominated and politically active organization. In the 1970's, the Church fought against the ERA, Equal Rights Amendment for women. Mormon women received their marching orders from their male leaders, who used the church service organization to work against the amendment's ratification. Political influence wielded by Mormon women helped defeat a gain for women's equality. Ironically, during this time the Church increased its emphasis on women's "proper role," stressing wifely submission and domestic duties.

Mr. Johansen must have suffered not being able to talk about how Utah became a state in his Utah history class. Had he been free to speak, he could have told us that within the city of my junior high school, Ute Indians, men, women and children were gathered up by Mormon settlers, held in captivity, then upon the order of Salt Lake Mormon leaders, slaughtered.27 This atrocity occurred within shouting distance of the very classroom in which Johansen did "not" teach us Utah history.

In yet another irony, Utah gets its name from the Native American tribe slaughtered by Mormon pioneers, the Ute Indians. Could Mr. Johansen dare explain where Utah got its name? Could he speak about any of the numerous abuses perpetrated upon the Indians of the Utah territories by the hands of Mormon settlers? Could he have the courage to mention the bloody Utah reformation, which led to an atmosphere, which culminated in the slaughter of over 120 men, women and children at Mountain Meadows in South Central Utah? (Those younger than age 8 were spared and adopted into Mormon families, as it was thought they would not have sufficient memory to be able to testify of the massacre.) Could he dare recount the murders of the Aikin party in the spring of 1857 by Danites Orin Porter Rockwell and William Hickman?28 Alas, Mr. Johansen would be relegated to take solace in the knowledge that he firmly implanted, in the incoming innocent, a sure understanding that Utah is a major producer of copper.

I do not blame the neglect of my seventh grade Utah history teacher to mention Mormon history. Had he exercised his constitutional right to free speech, it most assuredly would have ended with academic and social death, not to mention excommunication and public shunning. Such practices continue to this day. Six BYU professors were fired, and then excommunicated or disfellowshiped for attempting to teach actual Utah/Mormon history at BYU. They have become known as the "September Six."29

The Catholic Church forced Galileo to recant his heretical theory; that the earth revolves around the sun. Their prevailing doctrine maintained the earth as center of the universe, with all else revolving around it. Galileo famously said: *"And yet it moves."* In that same light, Utah's history moves, inextricably linked to Mormonism, and bound by a wall of silence to most of its inhabitants.

Utah history is dynamically unfolding before our very eyes. Brigham Young taught:

*"Shall I tell you the law of God in regard to the African race? If the white man who belongs to the chosen seed mixes his blood with the seed of Cain, the penalty, under the law of God, is death on the spot. This will always be so."*30

In 1978, Mormon leaders finally acquiesced and removed the racial ban against African Americans, and Blacks worldwide, to hold Mormon Priesthood.31 Outside pressures forced the Church to change their discriminatory policy toward Blacks. The threat of an NCAA boycott against BYU basketball, due to the Church's discriminatory stance, immediately preceded the 1978 revelation. At the same time, Jimmy Carter and the IRS made it clear to Prophet Kimball that the Church's tax-exempt status would be revoked unless their racist policy changed. To add insult to injury, the Church had just completed a temple in Sao Paulo, Brazil, and Church leaders could not tell which members carried "black blood." They were not sure which members to keep out.32

Yet even today, powerful forces strain to retain old policies, as Blacks and Latinos are not reflected in the upper echelons of Mormon Church leadership, and women are still subservient to men.

Mr. Johansen was relegated to bits and pieces of almost meaningless factoids. The wall of silence that stood firm against the backdrop of my childhood remains today. Waves of pupils, who should be planted in fields of amber grain, are instead seeded with misdirection and silence. Tough upperclassmen and silent history teachers are no match for the fertile Mormon grounds upon which Bountiful reaped a harvest of abuse by proxy for incoming innocence. When I turned 14, silent tongues withheld a meaningful history from me, leaving me in the dark. When Joseph Smith turned 27 he rewrote his own history. Smith retroactively claimed, that at age 14, he received further light and knowledge from God. Mr. Johansen never was the problem.

A child raised in Utah must tread a path past hundreds like Mr. Johansen. I remained ignorant to the true history of Utah and the Mormon Church for the next 33 years of my life. Throughout my secular education and matriculation at universities other than BYU, my critical thinking toward religion was kept in check by weekly recitals of our shared Mormon illusions. We endured our three-hour meetings on Sundays, along with intentionally endless lists of requirements to become perfect. This tactic, employed by cults, keeps adherents too busy to stop and think.

In many ways, I am the product of secret oaths of silence taken by those who passed before me. Worse yet, I actively soldiered and blindly propagated a false Church history to anyone who would listen. I did so under the banner of Mormonism.

*"We are instructed to be like children, who are willing to be taught and then to act without first demanding full knowledge."*33

The active allegiance to blind faith, supported by a culture bent on maintaining ignorance through information control, goes a long way to explain my young and unreasoning mind. But does it explain how I, as an adult, set aside reason and credulity for a rather bizarre set of claims made by an adulterous man named Joseph Smith?

CHAPTER 8

The Forer Effect

You'll never discover the truth until your desire to "know" supersedes your desire to "believe."

All the forces of evil combined for a perfect accident. The truck wore slick back tires. The windshield wipers groaned against crystallizing ice. The brake cylinder dripped its last hope for a moderate stop, and the 17-year-old wheelman sat underdressed in the face of hardening grey skies.

The two-toned green Chevy truck rotated violently on the slick black ice. It spun in front of oncoming traffic. An adrenaline rush pumped fear through the vocal cords as pleas for heavenly help finally found an ear in the form of a solitary wooden post. The passenger side door slammed violently against the wood, the only obstacle between the road and a steep canyon below.

After high school, I attended one semester at the University of Utah. I loved to ski and tinker with my car. My grades reflected my utter lack of commitment to higher education. After one semester I quit school and worked full-time instead. I needed to save money for my upcoming mission.

I pushed wheelchairs for a night job at St. Marks Hospital. I felt fortunate to have found a full-time day job delivering parts all over Salt Lake City for the Utah Power and Supply Company. Between these two jobs I earned more money for my mission than ever before. I skied on weekends and ran with friends between jobs. I attended the farewell meeting (a church meeting to say good-bye to young men or young women departing for their missions) of my best friend Gary. Watching him speak in front of his large home congregation made me feel inadequate for my upcoming mission.

Full of hormones, I asked Gary if I could date his ex-girlfriend while he was gone. Her name was Cindy. Cindy's clear, fair complexion stood in sharp contrast to the long loosely curled black hair that draped her shoulders and back. Gary gave me his blessing but warned me that she liked to kiss a lot. Not having dated a girl who liked to "kiss a lot," made me feel a certain inclination to date her. After all, Gary was my friend and he was still worthy to go on a mission.

Cindy kissed like a mad fool. She scared me. In one very uncomfortable moment, only the console on my 72 Camaro, stood between me, and my curly-haired passenger's burning desire. Having barely escaped attack, I never called her again. I understood Gary's warning.

I share my brush with Cindy's front seat assault only to invite you into the mind of a young man preparing for a mission. Had I partaken in Cindy's wanton desires I knew there would eventually have been rather unpleasant consequences. I knew at the very moment she grabbed my hand and tried to place it upon her breast I would have to confess the whole sordid affair to my bishop. I knew my pending mission might be postponed due to immoral behavior and I feared the shame it would openly bring. Despite this near miss, I did not feel properly prepared to serve God on a mission. I still felt I was not good enough.

One Saturday morning I secretly fasted and prayed to God. I asked God to help prepare me for my mission. The following Monday at 4:30 p.m. my work truck began to spin out of control.

Wasatch Boulevard winds high along the mountainside

overlooking the Salt Lake Valley. As the truck hit the sole wooden guardrail, I felt an immediate sense of relief. My prayers had been answered, until the guardrail gave way and the truck slid sideways off the edge of the mountain. My seat belt remained unfastened.

The next few minutes played out in slow motion. My body flew back and forth like a heavy shoe in a dryer. The wheel wrenched out of my hands. The truck progressively built up speed as it tumbled down the uneven canyon wall. Mercifully, my mind went blank as my body exploded through the driver's side window. I landed on a pile of rocks, which awoke me to my predicament. My head faced down the slope and I watched the tops of trees shake and bend as the truck made its grisly way down the canyon. I could not see out of my right eye, and I could not move. I knew other motorists saw me go over because I had circled right in front of oncoming traffic. I lay motionless in excruciating pain.

Within a short time I heard rocks shifting above me. The panicked voice of a man out of breath blurted, "Are you alive?" By the time he reached me snow flurries had dusted me in white. A stream of blood pooled around me.

A rescue team eventually carried me out of the canyon and whisked me off to the very hospital where I was scheduled to work that same evening. Only persistent pain alleviated the embarrassment I felt when scissors snipped off my clothes in front of the cute emergency room nurses with whom I flirted just days earlier. The fact I was shivering and lost a lot of blood did not add to my confidence. They carted me off to intensive care for one night, followed by special care for a week, then moved me to a regular hospital room for two more weeks. While in the hospital, I asked my dad and brother-in-law to give me a priesthood blessing to heal me. They did, and I believed I would be made whole. My dad asked me if I wanted to sue the company for their neglect of the work truck. It had bald tires and a broken master break cylinder. I was just happy to be alive. I felt it would demean me to even entertain such a thought.

Besides, my boss had brought me flowers along with a get-well card. In addition, I secretly believed if I sued him, then God would not honor the blessing to make me whole again.

I could not work as my right eye remained under bandages, and I carried my right arm in a sling. I also wore a brace to stabilize my back. I remained in this condition for several months, during which time I read the Book of Mormon and other Church scriptures. In an odd way I believed God directed this horrific accident to help me prepare for my mission. I held extreme confidence in the blessing my dad gave me in the hospital.

I felt disappointed when the bandages were removed from my face. I could no longer wrinkle my most expressive eyebrow, and it hovered above its normal resting place. I also had a large scar, which ran down my forehead and across my cheek. This depressed me for several weeks until an old perfumed lady at the drug store told me the scar made me look handsome.

All Mormons know the meaning of a "Patriarchal Blessing." It is a special blessing given by a distinguished older gentleman in the Church who has specifically been called to render such blessings. They are given to kids around age 14. Children look forward to this blessing as it is purported to be a special message from God directed specifically toward that individual. It is recorded on paper and carried by its recipient for life. It is used as a spiritual guide.

My patriarchal blessing told me everything I hoped to hear. The Patriarch told me I would go on a mission and be successful; I would return home and find a special person to marry; I would have children; I would have grandchildren who would rise up and honor my name; and I would become a leader in the Church. My entire life I assumed these things came to pass because God inspired my Stake Patriarch. My patriarchal blessing was a special revelation just for me.

When my eyes opened to the reality of the history of Joseph Smith, and current motives of the church he established, I asked myself how my Stake Patriarch could have known so much about me personally if he was not a man of God? I found the answer in "The Forer Effect."

In 1948 Bertram Forer, a psychologist, gave a personality test to his students. He then gave them a personality analysis supposedly based on the test's results. He invited each of them to rate the analysis on a scale of 0 (very poor) to 5 (excellent) as it applied to them. The students gave themselves an average of 4.26. This indicated this test was highly successful in predicting their personalities. He then revealed each student had been given the exact same analysis, or results, which he randomly picked out of the horoscope column of his local newspaper. The analysis all students received reads as follows:

"You have a need for other people to like and admire you, and yet you tend to be critical of yourself. While you have some personality weaknesses you are generally able to compensate for them. You have considerable unused capacity that you have not turned to your advantage. Disciplined and self-controlled on the outside, you tend to be worrisome and insecure on the inside. At times you have serious doubts as to whether you have made the right decision or done the right thing. You prefer a certain amount of change and variety and become dissatisfied when hemmed in by restrictions and limitations. You also pride yourself as an independent thinker; and do not accept others' statements without satisfactory proof. But you have found it unwise to be too frank in revealing yourself to others. At times you are extroverted, affable, and sociable, while at other times you are introverted, wary, and reserved. Some of your aspirations tend to be rather unrealistic."

The Forer effect refers to the tendency of people to rate sets of statements as *highly accurate* for them personally, even though the statements could apply to just about anyone.1

His test has been repeated hundreds of times with psychology students and the average is still around 4.2 out of 5, or 84% accurate. Later studies have found subjects give higher accuracy ratings if the following are true:

The subject believes the analysis applies only to them.
The subject believes in the authority of the evaluator.
The analysis lists mainly positive traits about them.
The analysis says things people want to hear.

In short, Forer convinced people he could successfully read their character. The Forer Effect explains why I believed my patriarchal blessing. Indeed, my blessing met all the criteria above.

As children we are told not to share our patriarchal blessings with anyone else, supposedly because they are a sacred gift given only to us, by God. I have since come to find out children are asked not to share their blessings with others because they are so similar. This, of course, takes away from the mystique surrounding this fortune telling effect. The Forer Effect also explains why so many people believe pseudo sciences "work" such as astrology, astro-therapy, biorhythms, cartomancy, chiromancy, the enneagram, fortune telling, graphology, rumplogy, etc. It is also called the Barnum effect, cold reading, confirmation bias, Myers-Briggs Type Indicator, selective thinking, self-deception, subjective validation and wishful thinking.2-8

It explains phrenology, predicting your strengths based upon the bumps on your head, a con my grandfather Reuben and his parents fell for in Australia. It explains virtually all priesthood blessing given by Mormon men to people in times of distress. Mormon men are taught they have special priesthood powers. They use these "heavenly" powers in the following way:

The Priesthood authority figures place their hands upon the head of the sick or afflicted, at their request, thereby showing they, the sick, already believe in Mormon priesthood powers.

They then call the sick or afflicted by their full name, making the blessing appear specific to them.

They state they are giving the blessing by the power of the Holy Priesthood of God, reinforcing the belief in the authority in the mind of the recipient.

They pronounce a blessing upon the recipient, which usually tells them they will eventually get better, which is exactly what they want to hear.

They reconfirm God is specifically aware of them and is watching over them, again making the blessing specific to them and telling them what they want to hear.

They close the blessing with the usual just-in-case caveat, which states, if it does not work, it is not God's fault, but the recipient's fault, due to their lack of faith.

They close in the name of Jesus Christ, reconfirming authority.

I have been sick dozens of times in my life. With or without a blessing I survived. I witnessed a baby die shortly after she received a blessing promising a full recovery. Perhaps the infant just didn't have enough faith?

I practiced the "Forer Effect" without even knowing it. I personally gave dozens of priesthood blessing to the "sick and afflicted." I gave them during my mission and many times since. Though I always approached them with humility, I usually said what they wanted to hear and told them the Lord loves them, and added the required escape clause, that all blessings are predicated upon the faith of the recipient. Most people regained their health. A few did not.

Priesthood blessings contain all the elements employed by confidence men in exploiting the gullible and innocent. Patriarchal blessings are both calculated and cruel. They are calculated in their Forer-Effect pattern. They are cruel in that they write the future story of a child's life and intermix it with the specific interests of a man-made religious organization, the Mormon Church. Finally, they add the ultimate cruel caveat. If any of it does not come to pass, then the fault lies in the child and not in Church authority.

After I left the Church, I studied the history of priesthood blessings. One can easily obtain the blessings of famous early church leaders. Many of them contained promises they would do missionary work on the moon. This common theme seemed to prevail in 1840's era blessings. They reflected Joseph Smith's teaching that the moon was peopled with tall individuals who dressed like Quakers, and of course, they deserved the same salvation afforded to all mankind. None of these absurdities were mentioned during the 47 years I attended Sunday school and priesthood classes, and yet, I received specific instructions detailing the steps of "successful" priesthood blessings.

Psychologist Barry Beyerstein believes "hope and certainty evoke powerful psychological processes that keep all occult and pseudoscientific character readers in business. We are constantly trying to make sense out of the barrage of disconnected information we face daily. We become so good at filling in to make a reasonable scenario out of disjointed input that we sometimes make sense out of nonsense. We will often fill in the blanks and provide a coherent picture of what we hear and see, even though a careful examination of the evidence would reveal that the data is vague, confusing, obscure, inconsistent and even unintelligible."

I think this best explains the mental evasion we witnessed when we approached our own families with the evidence of the scandalous life of Joseph Smith. Not only did they immediately fill in the blanks with nonsense, but they really did not want to hear any truth that might shatter their illusionary Mormon world. The security and comfort that their world of certainty holds apparently is worth the price of mental captivity, which results in the exclusion of much beauty and opportunity surrounding them.

A perfect example of this adherence to an illusion occurred in my studies at BYU. All students are required to enroll in a Mormon religion class each semester. I majored in science and I also enrolled in an evolution course. My religion instructors railed against evolution. One of them openly called all the science professors "card-carrying Mormons." This is a derogatory term. It implies that while science professors carry the card to enter the temple, they remain unworthy to enter. Ironically, my name-calling professor of religion had little to fear with my professor of evolution. In my evolution course we learned how to classify animals according to their outer morphology or phenotype. We also learned the names of a great number of dinosaurs, along with the period of time they lived. Curiously, we did not specifically learn about Darwin's theory of evolution, which one might assume would be taught. I have since learned why this glaring lack of knowledge was withheld from me, and the good students at BYU. The Mormon Church owns BYU. Their Prophets and Apostles dictate that professors "not" teach anything contrary to the teachings of Mormon doctrine. This of course puts a serious damper on teaching evolutionary theory. In the interest of full disclosure, the class should have been labeled "How to classify extinct animals."

During my years at BYU, then Mormon Prophet, Spencer W. Kimball, said, referring to queries about evolution and dinosaurs: *"if it is not important to your salvation, don't worry about it."*9 Trite little thought stoppers such as this, govern internal Mormon vernacular. One need only believe what Mormon leaders dictate, and obey. Obedient men will be rewarded with endless wives, to impregnate and populate worlds without end. Obedient women get to service their obedient husbands, and bear children along side of their eternal sister wives. Linda informed me if Mormon women really thought about Mormon heaven, they would leave the Church in droves.

Other Mormon thought stoppers include: *"a Prophet*

will never lead you astray," "faith proceeds the miracle," "I know the Church is true," "don't delve into the mysteries," "milk before meat," "just have more faith," "we won't go there," "all men have short comings so we can't trust our own thinking," etc., all of which are designed to end conversations which may spoil the Mormon illusion. These sayings are so common and deeply rooted among the Mormon faithful; they magically spring to the front of the mind whenever a challenging thought threatens their illusion. I used these thought stoppers for years. They explain, in part, my past propensity toward a self-perpetuating ignorance.

A large sign decorates the entrance of BYU and proclaims "Enter to learn. Go forth to serve." In the interest of full disclosure it should read: Enter to learn *what we want you to know*. Go forth to *serve as we tell you to*.

Mormon claims are saddled with heavy contradictions. They teach moderation in all things, and yet they present the world in black and white terms. They affirm the virtue of free agency of men, and yet argue men are not worthy of a full understanding of their own history. They present ignorance as milk, and reserve meat as something never to be given. They proclaim charity to be the pure love of Christ and yet devote less than 1/5th of 1% (.002) of their holdings toward true charity.10 They feign humility, and when they do donate less then 1% of their holdings to charity they make public announcements and turn it into a PR campaign. They assert God loves all men equally, yet they teach God rewards only Mormons with the highest level of heaven. They declare families are forever, and yet they harshly divide a family's love with their exclusionary temple practices, including weddings, and inflammatory internal rhetoric toward all who are not Mormons. They engender homophobia and treat the gay community as wayward sinners. They use church funds to act politically against gay rights as witnessed in California's Proposition 8, and against women's rights as witnessed in their opposition to the Equal Rights Amendment. They wedge themselves between family members.

Bishops interview children bi-annually without parents present, thus usurping the natural authority between parents and their children. Fear, guilt and shame are rung as bells to collect devotion and lucre.

Mormon leaders demonize those who leave the church peacefully, and label the world as either Mormon or non-Mormon. It labels all other religions as abominations in the sight of God, and, according to Mormon prophets, the Book of Mormon refers to the Catholic Church as the great and abominable Church, and the whore of all the earth.10 Yet the ultimate irony is that Mormonism closely mimics the Catholic Church with its hierarchies of power, claims to divine authority, penchant for church construction and excessive wealth accumulation. They might as well call themselves the "Mini-Whore of the Earth." Their duplicity is grotesque, yet innocent Mormon children continue to feed on the warmth of soft words whispered into their ears as they stand on their tiptoes to reach the microphone, "I know the Church is true, I know Joseph Smith is a Prophet, I know the Book of Mormon is the word of God, and I love my mother and father." Only one of those statements is natural and true.

CHAPTER 9

Walk Toward the Light

The more a man knows, the more willing he is to learn. The less a man knows, the more positive he is that he knows everything.
Robert Ingersoll

A friend of mine invited me to visit him in the small mountain town of Snowflake, Arizona. He recently relocated there. Snowflake is a small dusty town with one traffic light and a whole lot of piety. Most of the population is Mormon. Mormon pioneers Erastus Snow and William Flake founded it in 1878. They were polygamist families who received letters in Box B, ordering them to colonize new frontiers for Brigham Young. My friend grew up in Snowflake. He is the proud product of a religious and cultural polygamist history. Even though he did not always live the life of the model Mormon, I nonetheless am proud to call him my friend. I was away from home visiting him when the weeping, wailing and gnashing of teeth began in earnest.

Linda revealed to her sisters and her mother, our feelings and concerns about authentic Mormon history. I arrived home to a considerably long conversation. Linda was in tears at the initial reaction of her family. Her mother lamented that she always thought all her daughters would be in heaven with her, implying Linda would be precluded from heaven since she did not believe the Church's version of the Joseph Smith story.

Up until this point, we were very careful not to give our Mormon neighbors reason to hate us. But even with our continued friendliness and lack of negativity toward the Church, our neighbors found ways to minimize and categorize us as problematic. We did not get the full banishing treatment from them because we did not reveal that our growing understanding differed from their childhood beliefs.

But now with Linda's revelation, emails from two of her brothers quickly followed, as well as from other family members. They accused us of being led away from the Church by Satan, and of sinning.

The people supposed to love us the most, let us down. We did not expect them to agree with us, but they caught us off guard with false allegations made against us. We stood not only wrongly accused and condemned for sins we did not commit, but one even offered to take our children from our "insane path," assuming us no longer worthy of parenting. Members are taught to link belief in Joseph Smith, with one's ability to be good parents and good people. It is a connection planted early in their lives, and deep within their psyche… *"I know the Church is true, I know Joseph Smith was a true Prophet, and I love my mommy and daddy."*

We understand such emotional pleas are simply a reflection of indoctrination by the Mormon Church. Now, living outside of Mormonism, we see just how ridiculous such inculcated and paranoid thinking becomes. I feel sorry for them, and the indoctrination they feel obliged to feed their children. I see the pattern of their lives in Mormonism from beginning to end, and wonder if they will ever break free to enjoy a life of self-autonomy and self-determination. Linda's family is full of great people with good hearts, but unfortunately, Mormon belief has misdirected some in their judgments.

They followed church protocol and circled the wagons. One shot out against us for not having allowed him to help us make "our own" decision. Another hid behind a diatribe of unsupported reasons why the Church must be true. Others only knew to shout out their personal feelings and beliefs. None, however, stopped attacking long enough to respond to our white flag. We simply requested they show us one single prophecy Joseph Smith made that came true. Our research revealed Smith, and his predecessors, changed his prophecies post-facto to try and make them appear fulfilled. It also revealed a great many, which were enormously incorrect and false. None could show us where our recounting of Smith's history was inaccurate. Only one brother, to his credit, apologized to us for his false accusations. The rest, who read the same false accusations remained silent, which showed the control the Church has over their minds. They knew and accepted the love we have for our children until they heard we no longer believed in the claims made by Joseph Smith. Rather than point their finger at Smith, who lived a life filled with frauds, abuse, and the deflowering of dozens of ladies, including teenage girls as young as 14, they blindly followed Church teachings and assumed we suddenly became evil.

To the credit of a few family members, we heard behind-the-scenes talk and actions of our family. Our secret family sympathizers called us and spoke of the weeping, wailing and gnashing of teeth expressed in our behalf.

First, the Church makes them feel like they have to condemn us for not believing as they do, and then they are made to feel guilty for our lack of belief. It sickened us to witness this first hand. We truly felt sorry they were made to believe and feel this way.

In the summer of 2007 we moved to California. In that same summer, Phoenix recorded the hottest temperatures ever with 100 days in a row over 100 degrees. The mercury topped out at 117 degrees on the day we headed to California with a loaded U-haul. Linda followed behind, driving our car. We left at the height of the heat. Both vehicles had air conditioning. The trip was supposed to take 7 hours. That would not be the case.

Just one hour outside of Phoenix I began to feel unusually sleepy. I wiggled around, turned the A/C cooler and took a few caffeine pills, which turned out to be a big mistake. Within 15 minutes my head began to spin and I pulled over to a rest stop. I felt nauseous and my skin was dry. I began to shake and I was barely able to walk back to Linda's car. She knew I was in distress, and I attributed the symptoms to a caffeine overdose. I progressively felt worse and asked Linda to take me to a hospital. The closest city was Blythe, California, a small town that lies on the California-Arizona boarder. As she drove I began to feel the life ebb from my body. I could not feel my legs. I lost control of my arms. To draw breath became a struggle. Death took hold of my body.

Linda called 911 as she drove. I struggled to tell her I was not going to make it to the hospital. As she received instructions over the phone I told her I loved her and if I had it all over to do again, I would not change a thing. I gasped for air as I also told her to let the kids know I loved them. By this point I had no control over my body. Linda wept as she spoke with the operator who instructed her to pull over and wait for an ambulance. She did, and as we waited, I told her I could see a bright light. She responded the only way she knew how. She told me to go toward the light.

This death was not painful. The prospects of giving up my body changed my perspective. To the observer, I completely passed out. Emergency personnel spoke over me as if I were unaware of everything they said. I pictured them in my mind's eye as they carried on conversations while they extracted me from the car and placed me in the ambulance. I made a comical mental play of it as they accidentally dropped the bottom half of me onto the pavement. They had not anticipated my 215-pound frame. Though I appeared unconscious, I was very much aware of my surroundings. The ambulance driver kept saying, "hang in their buddy," and, "you're scaring me." Along the way he kept giving me a sharp thump on the sternum, which I resented, as it was painful, yet I could not respond. He also kept shining a bright light in my eyes. During the 45-minute ambulance ride I reached a place where I had to decide if I were to continue to live or die.

I reasoned I might be of help to Linda at this particular point in her life. She had been under a lot of stress. She discovered her birth religion was based upon a mountain of lies. She left the Church. She was in the process of relocating to a new state. Her family had demonized her and now her husband danced with death.

I also thought I might be of some use to Jason. At 21 he lived at home and would not have local friends in California. I believed I could help him find friends, and if not, at least be his friend.

I also decided if I suffered a stroke and would be left paralyzed, I would not want to live as I figured Linda already had enough on her plate. I methodically went through this line of reasoning as I fought to draw breath. In the emergency room my heart rate fluctuated wildly between 230 beats per minute to 14 beats per minute. The diagnosis came in. It was severe dehydration. After hours of oxygen, fluids and monitoring, I finally squeezed the doctor's fingers. Struggling to utter speech, I inquired of the doctor if I would be left with any brain injury. He said, possibly swelling of the brain, but it would likely resolve in a few months. He was right. I experienced balance issues and motion sickness where I had none before. Those symptoms lessened over a period of months.

When my mother related our ordeal to my brother-in-law, who presides in the bishopric of his ward, meaning he is a high-ranking local Mormon official, his response was, "maybe he, [meaning me], should attend more church meetings."

How could a family member make such a thoughtless statement? I have, in the past, thought it hyperbole to refer to the Mormons as the "Morg," a Star Trek reference, (the Borg: a collective of individuals who have given up their personal identities to a machine whose sole purpose is to absorb everything in its path), and yet that is how the Church molded some members of my own family.

Lest I appear to be ungrateful toward help I received from others, I did have a different brother-in-law go out of his way to come to Arizona and drive our U-haul truck to California. My mother and father, along with my younger brother also flew down to Arizona to pack a second truck headed to Utah. It contained furniture, tools and other household belongings that would not fit in our smaller California rental home. I am in no way ashamed to say I very much appreciated their efforts. They were living what is real, to love your neighbor, or in this case, your family.

Linda was right when she told me to walk toward the light in my near death experience. My family walked toward the light on our way out of the Church. We pressed on to California, the elusive destination of the Fancher Party and the Parrish family. We cut against the pessimism of our bishop. We repelled the fear mongering of ward members who predicted the evils that lay in wait. We walked out of Mormon certainty, where our lives glittered brightly with the morning stars before our births. We escaped a life requiring us to bow our heads to Mormon threats and secret oaths. We refused to promote or idolize Joseph Smith, a historic prevaricator. We separated ourselves from friends whom we held dear for the sake of our children. We cast our lots to the winds of uncertainty, hoping only to float away from the fire. We left it all for one simple reason. The Mormon Church chooses loyalty and silence over truth. We will not. Apostle Dallin H. Oaks stated:

*"Truth surely exists as an absolute, **but** our use of truth should be disciplined by other values [referring to loyalty to the Church leaders].... When truth is constrained by other virtues, the outcome is not "falsehood" but silence for a season."*[1] *"When we say anything bad about the leaders of the Church, whether true or false, we tend to impair their influence and their usefulness."*[2]

"It does not matter that the criticism is true."[3]

A wall of silence should not separate men from truth. It should never be withheld out of loyalty to a church whose very foundation is built on deception. We will not burden our children with the yoke of men's lies. We choose a different legacy.

CHAPTER 10

A Land of Milk and Honey

*Pioneer: Someone who goes into previously uncharted territory with
the purpose of exploring.*

After a very strenuous move, our family landed in a rental
house, on a hillside, in a relatively small suburb city skirting the
South Bay area of Los Angeles. Prior to our move we researched
the school districts and crime rates. We found the school district
to be superior to those we left in Arizona. The crime rate was
particularly low when compared to Mesa. From a strictly
aesthetic point of view, Mesa is no more than a brown patch in
the desert when compared to the lush green trees and spectacular
ocean views afforded by our newly adopted town. We smile at
the fantastic views of Catalina Island, Santa Monica Bay and Los
Angeles. It is little wonder the housing prices here are three
times higher than in Mesa.

Would we find the non-Mormon people of California to
be the evil whoremongers the good members of our Mesa ward
had made them out to be? In retrospect, it seems like a silly
question to even ask. But there was a time when that proposition
remained open in our minds. Thankfully, it is a question made
only by cultic-thinking people clothed in mindless church-
promoted fear. We figured, in a worst-case scenario, we could
always move back to Mesa. We by no means expected people in

California to be perfect, but we hoped to find a more tolerant freethinking crowd.

Our 1954 rental home and driveway clings to a steep hillside overlooking Santa Monica Bay. It provides the perfect awe-inspiring backdrop for our new lives. Linda joined a book club hosted just a few doors down the street. She has met wonderful women with varied backgrounds, none of whom are Mormons. When she shares our life transition out of Mormonism, the women are surprised and amazed at our previously restrictive thinking and lifestyle. They sympathize with Linda and are dumfounded to learn we were shut out of our own daughter's wedding. Linda and I are both surprised at the number of people we have met since we moved here. We are equally surprised at how friendly and gracious they have been to us. We now recognize they love their children just as much as we love ours.

When we left the Church, many family members not only demonized us, but also expressed concerns about our children. We are unable to speak with a large number of them on any level, which remotely approaches religion. But, a few family members had already left the Church, either openly or in secret.

I have two brothers and four sisters. Karen is one of my younger sisters. She married in the temple, but found the experience so demeaning she never went back. Later, at age 26, she accepted an assignment to teach a monthly spiritual living class. In her own words:

"At that point in my life, I already had one foot out the door. But, given my rule following nature, I was trying to stick it out. You know, same ole story, caught up with culture, family pressure, and the voice in my head that says this is my issue.

To make a long story short, I found the sanitized church written lessons offensive. I was supposed to stand up and teach fluff and unquestioning obedience. So I decided to fashion my own lessons that were far more challenging and substantive.

None of which looked anything like the church promoting propaganda I was expected to peddle.

The day came when I was supposed to teach about the then prophet, Ezra Benson. All the usual church approved readings were proposed. I figured, however, if I was going to promote this man, I'd like to really get to know him. So I began studying available information, both authorized and unauthorized. Turns out, Ezra Benson was no friend to women or minorities. Moreover, he used his role as prophet to promote his own personal political and social beliefs, rather than the supposed teachings of Christianity. That was the final straw. I already had serious questions about Joseph Smith and Brigham Young. The ongoing personal corruption from church leadership, however, was it for me.

I returned home from church that day and told my husband I was done. I took off the garments, and as trite as it sounds, never looked back on my decision. I must say, I may not always make the best decisions. But that day, I was spot on."

Years later, Karen divorced her husband and took control of her own life. She lives with her life partner, Michelle. When news of her homosexuality reached our ears, the usual gnashing of teeth ensued. I even participated in family fasts for her, and we submitted her name on the prayer rolls of the temple. (Temples maintain a box in which prayer requests are submitted. When the boxes are full, a group of members surround the requests and prays for the recipients. It is similar to indulgence boxes of the Catholic Church). The fact we did not know anything about her private marital life did not matter. We just assumed Satan won her over, and why not, according to our leaders how else were we supposed to think? Apostle Boyd K. Packer:

*"The three greatest threats to the Church are homosexuality, feminists, and intellectuals."*1

After we left the Church, I was finally able to speak openly with Karen without the wall of silence between us. She dispelled many of the erroneous notions I held about homosexuality. I told her about my participation in family fasts held in her behalf. She was unaware of such fasts, but she smiled and thanked me all the same. I realized the family fasts and special family temple days were not for Karen. They were Mormon-inspired reactions, designed to circle the wagons of faith against thoughts of freedom beyond Church dictates. Karen stood oblivious to the "sky is falling" attitudes we universally expressed. This desperate scene of "henny-penny" panic replayed all over again when Linda announced to her family we no longer believed the claims made by the Church. We later learned Linda's family fasted and attended the temple in our behalf as well. I imagine this pathetic scene plays out over and over again, as thousands leave the Church each year. The unnecessary family grief and anguish that is ritualized by the Mormon Church is despicable.

My parents silently suffer the slings and arrows aimed in their direction by the church. They are in a catch-22. They live in Salt Lake City. They are surrounded by most of their children and grandchildren. If they show any doubt in Joseph Smith's claims, then they most likely would be demonized and no longer be allowed to be a part of their children or grandchildren's lives. We empathize with them. We understand the Church purposefully wedges itself in the middle of normal family relationships.

Our daughter Julie, who left our home six years prior to our awakening, came home to California to prepare for her wedding to a Mormon man. She loved him enough to marry him in the Mormon temple, knowing her parents would not be allowed to be there with her. For 4 months Julie lived with us while she and Linda made all the arrangements for a bright and festive wedding reception that would follow her temple marriage.

We happily hosted Julie and Simon's reception, but felt

sad to be locked out of her actual wedding. Linda's family expressed little sympathy for us as some of them openly stated it was our own choice to leave the Church. They are correct, we chose to leave the church, but they are incorrect not to sympathize with us as we vehemently disagree with any religious dictate that serves to separate the natural love between parents and their children. In an odd twist of fate, and at Julie's sole choice, she elected not to invite most of our immediate families into the temple. She told us she felt uncomfortable being surrounded by family members who judged us so poorly. That decision rested with her. When family members found they were not invited into the temple to witness her marriage, they again misjudged us and blamed us, only reinforcing the correctness of Julie's decision.

Julie's wedding was bittersweet for us. For the first time we knew how my grandmother felt when her baby daughter married my father, and she was made to wait outside the temple doors. While it hurt to miss our first daughter's marriage in the same temple in which we married, we nevertheless love and respect the man she chose to marry. We honored their marital wishes and will support them the best we know how, without compromising our newfound relationship with personal honesty over blind allegiance. We truly wish them nothing but the most beautiful and fulfilling lives possible, with or without illusions.

Linda's family and my family attended Julie and Simon's reception. We invited old friends from Arizona and new friends from California. Julie and Simon's friends attended from all over the US, a few came from overseas. After the reception, Julie and Simon flew to London where Simon works. We look forward to their happiness together. We fully respect their lives and will support them with love and freedom. We are happy Julie married such a wonderful man.

Our lives, in the normal non-Mormon world, continue to grow and unfold before us. We pick and choose our own paths. We attend street and city parties, concerts, dinner dates, ball games, dances, book clubs, school and charity events, exercise classes, cocktails, and festivals with diverse new friends and neighbors. Our Rolodex is becoming thick with names. The common denominator, they are all nice. They do not wish to offend. No one talks about religion. It amazes us. We enjoy our walks during the remains of the day. We speak of life's events as the sun sets over calm seas. The comfortable ocean climate and the refreshing sea breezes are new to us. It is invigorating to see people physically active and spending time outdoors.

After only one year here, Jessica has become a cheerleader in high school, and JD has done well in school, found friends and enjoys his baseball team. Jason drives to the local community college and attends classes. An interpreter signs the lectures. A professional note taker records his notes. We still feel challenged to help Jason find his place in the universe.

The most beautiful thing about our transition out of Mormonism has been the free and unfettered ability to speak openly with our children on any subject we desire. While sitting around the dinner table we openly discuss philosophy and the role of religion in human history. Jason, who suffers from cerebral palsy and is hard of hearing, asked: "Do you know when I realized the Mormon Church was false?" The question surprised us. With interest and intrigue we waited for his answer. He continued his protracted speech saying, "it was when I realized they didn't teach me anything new." This succinct, yet incredibly profound insight came from a quiet observer of life. I asked him why he didn't tell me sooner. He said, "I didn't think you wanted to hear it." He was right. My mind remained captured in the clouds of belief. I fell prey to Robert Ingersoll's prediction: *"The more a man knows, the more willing he is to learn. The less a man knows, the more positive he is that he knows everything."*2 Our church knew everything. I remained ignorant. Jason was right.

Until the desire to know supersedes the desire to believe, truth will remain hidden behind the illusion of belief, and those seeking truth will do so without the eyes to find it. With my blinders firmly in place, I tread the path of a bridled mule slavishly walking in circles within the religion of my birth. The Jesuits said, *"Give me a child under age 8 and I'll give you the man "I" want him to be."*

CHAPTER 11

Saving Jessica

*It is impossible to calculate the moral mischief that mental lying has
produced in society. When a man has so far corrupted and prostituted
the chastity of his mind as to subscribe his professional belief
to things he does not believe, he has prepared himself
for the commission of every other crime.*
Thomas Paine

In 1972, our family moved from Bountiful to Salt Lake City, only a few miles south. But from my perspective it may well have been hundreds of miles away. Cell phones had not yet been invented. AT&T ran all telephones, and long distance charges sucked up money faster than a hot slot machine. In short, I was cut off from all my childhood friends. I entered 8th grade at a new school in a much larger city. Yet, a silver lining appeared. I would have instant friends through my church.

Prior to the start of classes we attended our new Salt Lake City ward. I met four boys and five girls my age. I met them in Sunday school class. I met them at "Mutual." (Mutual was held on Wednesday nights at the local chapel and involved religious lessons mixed with fun activities.) I ran with them in our church-sponsored Boy Scout troop, which held weekly meetings at the chapel. It was nice to enter junior high school knowing at least a few other kids. I slowly began to gain friendships with other kids at school, as they naturally developed. I happened to ride a unicycle and found a friend who did the same. We became excellent friends and I became friends with his friends. Although they lived just up the street from me, they attended their ward/chapel, as required by the Church, and I attended mine.

On the surface it appeared I had two sets of friends. The "built-in ward friends" who lived closest to me, and the friends I selected at school. Two years of junior high school and three years of high school tarnished the silver lining of those instant friendships.

My upbringing in Bountiful stood bucolic against the vicious tongues and mischief of my built-in ward friends. A few of them exhibited cruelty and relentlessly made fun of a sweet, shy girl named Alice, in our Sunday school class. It infuriated me the teacher allowed this to happen in his class. How could these boys have such meanness in their hearts? Adult ward members crowned the very worst of the boys their "golden child." He was precocious to a fault. His father's gregarious nature and standing in the ward also elevated his son's status. Sometimes I ran with him so as not to be run over by him. Within the first few years of our arrival in Salt Lake, I avoided him altogether. His nighttime mischief and pranks manifest daily in the form of vandalism and theft. This bully became a popular kid in high school, and to this day I don't know why.

Ironically, the nicest boy in our ward was a semi-inactive kid whose mother and father separated. He also received barbs from the hellion. His mischievous nature adversely influenced other boys in the ward. The more I interacted with these boys, the less I wanted to be around them. As it turned out, the friends I chose at school helped me best navigate the awkward land mines of junior and senior high school.

I attended schools in the heart of Salt Lake City. The vast majority of kids were purebred, white Mormons. Nevertheless, plenty of kids had access to drugs and alcohol. Each morning smokers congregated just outside of the north doors of the high school. A few girls disappeared from the halls, as they became pregnant, and outspoken boys boasted of their sexual conquests. The sluts were revealed, whether they deserved the title or not, and on Sundays the same boys blessed and passed the sacrament.

Years later, as an adult, I learned the meanest of my instantly assigned ward friends had been accused of abusing a patient; stripped of his medical license; became hooked on drugs; and went through a messy divorce. The news didn't surprise me in the least.

As it turns out, Utah is over 75% Mormon, yet they have the highest male teenage suicide per capita, in the nation.1 During the two years Linda labored as Relief Society President, we had three teen suicides in our ward in Arizona. Why do Mormons have such a high male teen suicide rate? Could it be draconian church teachings, such as their teachings on masturbation, which are destructive to young men, fill them with self-destructive shame and guilt? A pamphlet entitled *"For Young Men Only,"* given to all 12 old boys in the Church, regarding masturbation, states:

"He [The Lord] has decreed serious penalties indeed for the misuse of it." "The signal of worthy manhood is self-control." "You are forbidden to use them now."

"You can quickly be subjected to a habit, one that is not worthy, one that will leave you feeling depressed and feeling guilty. Resist that temptation. Do not be guilty of degrading personal habits. If you can learn to master them, you will have a happy life." "If you misuse it, you will be sorry." 2

*"Immorality, including masturbation, brings generally a guilt deep and lasting. These guilt complexes are the stuff of which mental breakdowns come; they are the building blocks of suicide, the fabric of distorted personalities and the wounds that scar and decapitate individuals or families."*3

Physicians and psychologists treating suicidal young

men have stated that filling young boys with guilt and shame, over what is a natural process affecting nearly 100% of boys at puberty, is self-destructive and dangerous.4 To turn one's nature into a reason for self loathing is ignorant and dangerous.

This is a reoccurring theme. The Church wedges itself where it clearly does not belong. In this case, between natural male puberty, and what is unnatural, filling young boys with guilt and shame in order to control them. The outcome may be disastrous.

Young Mormon men are under many pressures to be perfect. Mormon church leaders unite in their directive that God demands "all" young men to fulfill a mission. Prophet Spencer W. Kimball said:

*"Every young man should serve a mission. It is not an option; it is your obligation."*5

The social pressures placed on young men to fulfill this obligation are intense. Young men who do not go on missions are universally looked down upon within the Church. Young women are taught to encourage boys to fulfill a mission, and to marry only worthy "returned missionaries." Parents feel obligated to send their boys on missions.

One of my Mormon friends has three sons. Two went on missions, one did not. My friend's voice waxes apologetic and fills with disappointment whenever he speaks of the son who did not go. His eyes lower and head shakes as if to hide a family shame. My friend absorbed all the subtle and overt cues beaten into him by an authoritative regime. He doesn't know how to be proud of a son who chose a different path. Again, the Church wedges itself where it doesn't belong, between the natural love of a father toward his son.

This cultural paradigm forces many young men to go on missions against their own wishes, just to appease everyone else. It may explain why thousands of missionaries have returned home prior to the end of their two-year missions. Missionaries, who return home early, are not given an honorable release from their Mission President. They are considered failures among their home wards. They are less sought after among Mormon girls for marriage. It is not far akin to the "lost boys" of the FLDS church.

Young women are not immune from ignorant piety gone awry. Prophet Spencer W. Kimball taught women are better off being killed, rather then allowing their rape to occur.6

Multiple studies, ranging from the CDC, Center of Disease Control, to MHA, Mental Health America, confirm that Utah holds the dubious distinction of the most mentally depressed state in the nation. These studies used suicide rates and anti-depressants data. Utah has the highest use of anti-depressants (i.e. Prozac, Zoloft etc.) in the nation.7 According to the findings:

*"In Mormon culture, females are supposed to accept a calling. They are to be constantly smiling over their family of five. They are supposed to take supper across the street to an ill neighbor and then put up with their husband when he comes home from work and smile about it the whole time. There is this sense that Mrs. Jones down the street is doing the same thing, and there is this undercurrent of competition. To be a good mother and wife, women have to put on this mask of perfection. They can't show their tears, depression or agony."*8

Does the Church minimize its role with this staggering problem? They put out a statement saying: "the high number of prescriptions is a result of people receiving the drugs *they need in Utah more than in other places."*

This awkward response does not address why so many people in Utah need to be medicated. A psychologist and assistant commissioner of LDS (Mormon) Family Services admitted:

*"Are there people who feel "I'm not living up to the LDS ideal," or "I'm not living up to my family's expectations?" Absolutely, there is no question."*8

This same Mormon psychologist then tried to minimize the problem by stating that outside the Mormon community:

"I saw people there, who were depressed because of *perfectionism,"*8

The Mormon Church does not want to take responsibility in causing this problem. Yet, recall that the first, of the Church's three openly declared goals, is to: "perfect the saints (its members)." Their prophets teach:

*"Personal perfection is an achievable goal."*8

*"The time to become perfect is now, in this mortality."*9

*"Forgiveness could take "centuries" and is granted based on a Mormon's humility, sincerity, works, and attitudes."*10

Setting impossibly high standards and rules are hallmarks of a cult. Developing lengthy lists of sins of commission (sins you commit by doing something), and sins of omission (sins you commit by "not" doing something), are designed to rob its members of their time, energy and sense of personal autonomy. It inevitably leads to unnecessary stress and depression, as members are never quite good enough. Ironically, members are programmed to vehemently defend the very system that starves them of their time, energy and money.

Utah quietly serves at the top of the list of "highest rate of bankruptcy" and "highest rate of white collar crime." Why is this happening in the heartland of Mormonism? The ABI, American Bankruptcy Institute, looked into it. According to ABI, the top five reasons people filed for bankruptcy were ease of obtaining personal credit and credit cards, loss of a job, financial mismanagement, medical problems and divorce. They found Utah has additional factors that placed it at the top of the list:

"In Utah, the reasons extend to larger family size, higher

charitable contributions and lower-than-average per-capita income levels. "11

Internal church growth has always been of prime importance to the Church. Babies born into the Church have a higher membership retention rate than do convert baptisms. The Church encourages young women to bear large families. They proudly announce the number of new births within their annual membership statistics. Women who do not have large families are considered selfish, or that something is physically wrong with them.

The *higher charitable contributions* refer to tithing. Paying tithing is required by the Church to stay temple worthy. It represents 10% of a member's financial "increase." Without paying tithing, members cannot enter into a Mormon temple. They cannot receive the secret signs, handshakes, passwords, new names, ordinances etc. required to go to Mormon heaven. Every December, all Mormon families are required to meet face to face with their bishop and declare whether they are full tithe payers or not. The Church itself is not bankrupt, but is considered one of the riches entities in America. The majority of its members cannot make the same claim.

Why all the white collar crime in Utah? Mormons are taught personal boundaries are evil and selfish. Members are led to "believe all things," and to be like little children, thus making them ripe victims to local scams.12 The last day I attended a priesthood meeting, in Mesa, I sat next to a member who was under criminal investigation for defrauding fellow members of the Church over $150 million. He bilked money away from anyone dumb enough to believe his claims. Greed inspired investors to bite at the 120% annual return he promised. He claimed to have connections with companies needing short-term "bridge loans," and that they would pay back with high interest rates. His victims included many of our ward members as well as other Mormons in Arizona. He exuded confidence and acted unscrupulously. He took money from a number of widows.

Before his pyramid/ponzi scheme went bust, a Mormon neighbor came to me and tried to get me to invest. This neighbor invested hundreds of thousands of dollars. I looked at him with incredulity. I asked him to show me proof that companies are willing to pay such high interest rates on short-term money. He had none. I asked him to show me proof his money did not go directly to a Swiss bank account. He chuckled and said, "This is the kind of investment where you just trust the word of the investment team." After all, they did have a very expensive office with all the trappings of wealth and success. I walked away thinking this man was one of the most gullible people in the world. Then I sat down and paid my tithing.

The Mormon Church, with its expensive buildings, trappings of wealth and success, pays dozens of apologists to blame these negative localized phenomenon, suicides, depression, bankruptcy, white collar fraud crimes etc., on anything but themselves. Yet interestingly, cults engender the exact same phenomenons.13

Mormon leaders recently mandated clear glass doors be placed on all internal chapel classroom doors where children are taught. They stopped allowing men to teach primary aged children alone. They did this to limit their liability to sexual abuse lawsuits, which have been brought against them. The Church also requires a witness to stand outside the door whenever a bishop or stake president interviews a female. The Catholic Church does not stand alone, when it comes to sexual abuse perpetrated upon innocent members by their clergy.

My father relocated our family from Bountiful to Salt Lake City to join a large medical practice. Linda and I relocated our family from Mesa, Arizona to California to escape religious persecution.

After we quit attending church in Mesa, we stayed in the same house for a year. Jessica had been accepted into cheerleading at her junior high and was elected as Class Treasurer. We wanted to let her have fun and experience leadership at school. We told our children we would be moving to California at the end of the school year. During this time, as I have stated, we received constant unwanted attention by the Church and its members. This unwanted influence extended beyond Linda and myself. Our children were targeted for assimilation regardless of our feelings upon the matter.

We understood this mentality because Linda, as Relief Society President, often received the assignment to re-activate less active members and I served as the head bean counter for the ward as the Membership Clerk. Our lack of attendance raised a giant red flag. The local leadership put on the "full court press" to reactivate us. We understood this pressure would come our way. We were, however, surprised at how deviously they applied pressure toward our children. When our children played at the homes of other members their parents would quiz them about us. These member neighbors, who always knew us as good upstanding Mormons, now felt compelled to make disparaging remarks about us. They did this without knowing the reason we quit attending. They just assumed, like the Church teaches, we had become bad parents. JD relayed to us how his best friend's mother told him we were evil and wrong not to allow him to attend church. Jessica, who was 14, also had girls in the ward rally around her with special interest. One of her friends, who previously had been somewhat distant, took particular interest and made Jessica her missionary project.

We were caught in the middle. We wanted to tell Jessica the reason we abruptly stopped attending. But we knew if we did, her inquisitive Mormon friends would pry out information and pass it along to their parents. The parents would tell our local church leaders, who would openly condemn us, and proceed to bring church disciplinary action upon us. It was a confusing time for Jessica. As her parents, we did not want her to feel the sting of being ostracized, which most assuredly would have come her way had we shared with her our findings. Already some of JD's friends were not allowed to play with him at our home. But by not telling her, she only heard her Mormon friends guess at the reason we stopped attending. Those speculations always involved "us" as the problem. We bit our tongues so she could have fun. Jessica did have fun, but she also began to close off to us. The last time we attended sacrament meeting Jessica received her Young Women's Award. We realized, afterwards, the mistake we made in allowing her to progress in the regimented church indoctrination programs for the youth.

At the time, we believed Jessica was born into the Mormon Church. Now we know Jessica Flynn was born into our family, not into a religion. And with that, allow me to reintroduce her.

Jessie arrived in this world with unusually big eyes. We wondered if she would ever grow into them. She immediately became passionate about jewelry, highbrow fashion and chocolate. By 14 she fully blossomed into a gorgeous young lady with beautiful brown eyes. Her natural facial symmetry, long flowing brown hair and lightly tanned skin make her a physical *knockout*. She possesses an overtly friendly disposition and naturally attracted lots of girl and guy friends. She loves to put on a show, and knows how to be dramatic. At times she takes things for granted, like her parents. At times she can be more social and less academic then we desire. She is, however, exceedingly bright and full of life. She is "our" daughter, not the Church's possession. The Church can fall under its own weight, shrivel up and die, and yet we will continue to love and support our daughter Jessica.

We added an additional garage to our home, which Jessica quickly claimed as a spot for her friends to hang out. Quite often a crowd of 15-25 kids roamed our home, eventually migrating into the cozy two-car carpeted garage, complete with couches, chairs and game tables. They listened to music, partied, slept over and played in the pool. We kept watch, scooted unwanted boys away and were happy to have them under our roof so we could monitor them.

Jessica's popularity shone at school. She was a member of Student Council, Student Body Treasurer, and a cheerleader. Nearly all of her friends were Mormons. Mesa was founded by

Mormon farmers and has a fairly prominent Mormon population. Our particular neighborhood contained a dense population of Mormon households. During our time in Mesa we lived in five different homes, which meant we attended five different wards. I operated a busy orthodontic practice and treated thousands of kids. We knew Mormons all around the city and they knew us.

When we discovered the Mormon Church is not what it claims to be, we came to the conclusion that our personal honesty must supersede any loyalty to a false church. We thought it best to leave our home and move to another state where we could get a fresh start. We knew if we simply moved further on down the road, Jessica's Mormon friends would naturally direct their missionary efforts toward her. We needed to put distance between her and Mormonism.

The second openly declared goal of the Church is: "to convert the world through missionary work." Most people have no idea the pressure placed upon Mormon youth to do missionary work. The Church maintains a plethora of meetings and activities designed to motivate young members to convert unsuspecting non-Mormon youth. The Mormon Church is the largest sponsor of the Boy Scouts of America program. While on the surface this appears innocuous, internally, the Church uses that platform as a missionary tool. When non-Mormon boys join a Mormon scout troop, they are taught more then what is in the scouting handbooks. Most of their scout meetings are held in Mormon chapels. Meetings open and close with Mormon prayers. When we stopped attending church, we allowed JD to continue his scouting activities. We finally ended his scouting when he brought home a camping list, which included not only a flashlight and sleeping gear, but also a Book of Mormon. Incidentally, I served as Assistant Scout Master for two years. When we huddled those boys around a campfire, in the mountains, we always brought a member of the bishopric to provide Mormon faith-promoting stories. As scout leaders, we often bore our Mormon testimonies to the scouts. Of course, Mormon-styled prayers ended our pow-wows just before dowsing the fire. Many a parent has lost a child to Mormonism through the Mormon-run scouting program. But the Boy Scouts program is only the tip of the iceberg for youth indoctrination and missionary work.

Mormon children look forward to attending EFY, Especially For Youth. It is an annual one-week program where kids sleep in the dorms at BYU, or other designated locations. They engage in exciting youth activities. They also endure heavy daily doses of Mormon indoctrination. We allowed Jessica to attend the year prior to our departure from Mesa. When we picked her up from BYU, the first words out of her mouth detailed how much more she believed Joseph Smith to be a true prophet. Then she proceeded to tell us how much fun she had. When asked what she had been taught about Smith's life, the same topical sanitized version of his life was regurgitated back to us. Linda and I instantly knew never to make that mistake again.

In addition to the EFY program, the Church also has a Young Men and Young Women organization. They are encouraged to invite their non-Member friends to attend. Mormon girls anticipate the excitement of annual "Girl's Camp." Each summer they head up to the mountains to engage in fun activities against the backdrop of nature, sleep in austere cabins or tents, then hold special faith-promoting lessons. The climax of camp is reached when all the girls are encouraged to follow their leaders and copy emotional testimonies, repeating the tired phrase; I know Joseph Smith was a true prophet, etc... In Mormonism, fun is justified when mixed with underlying theology. It is very much like the movie, "Jesus Camp."

The Mormon program called "The Trek" reenacts the trek the Mormon pioneers faced when crossing the plains. This program psychologically links early Mormon sacrifices to current Mormon members. The idea being, since pioneer Mormons sacrificed to come to Utah, current Mormons should sacrifice as well for the Church. It subtly allows new members to claim Mormon history as their own.

"Every member a missionary" is a favorite Mormon

motto. Virtually every Mormon knows it since it is repeated so often. Youth are lead to believe it is a mandate from the Lord. It serves to deepen the illusion that Mormonism is right, and the rest of the world is wrong, and members must convert them.

This holy mandate, every member a missionary, also applies to adult Mormons. They get a heavy dose of it every Sunday at church. Constant prayers are given in hopes of discovering which non-Mormon household within the ward boundaries would be open to conversion into Mormonism. Copies of the Book of Mormon are passed around and assignments given to present them to non-Mormons in the community. All Mormons know the "golden questions," "What do you know about the Mormon Church?" and, "Would you like to know more?" Adult Mormons covenant in the temple not to affiliate or sympathized with anyone who may hold opposing views to Mormonism.14 In other words, all your friends should be Mormon. The only exception to this rule is if a Mormon is actively trying to convert a non-Mormon. This is why if you are a non-Mormon, and have a Mormon friend, it is very likely your Mormon friend has already given you a Book of Mormon, or invited you to church. What most non-Mormons don't know is their interactions with their Mormon friends are often reported as missionary efforts in church on Sunday.

For three years I served the Church as Ward Employment Specialist. Every Tuesday evening I met at the Stake Center, a large chapel where several wards meet. I helped unemployed people look for jobs. We helped them build resumes. We directed them to a Mormon Internet database with job openings. We acted very friendly and encouraging. Now, as I describe this it sounds like an excellent service to the community. Of course, the real reason for this "community service" was missionary work. Prior to unlocking the doors at 6:30 we literally knelt and prayed to have a missionary experience with the job seekers who would enter our chapel. The man in charge of the program openly told us the only reason for this service was to gain new converts. He later became a member of the Stake Presidency.

Speaking of our Stake President, he appeared to be impressively obtuse. Linda not only helped provide for the funeral luncheons for the families of the children who committed suicide in our ward, but in addition, seven adults died during her tenure as Relief Society President. All these luncheons occurred in the ward chapel. The actual funerals and eulogies were held in the Stake Center. Our Stake President presided over most of them. All of the funerals he conducted were eerily similar. Instead of paying homage and eulogizing the memories of the departed, he turned the entire affair into one large missionary class in which he presented Mormon theology. Little time remained for family members to share their love for, and loss of, their departed. The Stake President commanded the bulk of the time, choosing to expound Mormonism to his captive audience. Even though I fully believed at the time, I still thought it slightly rude on his part to ignore the grieving family sitting at his feet.

I developed a friendship with a man in our ward. Our common connection was our love of flying. We arranged to go flying together the week before he discovered he contracted inoperable lung cancer. He lived another year and a half battling the disease. We shared fun and interesting times together. Both he, and his wife, did not want our Stake President to preside over his funeral, as they knew it would dissolve into a missionary lesson all over again. His wife asked the local bishop to preside, as she believed him to be more sensitive to the family's grief.

Before my friend died, he brought over a box full of pictures of his life with his family. Linda and I digitized them and made a movie of his life. He sat next to me and selected the songs he wanted to play in the background. The movie celebrated his life and was produced to give his children lasting evidence of his love and fun with them. Pictures of his wedding to his very lovely wife, and those of his five children portrayed a family full of love for one another. At the end of the movie he spoke into the computer's microphone and sweetly expressed love for his family.

We played these precious memories on a TV at his viewing. I wanted to feel closure and happiness for the brief, yet, fun times I spent with him. Instead, the Stake President decided to preside and, like a machine on autopilot, he presented the Mormon gospel all over again. His speech was so predictable that I knew just when he would reach in his pocket and pull out the rubber glove he used to illustrate the body; the glove covers the spirit, or his hand. I felt frustrated my friend's widowed wife's wishes were not respected.

The Stake President spoke at his own son's funeral. His son committed suicide. Even at his own son's funeral he robotically rehearsed the Mormon Plan of Salvation, glove and all. He also included that he received a revelation his son would be "restored to him." He informed everyone present his son had not committed a sin in taking his own life because he had been on medication for depression. I feel exceedingly sorrowful for this family, and all families, who have to deal with the loss of their child, regardless of the circumstances.

I attended the funeral of a young lady in our ward, who committed suicide. Drugs also influenced her. She was attempting to get off drugs when she took her own life. Again the Stake President presided over the funeral. Again, he recited the missionary discussions only this time he spoke directly to the parents. In this particular case, the father actively attended church and the mother did not. The Stake President focused on the mother and told her the one thing her dead daughter wanted was that she return to church, so they could be together in the afterlife. The duplicity and arrogance of this man seemed to know no bounds, yet in Mormonism it is expressly considered a sin to question the priesthood leader above you in the chain of command. According to him, his son would be restored to him in heaven, but her daughter's restoration required the mother to attend church. Of the hundreds of people who attended, no one dared say a word. *"It's wrong to criticize leaders of the church, even if the criticism is true."*15

Years later I came to understand why the Stake President

presented missionary rhetoric at every funeral he directed. As it turns out, he followed his chain of command. His excuse would be the same used by the post-war Nazis in Nuremberg. "I was only following orders." The specific order came directly from a high-ranking Apostle Boyd K. Packer, who instructed all stake presidents and bishops on the "real" purpose of funerals. Apostle Packer said:

"Another point of order: Bishops should not yield the arrangement of meetings to members. They should not yield the arrangement for funerals to families. It is not the proper order of things for members or families to expect to decide who will speak and for how long...bishop(s) should not turn the meeting over to them. We are worried about the drift that is occurring in our meetings...

*I have told my Brethren in that day, when my funeral is held, if any of them, who speak, talk about me, I will raise up and correct them. <u>The gospel is to be preached.</u> I know of no meeting where the congregation is in a better state of readiness to receive revelation and inspiration from a speaker than they are at a funeral."*16

     Apparently, my repetitively obtuse Stake President acted as an obedient servant of God who only followed orders from an even more obtuse Mormon hierarchy.

     I have shared just a few of the internal dynamics of Mormon programs and mentality to help non-Mormons appreciate our dilemma in trying to leave the Church. Mormons are not only made to feel guilty if they are not doing missionary work, but they are equally made to feel guilty to reconvert or fellowship those who leave the Church. Many within the Church find it simplest to label people like Linda and myself "apostates" and condemn us to hell, and why not, that is also Mormon doctrine. Either way, it is too much to ask for us to live among a community prone to pass pious, inaccurate judgments and malicious gossip. Today's execution of the penalty is social banishment and condemnation. Church leaders would eventually question members caught affiliating or sympathizing with us, and possibly deny them a temple recommend as a form of punishment and control.

As the school year came to an end, we finally called Jessica back into our bedroom for a talk. Linda and I sat next to her and explained many of the things taught in church simply are not true. We explained the inconsistencies, lies and schemes of Joseph Smith. We showed her Joseph Smith's plagiarism of "View of the Hebrews" to construct the Book of Mormon story. We showed how Smith lied about his ability to translate the Book of Abraham. We showed her an original 1831 book by Thomas Dick entitled "Philosophies of a Future State" and showed where Smith copied paragraphs out of Dick's book regarding the intelligences and the pre-existence and the planets, like Kolob, and all their rotations. Dick's book predated Smith's Book of Abraham. We told her all the conflicting versions of the First Vision Story, and about Smith's failed prophecies. This went on for over an hour. She cried a little than finally said: "I don't believe you, I believe in Gordon B. Hinckley, the true prophet." Both Linda and I had to catch our breath.

Imagine that, Jessica trusted a man, Gordon B. Hinckley, whom she didn't know from Adam, more then she trusted her own parents. Gordon B. Hinckley didn't know Jessica. Yet, she was so indoctrinated to believe in the head of the Mormon Church, she thought her own parents, who birthed her, raised her, fed her, love and truly support her, were lying to her. This exposed to us the ultimate betrayal of the Mormon Church. The love and authority that should naturally be accepted between a mother and daughter, and a father and daughter was stolen from us by an organization that can only exist based upon a sandy foundation of lies. We felt crushed. We were up against her Mormon identity that we helped create. Again, the Church wedged itself where it does not belong, between the natural love and trust of parents and their children.

Later on we again called Jessica back to our bedroom for

a talk. We told Jessica how much we loved her. We explained the Mormon Church called President Hinckley a "Prophet, Seer and Revelator," and yet he has never made a prophecy; has never "Seered" anything; meaning had the ability to translate languages, and has never "Revealed" anything not already known to the world. I told her Hinckley was no more a prophet than was I. Our reasoning with her was not getting through.

In an off-handed comment I told her the Church was building a two billion-dollar shopping mall in the heart of Salt Lake City. The two billion dollar price tag did not impress her, but it was as if a light clicked on in her head and she stopped sobbing and said: "No wait, the Church is building a shopping mall?" All the rest was mumbo jumbo to her, but if there is one thing Jessica understands, it's shopping malls. Suddenly her mind was open, her defenses lowered, and she asked: "Why would the Church build a shopping mall?" Of course, one question led to another, which is how Jessica began to see the big picture of deception and fraud not only practiced by Joseph Smith, but by the Mormon Church today. Thank God the Mormon Church is dumb enough to openly flaunt their excess wealth in an obvious commercial enterprise, at a time when the world is in desperate need of truly charitable donations. But Jessica is not out of the woods yet. She has a cell phone, and there are no extra fees for long distance.

After living in California for 11 months, we allowed Jessica to return to Mesa and visit her friends for her 16th birthday. We were torn between letting her see her old friends from Mesa and denying her the trip. We feared their parents would try to reconvert her, or demonize us again. Apparently our fears were justified.

Upon Jessica's return, I picked her up at LAX as midnight approached. As I drove her home we spoke of her fun with her friends. It is obvious she is very taken with them. Eventfully I calmly asked: "Jessica, do you know why your mother and I are prejudiced against the Mormon Church and not against the Mormon people?" She did not, and she became angry with me for even bringing up the subject. Her reaction told me she was uncomfortable taking about it, which was all the more reason we needed to clear the air and have common understanding. I told her we are biased against "all churches" that teach division among our human family. We are particularly intolerant against religions that invoke God as their justification to commit all, but themselves, to hell. I then asked Jessica if she thought she was going to hell because she is not Muslim. She said "no." I told her Muslims believe she will, simply because she is not Muslim. Mormons, like Muslims, teach the same fate to those who are not members of their faith. I then asked her the difference between her new friends in California, who are not Mormons, and her Mormon friends in Mesa. She replied, "I don't know?" I told her there is no difference. They are all the same. If there is a God, then God loves them all equally. Why then should we be any different than a righteous God?

Linda and I finally decided we would no longer act as enablers on behalf of the Mormon Church, or any other divisive religious institution, particularly where our children are concerned.

At some point in her life, as well as in ours, we just have to move on. Jessica came to "evil" California as a new tenth grader. She has already found a great number of friends. Once again she tried out for cheerleading, and she made it. In fact, the very night I wrote these words, she had friends sleeping over.

To be sure, Jessica deals with the same peer pressures and high school challenges I faced growing up in Salt Lake City. She desires the security of childhood while at the same time yearning for the freedom of adulthood. She is not immune from normal teenage angst.

Can we save Jessica from marrying into a closed system designed to disarm her sense of self and ability to reason? Dear God, we hope so. We would like her to think for herself and enjoy a life void of any cult-like influences. We would also like to attend her wedding. All the news coverage of the FLDS Church in Texas, and the cultic way they practice polygamy has been an eye opener for Jessica. She watched with great interest the zombie-like responses of the abused polygamist wives who knew only to repeat what their imprisoned prophet, Warren Jeffs, commands. The fact they believe in the Book of Mormon and live like Joseph Smith lived intrigued her. Jessica has read cult awareness books and the eyes of her understanding are beginning to open.

What Joseph Smith started, continues in the Mormon Church today. It contains nearly all the qualities and traits of a destructive cult.17 The Church usurps individual self-identity, suppresses information, and denies responsibility for self-rule. Loyalty trumps honesty. In Mormonism, women live a subservient role to men. Truth becomes whatever male leaders say it is, and questioning authority is forbidden.

Jessica is our daughter. She belongs to herself.

CHAPTER 12

The "D" Word

Filling in the Blanks...

Twilight now reflects in the eyes of my parents. Despite their graying hair and slowing condition they remain affable and enjoyable to be around. Dad's voice always rings with enthusiasm. A few years ago, Linda and I asked them to care for our children while we vacationed with another couple. They graciously flew down to Arizona to honor our request. Upon our return, we inquired about our kids' behavior, and according to Mom and Dad, they exhibited exemplary obedience. We dispersed the mandatory trinkets, jewelry and shirts to our kids, as a reward for their behavior. This custom followed all good reports after trips without our children.

The day after Mom and Dad left for Utah, we gathered around the kitchen table for a quiet family meal. JD, who was 9 at the time, then proceeded to tell us about Grandma's "bad" behavior. The tenor in his voice indicated his seriousness. He told us Grandma scared him. Sometimes he tried to avoid her. This surprised us. He continued saying, "Grandma was mean to Grandpa all week." Of course we had to get to the bottom of this. "JD, how was Grandma mean to Grandpa?" He replied, "she called him the D-word." Still confused, we asked JD, "What is the D-word?" He refused to answer. We informed him these special circumstances allowed him to say the D-word. There followed a long and pensive silence as JD garnered the courage to say it. His eyes dropped as he quietly said, "she called him a "Dick," and she called him Dick all the time."

We collectively burst into laughter and explained to JD that "Dick" is Grandpa's nickname. It is a nickname for anyone named Richard. A big sigh of relief overcame JD and his shoulders dropped in relaxation. He finally beamed, realizing Grandma was not mean after all. He told us that all week long he feared Grandma might start calling him a Dick. JD's behavior sparkled, even when he was not hiding from Grandma.

A similar incident occurred just a few years earlier. Jessica and JD found themselves in a tiff. JD marched over to us complaining about Jessica's harsh language. According to JD, she called him a "shellfish." He protested, declaring he was not a shellfish. Again we laughed as we explained the concept of being "selfish."

Our inquisitive brains automatically fill in blanks. The world in which we live varies from person to person according to how those blanks are filled in. Confucius said the purpose of life is education. He further taught that the underclass and poor could be educated. Local elite warlords of his day did not harbor such beliefs. They believed the peasants incapable of higher education. Confucius explained to his underclass followers that education should only stop when the lid is closed on their casket.

My father perfectly reflects Confucius' age-old wisdom. Though he cut his teeth during the depression, he sought education when and where he could. Between his various chores, such as selling eggs door to door, he read from Grandpa's small collection of books.

I enjoy listening to Dad's enthusiasm as he shares with me the latest scientific theory regarding quarks or the cosmos. He, like myself, prefers to read non-fiction. He considers himself a student of science. He achieved a dual medical degree in pediatrics and radiology. I have never seen Dad read a novel, but I have seen him read medical and science books for hours.

My dad is a left-handed Mormon enigma. Outwardly, he appears as the ever-obedient member. He accepted church callings, although he always managed to quietly avoid becoming a member of the bishopric. However, he never bore his testimony of Joseph Smith and Jesus Christ to us children. I never saw my dad stand up in a testimony meeting to bear his testimony. Occasionally, we held family prayers, the Church recommends these be done nightly, and he usually called on one of us kids to have the honor. As a child, I didn't think much of this.

My mother came down to my room each night and coaxed me out of bed to say my personal prayers. We took turns offering thanks and asking for blessing as we knelt side by side. I maintained this habit for 47 years. My father is cerebral. My mother is social and occasionally emotional.

In the hallways of my junior high school, the antitheses of higher education, I borrowed a book from a friend entitled: "A School Girl Sex Tease." As I suffered from dyslexia as a child, this perhaps, represented the first novel I would read cover to cover. I couldn't understand half of what was written, yet I pushed on through, and was proud of myself for having read a complete book. Sadly, I could not share my accomplishment with anyone else. This sadness abated the day Mom discovered the book in my room. She called me down to her room where she stood across from her bed. I stood in the doorway. She looked at me without saying a word. I wondered what she wanted. I then spied the book, in all its glory, lounging in the middle of her bed.

Mom grew up in a tough environment. She did not know her childhood father, and her mother often worked. She spent time alone. Older siblings watched over her. When thrust into the world of Mormonism, she bore a large family just as Mormon leaders recommend:

"Worldwide, the birthrate of Church members is only slightly higher than the world at large. Like the rest of the population, members of the Church must suffer the consequences of these

trends. We face a particular set of issues because the pool from which missionaries are drawn is in steady decline. The First Presidency has written, Marriage is ordained of God, and the paramount purpose of this sacred principle is to bring into the world immortal spirits to be reared in health and nobility of character, to fill the measure of their mortal existence."1

My parents dutifully answered the call with a large family. Mom endured nine pregnancies. Two of them miscarried. I was the third child out of seven. Our home often became hectic and chaotic. Dad spent an inordinate amount of time at the hospital, which meant Mom swam in a constant stream of laundry, supper, cleaning, teaching and discipline. She did a great job considering the lack of role modeling in her childhood. Mom drove us to all our functions. After I walked home from school, the first words out of my mouth were, "Mom, I'm home!" Mom grew into her role as a homemaker as we grew up. In my early childhood she swore when angered and often disciplined us with her favorite paddle, with the inscribed words: "Heat for the Seat." Occasionally when we hid her paddle, a belt or hanger removed the wind from our sails.

To my mother's credit she overcame the rough edges of her own childhood. She abruptly stopped swearing at us after I began to swear around age 9. Her disciple, at the end of a stick, also abated through the years. I don't know that my youngest sister ever felt the physical sting of her anger. Today, corporal punishment is illegal in most schools in America, but in my childhood it dutifully kept the peace. By the time I reached junior high, mom had long since withheld her hand in anger, although, when I spied my first paperback novel lying on her bed, an old childhood fear overcame me. I said nothing.

Mom broke the silence with the words: "Now Brent, you know sex is nothing like how it is portrayed in that book?" I didn't of course, but I lowered my head and said, "yes." She replied, "Good," after which I asked if I could go. She said "yes," and I scurried away. That episode encompassed the whole of my parent's birds and bees talk. The expressive detail of the tawdry book confused me. The unknown anatomical parts, mixed with the swear words shot out of mother's mouth in anger only further complicated the narrative. The rest of the blanks were filled in at junior high school. An unfortunate circumstance considering most of the kids attending my junior high school proved less informed than myself. Adults, as well as children, fill in blanks with the best information they are given.

I have only seen my father cry twice in my life. When I was 7, he tried to stop Mom from disciplining us children. We acted poorly and so did she. In her anger she ran Dad out of the basement. We all fell into an obedient, submissive state and followed her every command. When I had the chance, I crept upstairs to check on Dad. I startled him as he held his head in his hands and quietly cried. Upon seeing me, he immediately hugged me and told me everything would be all right, and it was not my fault. I did not see him cry for another ten years.

My younger brother and I had a sharp scuffle and Dad intervened. We both adamantly blamed each other for the tussle. Both of us shed tears filled with anger. Dad plopped us down on the couch. We straddled each end. Dad sat across the room. Amid our berating accusations toward one another, I noticed Dad started to cry. This immediately took me aback. I stopped finger pointing, and asked Dad why he was crying? He looked at me and said. "You guys just don't get it. It doesn't matter who is right or wrong." Surprisingly, his words immediately brought me calm. I looked over at my younger brother, who still sobbed recriminations toward me. I looked back at my dad, and I got it. My mind gave birth to a dispassionate objectivity. I calmly told my dad I understood. I desperately wanted my brother to experience the same epiphany. My father wished him the same. Being three years younger then myself, he stood just short of that breakthrough. I watched as my dad appeased him like one would a child, told him what he wanted to hear, then sent him on his way, happy. I then engaged my father in my first adult conversation. We spoke for quite some time, and I began to gain insights, which previously escaped my childhood perspective.

To the frustration of my mother, I began to listen to what she said, and then interpreted what she meant. I realized what people say and what they wish to communicate are often two different things. My relationship with my mother changed from that day forward. I honor her for vastly improving upon the upbringing she experienced. I hope to continue in the directions of her journey.

Education fills in gaps to create the broad and beautiful picture of life. We create our worldview based upon the pieces of the puzzle available to us, and how we put them together. At one time, I had all the pieces of the world-puzzle placed together correctly. The picture this puzzle revealed seemed to make sense. My family, and those with whom I chose to associate, agreed with it. But then I noticed one little piece of the puzzle out of place. As I looked closer, I began to see more and more pieces crammed together where they simply did not fit. I eventually sat back and viewed the puzzle from a dispassionate point of view. I realized the entire puzzle was put together incorrectly. What the picture wished to communicate to me, and what it actually said, were two different things.

I fully deconstructed the puzzle, piece by piece, and reconstructed it in the correct context and time line. My toolbox contained patience, reason, an unbiased perspective, and courage to touch the pieces. The pieces fit perfectly. The picture emerged graphically different then before. I desperately want my younger brother to have the same epiphany. My father wishes him the same. He is still three years younger than myself and stands just short of that breakthrough. I watch my dad communicate with him. He says just enough to send him happily on his way. I then engage my father open conversations. We speak, gain new insights, and ponder life's mysteries together.

When I arrived home from Peru, I choked with certainty. I wanted my dad to proclaim certainty regarding the Joseph Smith story. I pulled him aside and asked him why he never bore his testimony. He answered asking me what difference would it make in his life. He would still live the same values even without a spiritual experience. That answer did not sit well with me, and I brought it up with him from time to time. But I could not disagree with his logic. Dad found out the Church is not what it claims to be many years before I did. Every time I made a new discovery contrary to what we had been taught in Church, I called and shared it with my dad. He nearly always finished my sentences and understood the authenticity of the source information.

As I stepped over the wall of Mormon ignorance and into the light shed by reality, my dad supported me every step of the way. He did not condemn me, as did others in my family, quite the contrary. He told me, if he could do it all over again, he would have done things quite differently. I truly feel my siblings are missing out on a treasure, a gift to know our father's wisdom. It is a wisdom born in the depths of extensive medical training and a love for science. Regrettably, it is buried behind the Mormon wall of silence. The fact my father feels compelled not to speak openly with his own posterity only deepens my resolve to free my children from the mental bars that keep his wisdom at bay. I understand Dad's reticence toward openness. I understand any talk contrary to Mormon thinking is threatening to a members' psyche and may invoke the execution of the penalty.

Dad once told me that he has never had a close friend in whom he could fully discuss life's possibilities and purpose. He had a myriad of medical associates through the years, and many ward friends, but in Orwellian fashion, the confines of his thinking always remained susceptible to land on the desk of his local ecclesiastic leaders. He told me the closest friend he had, outside of Mom, was a ward member named Joe. Joe married Dad's first cousin, Marion. Joe did not believe in paying tithing. Joe believed it highly unlikely God would only reveal himself to less than one half of one percent of the world's population. This small speck of humanity represents all of the Mormons presence on earth. Joe garnered a genuinely nice disposition. He loved to tinker on cars. Joe brandished the formidable weapon of reason.

Dad loved that aspect about Joe, and many times wanted to discuss non-Mormon philosophies with him. But Dad said he always stopped short, as he did not want to upset Marion. Dad felt disheartened when Marion remarked that, upon her death, she would be assigned to a "worthy" husband to live with in Heaven. She made this Church-inspired comment less than a year after Joe's death. Another unholy wedge found its mark.

I consider my father a friend. I still highly value his insights, as he does mine. I guess we are just both lucky that way. We can challenge each other's thoughts without malice or limitations. I asked him how he could go to his grave without revealing his thoughts and feelings concerning Mormonism to his entire family. He writes, in email correspondences, that at this point he does not see how it would benefit him or his relationship with his grandchildren.

My dad is caught in the middle, born into a way of life not of his own choosing. I dedicated this book to my children, and to all who, like my father, are caught in the middle. But aren't we all? At some point, men and women should take hold of self-rule, and live with the responsibilities that follow. I love my dad. I consider him one of my greatest friends. Thank God, nature, or fate, that none of them has come between us. Father does know best for his situation, and I'm privileged to hear his deeper thoughts. He enthusiastically supports and pushes Mom, as she becomes relegated to a wheel chair. He reads out loud to her frequently, as her sight dims. He still does his own taxes and fixes every broken pipe and leaky faucet. My grandfather Reuben's frugality is in his genes. My dad is a skinny rail. He loves to hike. He grazes food, reads the paper and keeps the physical aspect of the home in order. Dad wants nothing more than to keep my mother happy.

I always look forward to visiting with Mom and Dad when they drop by our home in California. Recently they came to support Karen and Michelle. Michelle rode a bike from San Francisco to Los Angeles to raise money for AIDS awareness. Karen, and a group of her friends excitedly waited at the final ceremony where all the bikers crossed the finish line. Mom, Dad, my two boys and I watched Michelle cross the finish line. We are openly proud of her accomplishments. Michelle single handedly raised more money for AIDS awareness in one week, than the entire Mormon Church has raised for the cause to date. Yet, according to Mormon braggadocio, several Mormon chapels are being built every second of the day somewhere in the world. It is the Catholic history being repeated, only on a much smaller scale. My children belong to themselves, and just for the record, I told JD I also think it's weird whenever I hear Grandma call Grandpa, "Dick."

CHAPTER 13

A Legacy of Love

Be kind, for everyone you meet is fighting a hard battle.
Plato

Certainty sells. It can motivate and destroy. Roman Catholics marched with certainty against Greek Orthodox Catholics on the Crimean peninsula. Both churches remained certain God favored them in the conflict. With unwavering certainty, the Quakers spelled out condemnation upon the head of Grandmother Catherine. With equal certainty the Roman Catholics executed the penalty of excommunication, shunning and banishment upon Grandfather John for his love and marriage to Catherine. In a quiet reversal of fortune, we executed the penalty upon the religion of our birth. We excommunicated, shunned and banished it from our lives.

Linda and I recognize the allure of religious certainty, but we also understand its dangers. We now acknowledge the uncertain nature of life. Continents will continue to drift apart, ice ages will come and go, and evolution will march forward filling the voids in our ever-changing earthly environment. Uncertainty has always been there. Now we no longer require a religious leader to explain the unknowable, or to pretend occurrences of nature are acts of God or the Devil. We slapped the hand of our childhood mythology. We let go of Mormonism on principle. We could no longer be true to ourselves while at the same time holding hands with a religion that continuously makes self-serving claims that simply are not true.

I respect our ancestors. They acted with conviction and courage. My great-great grandfather, John Flynn, fought in the Crimean War. The time and place of his birth dictated the direction he pointed his rifle. I do not agree with any war whose justification is predicated upon divine dictate. The only war I can justify is one that fights for equality and basic human rights. But I do not fault or besmirch John Flynn's life. Rather, I feel an element of sorrow for the suffering he endured due to the negative impact of religion on his life. The dogmatic dictum of the British Army, along with the Catholic execution of the penalty, destroyed much of his life. I'm proud John Flynn had the temerity to marry a Quaker girl. I'm proud he placed distance between his heavy-handed religious overlords and took courage and personal authority to pursue a different life in the Land Down Under.

I feel sorry for Catherine, John's wife. The heartaches she bore seem too much for one life. At age 17, the first love of her life died, gunned down in an unnecessary religious war. She married a Catholic man, suffered through his excommunication, and received all the barbs and misapprehensions directed toward a non-believing Quaker. She survived John by 30 years. She raised her children alone while trying to leave them a legacy that made sense. Catherine had a tough go of it.

Michael, like my father, lived a life trapped in the middle. Being the youngest son of Catherine he gave into the prevailing religion that dominated life in Australia. He raised his children in the quasi-secular Church of England. Michael's limited pioneer quest kept one foot in the generally accepted church, and the other firmly planted in the soil of skepticism. Michael's mistake occurred when he failed to inoculate his children against the potential evils of cultic religions. The key to this failure can be found in the writings of Ethel, Reuben's wife.

She wrote: *"His parents did all they could to persuade him against the* [Mormon] *church but he would ask them to answer questions concerning life and salvation, they could not give him the satisfactory answer that he found in his new religion."* Mormons gave Reuben what all children desire, certainty. They provided a pat answer to all life's mysteries. In How We Know What Isn't So, author Thomas Gilovich writes: *"People will always prefer black-and-white over shades of grey, and so there will always be the temptation to hold overly-simplified beliefs and to hold them with excessive confidence."*

If only Reuben had understood the life of his grandmother Catherine, who suffered the consequences of religious certainty. Michael, nevertheless, lost his young son Reuben to a zealous Mormon illusion based on the other side of the planet.

As to Reuben, my grandfather, I hold mixed feelings. I am exceedingly proud he accomplished all he did with his limited education. In his earliest memory he recounted the shock of seeing a midwife take a large pair of scissors and snip the umbilical cord attached to his younger brother. After that, he said: *"Well, I had to unlearn other things such also as Santa Claus and Jack & The Bean Stalk."* Reuben understood these stories to be false, yet he believed in the fairy tales told by Joseph Smith. He believed because he wanted answers to the unknowable. He fell victim to the Forer Effect. Linda and I have now seen the midwife snip the umbilical cord, we studied Smith's history. We now understand the genesis of his fairy tales. We, like Grandpa, must "unlearn other things." Unfortunately, Grandpa lacked the history behind the tales.

It is striking to read Reuben's five personal histories and see the bulk of his notes regurgitate dogmatic Mormon doctrines. Most of his memoirs begin with him joining the Church. As his histories developed, he began to incorporate Smith's fairy tales into his own memories. He began two histories with the words: *"I was born of goodly parents,"* the exact words Smith used to begin the Book of Mormon. At one point in his history Reuben wrote: *"we moved a number of times to a new home which up till I was about 12 years, caused my sister and I to go to different churches such as the Church of England, Baptist, and Salvation Army Sunday School... At about 12 years I quit going to church as I did not like it, though I, at times, wondered what it was all about."* Most Mormons will recognize this as a reflection of Smith's stories about himself.

Did Grandfather Reuben ever really claim his right to define moral authority on his own terms? Most of his writings defer directly to Mormon hierarchal discourse. His prosaic justifications were not his own. His lack of accepted self-authority and autonomy exposed his Achilles heel in life, which at times weakened his perspectives toward the tender mercies he may have otherwise experienced.

His excitement to reach America left melancholy in his wake. His family in Australia could have received considerable aid and succor with his strong and capable hands. What did his invalid older sister, Muriel, have to gain with his departure? How were his mother and father blessed with his permanent trip to America? According to one of Reuben's histories, his justification for going to America primarily rested in the ability to do missionary work. Once in Utah he urgently pressed the local authority to grant him a temple recommend. They told him to wait six months, since many new arrivals became disenchanted with Mormonism after only a few months. Grandpa persisted, declaring: *"my dead ancestors could not wait six months."* I completely understand his sense of urgency. My mission leaders instructed me to "run" from door-to-door, as the Second Coming was imminent. But what of the living still drawing breath on earth? In Australia he lived in the mission field of humanity. His family loved him and connected hopes and dreams to their children. The familial dynamic inevitably changed with his departure.

I always wondered why the Church sent Grandpa to Tonga to build a college instead of another chapel. Grandpa's history answered that mystery. He stated that after the completion of the Church's Liahona College, he: *"received a letter from the Tongan government to get out of the country within 30 day."* It seems the royal family of Tonga was fed up with all the incoming sectarian churches, even churches posing as colleges. Linking secular education with missionary work has served the Church well. Witness the hundreds of Church owned seminary buildings constructed next to public schools.

Having said that, I am still proud Reuben was a man of conviction. It infuriates me any religious organization would take such unscrupulous advantage of an honest soul such as his. I am also grateful he took the time to record his history. Reading it broadens my perspectives and adds to the meaning of my life. I add my history here to his, in hopes his great-grandchildren, my children, will continue to broaden their perspectives, acceptance and understanding of all people.

I regret being born and indoctrinated into the world of Mormonism, but I certainly do not regret being raised in America. Nor, do I regret my beautiful wife, marriage and children. That part of grandpa's legacy affords me delight. It would have been nice to come to America strictly for its secular freedoms, rather than be closeted into the closed authoritarian system of Mormonism.

My father represented the first full-generation Mormon in our family. He baptized his wife, my mother, while in the mission field. He later married her in a Mormon temple, then immediately started their family. Even with all the rigors associated with medical school and the various commitments and residencies, they whispered into the ears of their young children, my siblings and I, the recommended indoctrination. His three sons all served two-year missions in foreign countries. One of his daughters also served an eighteen months mission. All seven of us kids married in Mormon temples. We worked hard in school and accepted church callings along the way. We passed the essential program to our children; filling them with fear of the world; safety in the Church; and a false history of Joseph Smith and Brigham Young. We passed along stories of non-

Mormons who did not have things work in their favor for lack of God's spirit in their lives. We all learned to rationalize away scenarios, which contradicted Church doctrine or history.

My mother left a broken home when she accepted Smith's gospel. She confided in me that she really sought a stable family environment with the presence of a father and a less angry mother. Though I now see the folly of the message my father, as well as myself, presented to unsuspecting investigators of the Mormon religion, I very much admire and respect my mother for following her understanding and her hope for an ideal family. Her life has come full circle and she now has a deeper understanding of what she gave up as a result of her venture into the religion. She laments the fact her own mother, my grandmother Clarke, stood outside of the temple on her wedding day. My mother now wonders how she could have so easily accepted such an unfair situation. Her new church family placed a wall before her mother, siblings and stepfather. She now corresponds with her last remaining sibling, Cam. He is 94 years old. Mom has not told him he was right about the Church when he called it a cult over 50 years ago. Ironically, I was named after Cam. My middle name is Cameron. I am more proud of my middle name than ever before. I don't recall ever meeting Uncle Cam. He was not a part of our "Mormon" family. What a shame.

Linda and I suffered the same fate as my mom's mother. Since we left the Church, we were not allowed to attend our daughter's wedding in the Mormon temple, the same temple in which we married. At the time of our marriage, Linda's uncle, a non-Mormon, waited patiently outside. We did not think anything about it. We just figured it only a matter of time before he too would see the light and join the only true church on earth. We were wrong. We now have felt the sting of divisive exclusivity engendered by the Mormon Church. Their wedding policy is evil.

Just four years prior to her death, Richard Flynn carried his bed-ridden mother-in-law into the waters of baptism. Dorothy listened to the missionary lessons while she lay dying in a nursing home. Her feeble body never attended meetings, but the Church finally possessed her as well. When she passed, Richard and Sylvia dutifully performed her required temple ordinances, posthumously, so she too would be received into Mormon heaven.

Mormons must convert the world, the living and the dead. I lived under this prime directive for 47 years. I see this same self-centered worldview when I read the words I penned while serving a mission in Peru. I cannot read my own Mormon history without embarrassment. The sheer naiveté and ignorance, mixed with the arrogance of certainty I professed is dumfounding. The atrocious grammar only accentuates the point. I took upon myself the personification of the young and brash Joseph Smith, speaking to the world with boldness. The difference being, Smith knew better, I did not. The end result, however, remains the same. We both lied. He lied for his own aggrandizement. I lied for the aggrandizement of his Church. I apologize to the people of Peru. My only excuse is "I was just following orders." I acted no better than my obtuse Stake President.

Unfortunately, we cast a wide net. We trained to view everyone as a potential baptism. Meeting high baptism goals stands supreme for all Mormon missionaries. My companions and I taught approximately 3,000 lessons over a two-year period, and to my regret I personally helped baptize 51 people. I take solace in the knowledge that the vast majority of Mormon converts quickly fall away from the Church. I know I split up families, and for that, I feel the most sorrow.

Ironically, my own mission taught me how fleeting belief can be. I served as a zone leader in a medium size town named Juliaca. It is a dismally brown, wind-swept city surrounded by barren lifeless plains. When I first arrived there, only seven people attended church. I tracked down the inactive local leader. He served as branch president for several years. He shrugged his shoulders as he informed me the town had over 300 families already baptized. Five of the seven people who attended when we arrived had been baptized in the previous month.

The Mormon experience only works when the entire family participates in the same-shared illusion. This is why Church leaders organize meetings with constant sharing of testimonies. Orally sharing a commitment to a belief with family and neighbors further commits oneself to that belief. It becomes a strong reinforcing mechanism powerful enough to deceive oneself into repeating illogical reasoning to support the professed belief. For years, I practiced mental gyrations, minimization, and rationalization to justify my commitment to nonsensical beliefs, such as magic rocks, magic compasses, golden plates, and nonexistent Lamanites.

This self-deception is not a thing to take lightly. I posed a simple question to some of my closest friends, who still adhere to Mormon illusions: "If God almighty, with all the angels, came down from heaven and stood before you and said to your face, "Joseph Smith is not a prophet," would you believe him?" Surprisingly, every time I ask this question I get a similar reaction... a pause. It is the pause of a mind searching for an answer that will somehow still allow Smith to be a prophet. I have heard Mormons respond, after the pause, saying such a scenario could never happen. Yet ironically, that is the exact same scenario claimed by Joseph Smith, that God came down and visited him, which is what they want so desperately to believe in the first place.

I once asked two family members, strong believers in Mormonism: "If you found out Joseph Smith chopped up babies every day of his life and ate them for lunch would you still believe he was a true prophet of God?" Both agreed they would. This is the strength of their shared illusion. One of them, after doing the mental "hokey pokey," reasoned that if Joseph did it, then God must have told him to do it, so it must be right. Any non-Mormon would call this an obvious case of brainwashing.

This adherence to sheer craziness is likely why most converts to the Church actually leave rather then continue to express illogical beliefs. However, children born into

Mormonism are so deep into the rabbit hole of illusion that any belief proffered them by their leaders is correct, regardless of how contradictory or nonsensical it may sound.

I have begun to peer through the exaggerated fears, past the wall of silence, and view the world with better appreciation of our collective history. I particularly appreciate brave individuals who sacrificed a comfortable life to share with the world a perspective of openness. I speak now of men like Thomas Paine, Voltaire and Benito (Baruch) Spinoza. Sacrifices of men such as these laid the very foundation of our current American constitution built upon individual freedoms. A constitution "of the people," not "of God," or any of man's interpretations of God.

Baruch Spinoza studied in rabbinical school to become a rabbi. While studying the Old Testament he discovered inconsistencies, duplication errors, impossible anachronisms and fatal contradictions in the text. When he pointed out the errors to his superiors, they admonished him to keep his discoveries to himself. He did not. The Jewish leaders of his synagogue knew the survival of their small community in Amsterdam depended on avoiding scandal. They offered Spinoza hush money if he would renounce his growing heretical views in public. He would not take it. Jewish leaders then invoked the execution of their penalty. Before the ark of the synagogue in Amsterdam they excommunicated him. The verdict read, in part:

"Espinoza should be excommunicated and expelled from the people of Israel...Cursed be he by day and cursed be he by night; cursed be he when he lies down and cursed be he when he rises up. Cursed be he when he goes out and cursed be he when he comes in. The Lord will not spare him, but then the anger of the Lord and his jealousy shall smoke against that man, and all the cures that are written in this book shall lie upon him, and the Lord shall blot out his name from under Heaven."[1]

Although cursed by the Jewish religion of his birth,

Spinoza wrote *"The Tractatus Theologico-Politicus,"* (English translations-Theological-Political Treatise) in 1670. His book not only pointed out inherent textual errors, but also included ethical problems within the text. It undermined not only Jewish authority, but Christian authority as well. All religious leaders of the day roundly condemned him. Rather then defend erroneous religious texts, they choose to use ad hominem arguments to attack him. They conveniently labeled him the "Atheist Jew," even though he was no longer a member of the Jewish community, and he professed a belief in the God of nature. He humbly kept to himself working as a lens grinder.

After his death, friends found another manuscript written by Spinoza in his desk. They published his work posthumously and it spread like wildfire throughout Europe. In his book, *"Ethics treatise on the Emendation of the Intellect,"*2 Spinoza single-handedly laid down the philosophical pretext for future democratically elected governments, which recognize the basic rights of individuals. His arguments formed the ethical foundation used by the Founding Fathers in the creation of the Constitution of the United States. I highly value my individual liberties and freedoms granted me by the Constitution. It is no exaggeration to state that Spinoza's quiet efforts afforded the lives of hundreds of millions of people with individual freedom. He wrote the book on Ethics. He wrote what it means to love your neighbor in a society, without adding divine justifications predicated upon man's interpretation of God.

Men like Joseph Smith, who usurped individual and mental freedoms, disgust me. Their self-proclaimed authority comes from a God of their own imagination. Ultimately, their tawdry self-serving motives become exposed in their private behavior, amassing wealth and telling lies. But despite such men, I have hope.

Epiphanies happen and magically a mind is set free. It happens to members of the Mormon Church. It happened to me. As I broaden my horizons by reading books, such as "Infidel," by Ayaan Hirsi Ali, I recognize it happens to members of other belief systems. The mind suddenly realizes the religious illusion is not what it professes to be. It is both terrifying and liberating. It is confusing and thought provoking. It offers unprecedented growth and challenges. Though it happens around the world, the awakening still must be dealt with in a real and personal way. Regretfully, there does not appear to be an easy way for humans to relate to one another without running headlong into the pretentious, self-serving barriers cultic religions create.

How do you "snap" a person who does not want to leave the comfort of a pernicious illusion? A person who doesn't want to be snapped will resist it, because, without the illusion, their self-identity and current sense of certainty would be destroyed. The grasp of cultic indoctrination only allows for a "self" defined by the cult. Any other self is to be demonized, ostracized and feared. Often physical interventions require distance and time to free people from cultic thinking.3 Most members won't come out of it until they are ready, or until they accidentally begin to think for themselves.

The Mormon Church accomplishes what cults, in the pejorative, aspire to achieve, total domination of thought and will. Grandfather and I thought we knew unknowable things. Since the advent of recorded history, post-death information has both inspired and plagued the mind of man. We further asserted to know a history of Smith neither of us really knew, a history that "is" knowable.

Shortly after Linda informed her sister of our findings in church history, she asked Linda not to become one of those "bitter" Mormons who leaves the Church. When Linda and I married in a Mormon temple, I agreed to: *"receive her unto myself to be my lawful and wedded wife..."* and she agreed to: *"give herself to me to be my lawful and wedded wife, and for me to be her lawful and wedded husband..."* These commitments we made to one another. But within the same sentence, we also made a commitment to the Church. The actual secret temple wedding reads as follows:

"Officiator: *Brother Brent, [naming groom] do you take Sister Linda [naming bride] by the right hand and receive her unto yourself to be your lawful and wedded wife for time and all eternity, <u>with a covenant and promise that you will observe and keep all the laws, rites, and ordinances</u> pertaining to this Holy Order of Matrimony in the <u>New and Everlasting Covenant,</u> and this you do in the presence of God, angels, and these witnesses of your own free will and choice?.....Groom: (says) Yes.*

Officiator: *Sister <u>Linda</u>, do you take brother <u>Brent</u>, by the right hand and give yourself to him to be his lawful and wedded wife, and for him to be your lawful and wedded husband, for time and all eternity, <u>with a covenant and promise that you will observe and keep all the laws, rites and ordinances</u> pertaining to this Holy Order of Matrimony in <u>the New and Everlasting Covenant</u>, and this you do in the presence of God, angels, and these witnesses of your own free will and choice?.....Bride: (says) Yes.*

Officiator: *By virtue of the Holy Priesthood and the authority vested in me, I pronounce you Brent, and Linda, legally and lawfully husband and wife for time and all eternity...and I seal upon you the blessings of kingdoms, thrones, principalities, powers, dominions and exaltations, with all the blessings of Abraham, Isaac and Jacob and say unto you: be fruitful and multiply and replenish the earth...together with all the blessings appertaining unto the <u>New and Everlasting Covenant</u>, I seal upon you by virtue of the Holy Priesthood, through your faithfulness, in the name of the Father, and of the Son, and of the Holy Ghost, Amen."*[4]

That's it. This is the entire temple wedding that non-Mormons and non-tithe payers are not allowed to witness. This is what young brothers and sister are not allowed to see or hear. It is administered in an assembly-like, cookie-cutter fashion. Wedding rings and affectionate phrases such as "you may kiss the bride" or "honor, love and cherish one another" are not part of the official ceremony. Indeed, we promised to: "<u>observe and keep all the laws, rites and ordinances in the New and</u>

Everlasting Covenant." The "New and Everlasting Covenant" means accepting plural, or polygamous, marriage.5 In addition, the Church defines it as accepting all of their rules and ordinaces.6 It seems like we married the Church more than we married one another. The Church became our "third spouse." Temple marriages create a love triangle.

Linda and I worked hard to *"receive"* one another as husband and wife. We worked hard to honor the commitment we made to the Church. We gave the Church our time, talent, money and affection. When we learned the Church was not what it claimed to be, we felt shocked, betrayed and angry. It was as if we discovered our third spouse had been cheating on us for the past 25 years. It hurt deeply. It led to the divorce against our "church spouse," who remains unrepentant. Imagine the pain incurred in a divorce, where the deceptive, cheating spouse is caught, then blames the innocent spouse for having discovered the infidelity. Now imagine someone telling you not to be bitter against the unrepentant cheating spouse. This is exactly what the Church wants its members to think. Members assume the Church is true because they believe it is true. For whatever reason, desire, denial or ignorance to the facts, most members have not yet discovered the infidelity of their cheating church partner. When that illusion is finally broken and they begin down the road of self-determination, only then will they fully realize the impossibility of not harboring some resentment toward the cheater. Only time, understanding and compassion overcome such deep wounds. Glib statements, such as, "well at least don't be bitter," do nothing to mend a broken heart, or in our case, two broken hearts. Mormon temple weddings are the greatest wedge the Church drives between the natural love of a husband and wife. It places a plethora of dogmatic demands on the couple, all of which sprung from a sea of lies that serves church interests outside the marriage.

I am saddened for my siblings who continue to believe their families can only reach heaven through obedience to Mormon authority. This is the biggest stick of fear swung before their eyes. It keeps them obedient to church dictates. It is to believe God's hands remain tightly bound behind his/her back unless the Mormon Church provides secret signs, tokens, handshakes and new names, etc.7 Secrets that keep changing, since the day Smith plagiarized them from the Masons.8 It is the Catholic system of indulgences, combined with acts of faith, to free souls from purgatory revisited all over again. Only this time hidden behind secret temple walls and reinforced by a code of silence.

Mormon doctrine threatens members who leave the Church, and "deny the truth" with eternal suffering in hell. This fear-inspiring indignation is clearly stated in their current cannon of scriptures and could easily be mistaken for similar condemnations slipped through the lips of Quakers, Catholics and Jews. Mormon doctrine states:

"Thus saith the Lord concerning all those who know my power, and have been made partakers thereof, and suffered themselves through the power of the devil to be overcome, and to deny the truth and defy my power—

They are they who are the sons of perdition of whom I say that it had been better for them never to have been born; For they are vessels of wrath, doomed to suffer the wrath of God, with the devil and his angels in eternity; Concerning whom I have said there is no forgiveness in this world nor in the world to come"...

These are they who shall go away into the lake of fire and brimstone, with the devil and his angels".... "they shall go away into everlasting punishment, which is endless punishment, to reign with the devil and his angels in eternity, where their worms dieth not, and the fire is not quenched, which is their torment."9

"These are they who suffer the wrath of on earth. These are they who suffer the vengeance of eternal fire. These are they who are cast down to hell."10

"And in his hot displeasure, and in his fierce anger, in

his time, will cut off those wicked, unfaithful, and...unbelievers;
Even in outer darkness, where there is weeping, and wailing,
*and gnashing of teeth."*11

In addition to these common age-old fear tactics,
directed toward nonbelievers, current Mormon scriptures also
paint a bleak picture for all people who do not accept the
Mormon Gospel:

"Behold, and lo, there are none to deliver you; for ye
obeyed not my voice when I called to you out of the heavens; ye
believed not my servants, and when they were sent unto you ye
received them not. Wherefore, they sealed up the testimony and
bound up the law, and ye were delivered over unto darkness.
These shall go away into outer darkness, where there is weeping,
*and wailing, and gnashing of teeth."*12
"And there shall be weeping and wailing among the
hosts of men....I will take vengeance upon the wicked, for they
will not repent; for the cup of mine indignation is
full... Wherefore, I the Lord God will send forth flies upon the
face of the earth, which shall take hold of the inhabitants thereof,
and shall eat their flesh, and shall cause maggots to come in
upon them; And their tongues shall be stayed that they shall not
utter against me; and their flesh shall fall from off their bones,
and their eyes from their sockets; And it shall come to pass that
the beasts of the forest and the fowls of the air shall devour them
up. And the great and abominable church, which is the whore of
*all the earth, shall be cast down by devouring fire."*13

It is little wonder Mormon families impulsively react
with weeping and wailing upon hearing the news that loved ones
no longer believe in Smith's claims. The legacy they inherited
limits their acceptance of different perspectives and entices them
to propagate divisive dogmas that cause real hurt and pain.

Mormonism is not the only religion consigned to execute
a penalty toward those who leave. In the world today, there
remain religions that openly stone to death those who leave their

faith. In more civilized countries the stoning only destroys social standing. In truly enlightened countries, stones remain on the ground and are used to build bridges of understanding.

Twenty-two years ago a nurse caught up to us in a cold Nebraska hospital. She informed us our newborn infant, whom we held in our arms, was probably deaf. At that point, we were already in a state of shock, having just learned from the doctor the extent of Jason's brain injury. The doctor left little room for hope. Linda and I learned to interact with Jason using "total communication." This involved signing to him as well as speaking to him. For the first year and a half we diligently signed as we cared for him, not knowing if he would ever sign back.

In order to feed Jason, we propped him up in a highchair with rolled-up towels at his sides. Cerebral palsy kept his tiny hands tightly clenched in a fist. As always, Linda enthusiastically spoke, and signed, "Time to eat".... "Isn't that delicious Jason?".... "Would you like some more?"

One day, while eating at McDonalds, Jason looked up at Linda and brought one fist up to his mouth and crudely tapped on his lips with a look of determination and defiance. Linda's eyes widened as her mouth dropped. Had Jason just signed his first word... "food?"

Filled with excitement, Linda quickly rifled another french fry in his mouth, and then paused just long enough to see if he would do it again. Sure enough, he again struggled to bring his fist to his mouth and tapped his lips. Linda screamed with joy. She rushed home to share Jason's breakthrough with Julie and me.

Despite the negative predictions of the doctors, Jason found his voice. We then sat back filled with excitement. But Jason was not content. He soon bumped his fists together, crudely signing the word "more," after which he brought one fist up to his lips. "More food!" Jason's ability to understand startled us, but for him it represented a new beginning in a life of exploration. In like manner, we crudely bumped our fists together, discontent with the false and stifling predictions of our religious leaders. The legacy we leave will never stand in the way of those tiny fists.

I love all my children. I am proud of Julie. She is a beautiful thinker with a fun zest for life. She recently gave birth to our first precious grandchild.

I am proud of Jason. He is my first-born son, my friend and hero with a heart of gold. I came back from death to be his friend. While Linda assisted Simon and Julie in London, after the birth of our first grandchild, Jason and I stayed home and played chess each night to determine who would wash the dishes the following day. I now play chess wearing dish gloves.

I am proud of Jessica. She is rising to the challenge to understand and accept all people at a pivotal and difficult point in her young life. I am proud of JD. As I drive him to his baseball games, practices or school, I marvel at what his life can be.

I told JD I'm jealous of him. I wish I could start over in a life without divisive dogmas cluttering up my head. He is free to embrace all aspects of science and the arts, without denying facts that don't agree with someone's "true" religion. I hope and wish the same for all my children and posterity, that they remain mentally free to enjoy this beautiful journey of life. I hope to set James Dean's feet upon a path whose legacy leaves love and acceptance for all neighbors along the way.

CHAPTER 14

A Letter to James Dean

*The most formidable weapon against
errors of every kind is Reason.*
Thomas Paine

Dear JD,

Your mother and I made a mistake. For the first 11 years of your life we raised you in the religious tradition of Mormonism. Your mother and I believed with all our hearts the things taught by Mormon leaders were true. We wept when we discovered they lied to us.

We have since become aware that the fundamental philosophy of Mormonism is the same as most religions. They pretend to have a special connection to God. They profess to know God's will for you. They claim to hold the keys to heaven.

Religions rely on books of scripture. Muslims have the Koran, Jews have the Torah, Christians have the Bible, Hindus have the Vedas, Shinto has the Kojiki, Taoism has the Tao-te-Ching, Confusium has the Confucian Canon, and Sikhism has the Granth. Even small religions like Mormonism have books, such as the Book of Mormon.

The purpose of all these holy books is the same, to make the reader become obedient. Religious leaders need you to become obedient so they can control you. To show you are a true believer, that you have faith, religious leaders will require you to prove it, by giving them your time, talent and money. JD, it is not in your best interest to give away your life's time, energy and money to simply build up a religion created by people.

I am going to share with you a few secrets religious leaders don't want you to know. Religious books contain two basic parts. One part is what I call the "love-your-neighbor" commandments. The second I call "belief" commandments. The love-your-neighbor commandments are good. The belief commandments are not.

The love-your-neighbor commandments are written in heroic and empathetic stories. Every one of the sacred texts referenced above recommends you "not" kill, cheat, steal, lie, commit adultery, covet, etc. They all ask you to be kind to the sick and needy, and share with the less fortunate. They correctly recommend you deal fairly and justly with your neighbors and extend mercy to them.

Love-your-neighbor commandments are good and have been around for millions of years. They predate Joseph Smith's Book of Mormon. They predate Jesus Christ's New Testament. They predate Moses' Old Testament. They are inscribed in Ancient Egyptian law. The love-your-neighbor laws predate writing. They have been practiced for millions of years, and are even practiced by millions of different animals, within their own species.

It is absolutely in our own best interest to love our neighbors. If, for example, we don't love them, if we allow lying, cheating, stealing or killing to occur in our neighborhoods, then the same may happen to us. It is in our best interest that society works together for our common self-interest. This is self-evident. It does not take a holy book to tell us this. An ant cannot read, yet they understand the benefits of working together under common rules. Secular governments, like the United States which do not endorse a religion, have set up laws promoting fairness that reflect ancient love-your-neighbor rules. As Thomas Jefferson penned, "We hold these truths to be self-evident."

These love-your-neighbor rules truly are ancient and a part of natural evolution. Sharks have sharp teeth, but they usually don't eat their own species. Humans have sharp minds, but they don't eat each other. There are of course exceptions, like when humans and other animals run out of food. Under those conditions we have been known to eat each other, but generally, that is not the case. In order for any complex species to survive, they must foster an environment, which is conducive to procreation and the safety of the incoming generation. People inherently know this to be a true concept that works toward our self-interest and self-preservation. Animals who work against themselves become extinct.

Unfortunately, holy books also contain belief commandments. The belief commandments define what God is and how one should love and worship God. They say, "to love God," one must be obedient. Then, of course, they go on to expound a hundred things one must do to please God. This is where the great religious fraud occurs.

Readers of holy texts inherently recognize love-your-neighbor commandments are good and ultimately in our self-interest. However, readers mistakenly think belief commandments are equally good, when in fact they are not.

Like all magic acts, the trick is quite obvious once the secret is revealed. Religions emphasizing belief commandments capitalize (take in money) using this simple sleight of hand. Most holy books intermingle things all humans intuitively know to be true, such as to love your neighbor is in your self-interest, with things that are completely not knowable to humans like the various Gods, or mythological Gods and their apparent egotistical desires to have us worship them. People read a part of the holy books they know to be true, i.e. the love-your-neighbor parts, and they assume if that part is true, then the rest of it must be true as well. Hence, millions of people around the globe fall victim to the holy book sleight of hand. They readily get sucked into a religion full of rules and acts of faith required to worship, one God or another, not realizing only half of what they read in holy books is true.

It is interesting and telling that most holy books have the same love-your-neighbor teachings, but they vastly differ when it comes to the secrets about God, and the rituals God requires of you to reach heaven, paradise, nirvana, enlightenment, etc. The inevitable outcome is to convince you that you are never quite good enough, need to try harder, pay more money, and be more obedient to the religious/spiritual authority. It is a vicious cycle which collects the innocent and ignorant, then victimizes believers with mental deception leading to wars and poverty. In the name of one God or another, based solely on belief commandments, men commit unspeakable atrocities toward their neighbor.

Ironically, religious institutions, as opposed to individuals, are not required to love their neighbors. They become a divisive tool to separate you from your neighbor. Religion shows its evil face when belief in a God becomes more important than loving behaviors toward a neighbor who has a different belief in God. Mormonism is no exception to this rule.

Joseph Smith taught all other religions are an "abomination"1 before God. Which is similar to many other religions' teachings. They believe their conception of God is right and everyone else is wrong. Perhaps the only thing unique about Mormonism is the endless multiplicity of lies required to maintain the belief of its members. As science discovers errors in the Mormon story, Mormon leaders simply create new lies. They use revelations to hide or justify the exposed lies. This is why the Book of Mormon has been constantly revised since the day it was first published in 1830, even though Smith claimed it came directly from God, word for word. Mormon leaders, like many religious leaders, pretend to care about the "God part" of their holy books. In truth, they care most about retaining power, hence the myriad of holy books, rituals, interpretations, etc. As long as you bow your head and do their will, religious leaders will be happy. JD, life is too short to keep charlatans happy. Most people recognize this pattern in all other religions except their own.

It is true the human mind cannot know all things. There are things we don't know and things we don't understand. This naturally requires life to contain elements of uncertainty. People desire an understanding of the world around them. People don't like uncertainty. People innately want to think someone smarter than themselves will protect them in times of uncertainty. In 1740, David Hume explains this philosophy. As a side note, you may someday explore the richness of philosophy, and when you do, check out Spinoza.

Religions sell certainty. If something good happens in your life, religious leaders tell you God blessed you. If something bad happens in your life, they tell you God punished you, or God is testing you to see if you will obey what they, the religious leaders, dictate. The absolute truth of the matter is religious leaders do not know the mind or will of God or the Gods. They only pretend to know because certainty sells and lines their pockets with money, power and sometimes sex.

Your mother and I don't claim to know any ultimate secret truth about our existence. We just know that we are. We exist, and truth is not a lie. We are sorry to have dragged you to church during the formative years of your life and filled your head with all the nonsense concerning dead and living Mormon prophets. We are glad you love your neighbors. We clearly see those self-protective traits are naturally taught at home and expanded upon in civics or ethics classes taught around the world. I'm sorry the Bishop talked you out of your $25 dollars. He said it belonged to the Lord. The Mormon Church is not the Lord, nor is any man-made organization. JD, you are your own Lord and must act accordingly.

We hold open the possibility of God, but we will not follow a dishonest God, nor a God defined by other men. Some people are preoccupied to know God's will. They pray constantly and suffer through all sorts of bizarre rituals trying to figure out what God wants them to do. JD, love your neighbor and you'll be on a sure footing. Worship God through holy books and you'll be wasting time. You will lose money, think less of yourself, and engender animosity toward all other belief systems and people in the world. Don't listen to imposters of reality.

So now you know the secret destructive power behind religion. Religion only serves our culture in a positive way when they teach correct love-your-neighbor ethics. Religions are most destructive when they confuse love-your-neighbor ethics with belief commandments that supposedly serve God. A perfect example of this is when Mormon Prophet Brigham Young declared, "*This is loving our neighbor as ourselves; if he needs help, help him; and if he wants salvation and it is necessary to spill his blood on the earth in order that he may be saved, spill it.... That is the way to love mankind.*"

JD, had Brigham Young stopped his preaching at: "if he needs help, help him," and left out his evil ideas involving his concept of salvation, then the lives of hundreds of Mormons would not have been destroyed in a religious blood bath justified in the name of God. Religious leaders know no more about God than you.

The good news, JD, is that there exists a wealth of knowledge we can acquire in this life. Science and technology progress despite any underlying pretext from a panhandling God cloaked in the greedy or misguided robes of a "holy priesthood." The world is your playground, full of fun and adventure. It abounds with opportunities to love your neighbors. I recommend you help the poor and the needy, but help them directly with your life's efforts. Don't give your money to a church that will simply keep most of it. That's another mistake I made. I gave hundreds of thousands of dollars to the Mormon Church, and what did they do with it? They built more churches to collect more money, to build more churches, etc. I wish now that I gave it to the needy and not the greedy.

Again, I apologize for giving away so much of your

inheritance to a wasteful endeavor. Religions teach it is your duty to worry about life after death. They are quick to help solve this mystery by taking your money, time and talent. What a waste. I hope these words will save you the 47 years I wasted chasing my tail in the Mormon Church.

I simply believe all good people "go to heaven" regardless of belief or non-belief in any God or God mythology.

JD, I would also like to discuss with you a word people define incorrectly to fool you. The word is "morality" or "good." What is moral? What is good?

Good equals self-interest. If you cut off your hand we would call that bad, or against your self-interest. If you spend your life extending a helping hand to others we would call that good, because eventually one of those people will extend a helping hand back to you. Generally this is thought of as Karma, or what goes around comes around. It is because our human species has worked together so effectively; we have become the dominant animal on the planet.

Doing "good" has always been in our self-interest. It not only has preserved us as a species, but it makes us feel good inside which reinforces the preservation of self. Being good avoids the pitfalls of being bad. It is not in your self-interest to be bad and end up sitting in a prison cell. It is not in your best interest to lie, cheat or steal because all those behaviors bring negative consequences to your life.

The only commandments you don't have to worry about are the belief commandments. They change from religion to religion. Indeed, they even change within the same religion over time. If you fully comprehend this important secret, then a huge load will lift off your shoulders. There is an endless supply of belief commandments, which have nothing to do with loving your neighbors.

My fatherly advice is, do good. Allow people to believe as they may, but personally don't feel beholden to any religious group or cult. When you adhere to someone's belief, you immediately exclude yourself from the rest of your fellow human family and all the richness of life and understanding that can be mutually shared.

All the belief in the world will not change what will or will not happen after you die. Don't let anyone fool you when religious leaders pretend to know secret things that occur after death. Belief won't change a thing. Doing good will, especially in this life.

People lie for a variety of reasons. JD, a lie never sits still. It only knows to grow and destroy everything in its path. A lie follows its creator.

Shortly after the Mormon Church was organized, early members began to compete to see who would lead. Hiram Page acquired a seer stone of his own and started receiving revelations contrary to Joseph Smith.2 The Whitmer brothers and Oliver Cowdery believed Page's revelations. Joseph Smith then conjured up a revelation that Hiram's seer stone did not work.3 Later, Oliver Cowdery claimed he received revelations. Then Smith claimed another revelation, telling Oliver that only Smith gets to have revelations.4 Then a member, John Noah, claimed to be a prophet and Smith expelled him from the Church.5 Following that, a woman named Hubble claimed to receive revelations and some members believed her. Joseph Smith again received a revelation that only he gets to receive revelations.6 Others continued to challenge Smith's authority. Many dissented because they wanted to be the boss. Were this not all true, it would be comical.

In order to retain his authority over the Church, Smith created an enormous lie, a lie that would follow him the rest of his life. A lie he expanded and changed in years to come. In 1832 he claimed, for the first time, that some 12 years earlier he concluded all religions were false, and he needed forgiveness from his personal sins. He further said he went into the local forest where Jesus met him and forgave him of his sins. He created his "face-to-face" lie about Jesus in order to retain the upper hand of authoritarian rule over his new church.

Truth remains constant whereas a lie becomes a dying

creature. Once a lie is created it must be fed. The liar must not only remember the lie, but is consigned to remember the details of the lie and the reason for the lie. In addition the liar must recall to whom the lie was delivered. When truth surfaces to reveal the lie, a new more all-encompassing lie must be created to hide or prop up the failing first lie.

Until he penned it in 1832, no one, not even members of his own family or friends, had heard this big lie, supposedly meeting Jesus in the woods some 12 years earlier.7 The lie worked its temporary magic and for a time no one threatened Smith's standing as the head of his new church. But the lie festered and began to grow. In 1834, he recounted the same lie to a newspaper. He began to change the lie to make it sound more credible. He added angel visitors to make him appear even more important. Then in 1838, he penned an even greater lie to give strength to the old one. This time he changed many more details.

He claimed that, not only Jesus visited him, but also God the Father showed up to make the introduction. He had to alter the original lie since his new belief required God and Jesus to be two separate beings. (Incidentally, he also retroactively altered many lines in the Book of Mormon to correspond with his new definition of the trinity.) Smith claimed, in a later 1838 version, that Jesus personally picked him to be the instrument to create His church on earth, and all other church creeds represented an abomination in His sight. By adding these personal instructions from Jesus, to himself, he managed to keep all other claims to church authority at bay. It just so happened, in 1838 Smith was caught in a bank scandal and lost his credibility among the faithful. Half of his 12 apostles apostatized (left the Church), due to Smith's bank fraud. They included his counselors. Smith's new 1838 version of an old lie was needed to put to rest the tide of suspicions that arose when many questioned his revelations and authority to lead.

Smith notoriously lied about his marital infidelities. He lied to his wife, his church, the public, and to his secret wives. In the last 3 years of his life he bedded, in secret matrimony, nearly every woman he could get his hands on. Over 30 women, identified by affidavits supplied by Brigham Young, exposed his philandering.8 When his amorous attempts failed, Smith introduced yet another lie. He claimed he was only testing the virtue of the women.

Joseph Smith had a counselor named Sidney Rigdon. Sidney had a daughter named Nancy. Smith tried to marry Nancy in secret. Nancy would have no part of it. Dissembling Smith created yet another lie. He told Nancy if she would not marry him, an angel with a flaming sword would kill him. Nancy would still have no part in it. Smith told her if she revealed his advances toward her, he would discredit her in the community by destroying her reputation. Smith later softened his rhetoric toward her and wrote her a letter, which justified his sexual advances. When Sidney learned the truth from Nancy, he angrily approached Smith, who denied all his actions toward his daughter. Sidney reached in his pocket and produced the letter Smith wrote to Nancy. Smith was caught in yet another bald-faced lie, and it spelled the beginning of the end of a life filled with lies.9

Smith's addictive impulse again struck when he tried to marry Jane Law. Jane was married to William Law, another counselor to Smith. Jane would have no part of it and told her husband. William's education, as an attorney, superseded Smith's wily cunning. Smith's secret marriage proposal to Jane angered William. William pressed Joseph to repent and renounce his secret marriages to the various married women and young girls of the community. Joseph would not. So on May 23, 1844, William filed suit against Smith in Hancock County Circuit Court, at Carthage, charging Smith had been living with Maria Lawrence "in an open state of adultery" from October 12, 1843 to the day of the suit. In response, Smith did what he knew best, he publicly lied, denying his adultery and polygamy in a speech he delivered on May 26 saying: *"What a thing it is for a man to be accused of committing adultery, and having seven wives, when I can find only one."*10 (Brigham Young later confirmed

Smith secretly married over 30 women at the time he made that public prevarication.11)

William Law then helped organize a newspaper, the Nauvoo Expositor. On June 7, 1844, its first and only edition was published. In it, William and others threatened to expose all of Smith's secret marital affairs publicly unless he repented of his illegal and immoral behavior with women of the community. Rather than face up to his life of lies, Smith angrily used his power as town Mayor. He declared the press a "public nuisance" and ordered its destruction.12 He then sheepishly fled in the face of an impending arrest, for destroying a free press. He surrendered and ultimately died at the hands of angry citizens who would bear no more of his lies and adulterous behavior. Karma, what goes around comes around. Smith's lies and bad behavior directly led to his death.

It is accurate to say Smith's lies grew and caught up with him. It is accurate to say all lies grow and catch up to us. JD, I recount the devastating effects Smith's lies had upon him to underscore the dangers of living a lie. Lies are not in your self-interest. They are not good. I also retell the sorry story of Smith's life so you may fully appreciate the legacy I wish to leave you. It is to expose the truth of Smith's lies, so you are not consigned to a life of repeating or defending them. Truth is never a lie. The Mormon Church today still conceals these facts from the world and, more abhorrently, from their own members. Learn from my mistakes. Learn from Smith's mistakes.

JD, if you no longer feel obligated to perpetuate Smith's heritage of lies, then I feel that I may die in peace. My legacy disentangled you from a pernicious religious lie, stamped upon both you and me at birth. You are no longer caught in the middle.

Your church is your mind.13 It is a beautiful thing. You carry it wherever you go. Only you own it. Perhaps the greatest "execution of the penalty" occurs when you allow others to replace your church with theirs. You are your "true" self when you think for yourself.

I love you and hope you have the most wonderful life experience possible. You are a wonderful young man, with a terrific body and an open mind. The world lies at your feet, waiting to be discovered. Your neighbors will benefit from your existence. The world is full of good. The world also contains pious posers who will try and take advantage of you. Knowledge and reason are your best protections. Smile and enjoy the ride. I look forward to your contributions and happiness.

Come what may or may not, I love you.

Dad

P.S. As I openly learn about the world around me, I am continually amazed. I hope you remain open for the same experiences.

Epilogue

There are worst things than dying, like not living.
Brent C. Flynn

My own journey out of my birth religion is a part of who I am. I find most of the stereotypes imprinted deep within my psyche by religion are false. People of every ethnicity desire the same. Their hopes and dreams reflect mine. Labels offend them as they do me. Diversity stimulates and enriches my life.

Even with the added responsibility required in thinking for oneself, our experience has been one of quiet excitement. I am relieved not to feel compelled to support the baggage of the Mormon Church. It is what it is. It is not what it claims. I will never carry its water again.

Knowledge always runs faith out of the building in shame. Instead of the constant preoccupation with the unknowable afterlife, I am now more interested in this life and the lives of those around me. It makes me want to reach out and touch nature and understand that which is knowable. I hope to erase as much faith from my life as knowledge and time will permit. I am especially happy because of the excellence of my partner and wife, Linda, who shares my journey. Her companionship and love is real. I admire and respect her. We are both exceedingly happy to remove ourselves from the twisted love triangle we once had with the Mormon Church.

My parents and grandparents accepted Mormon claims on faith. They were not given information exposing the true lives of Joseph Smith or Brigham Young. Had they been given full disclosure regarding Smith and Young's history, they would have scoffed at the very notion of becoming a Mormon.

The Mormon Church never really cared about my ancestors or their rights. They never cared about my family or me. Even when we learned of their current and past frauds, and tried to amicably leave, they made it difficult for us. We asked to be left alone. They did not respect our privacy. We moved to another state to escape their grasp. Within short order, they tracked us down through other members, a skill I acquired while fulfilling my duties as Ward Membership Clerk.

They first sent the local High Priest Group Leader. He showed up on our doorstep armed with pamphlets and a message from the local bishop. I politely informed him our family was not interested in attending church. He all but ignored me, and said he had already made arrangements for home teachers (men assigned to teach and watch families), and visiting teachers (women assigned to teach women), to come by for a visit. I repeated our desire to be left alone. He then quipped we would have to speak with the bishop to make any changes. He smiled as he walked away, having completed his assignment.

We fully understood, as long as our names appeared on church records, they would never leave us alone until they either demonized us or received our devotion and money. The next day we sent a certified letter directly to Church headquarters in Salt Lake City, requesting our names be removed from their records. In a bizarre response, the Church said they could not remove our names, stating it was not their problem, but a local "ecclesiastical matter." Having been the Membership Clerk, I knew this to be another prevarication. In fact, local wards cannot delete member records without the approval from Salt Lake leaders.

In the end, we sent 4 different letters and waited over 6 months for the Mormon Church to finally agree to remove our names from their organization. Correspondences from the Church, to our family, were condescending and demeaning. In addition, they would not remove the names of our minor children unless each of them individually signed the request.

Four months after we formally asked to have our names removed, JD told us a boy from school approached him and wanted to know why he did not attend church. JD asked him what he was talking about. The boy informed him the Mormon Sunday school teacher called out his name in church each week, and consequently marked him absent. Upon hearing this, my civility toward the Church finally broke. Despite being disparaged, invade and shunned by members of the Church in Mesa, we retained our civility and quietly withdrew, moving out of state to begin a new life. I now stood disgusted with the cultic grip and underhanded delay tactics employed by the Church.

The Mormon Church is a "legacy theft." It intentionally robs its members of their time, talent and money. It stamps a precast and self-serving legacy upon all who are deceived by their false stories and pious rhetoric. It employs multiple psychological techniques to control the mind, and purposely places unnatural wedges between loving family relationships. It is especially harmful toward innocent children who are raised under its pretentious illusion. It restricts personal growth by requiring adherents to defend silly, outdated and false nonsense. It teaches racism from the pulpit; when in fact, Blacks did not descend from the evil seed of Cain, and Native Americans are not descendants from the evil seeds of Laman and Lemuel. It subdues and minimizes the intelligence and capabilities of women. It attempts to retain its membership by damning to hell any who dare leave its self-proclaimed kingdom. It is a cult.

I contacted an attorney and threatened the Mormon Church with legal action if they would not immediately remove our names from their records. In addition, I demanded a full accounting of all the monies the Church collected from us. Mormon Prophet Hinckley publically declared that members are entitled to a full accounting of their donations. Of course, this is yet another Church lie. They do not give an accounting of their donations to the public, or to their membership. However, shortly thereafter, we received a two-sentence form letter from Church headquarters, stating:

"This letter is to notify you that, in accordance with your request, you are no longer a member of The Church of Jesus Christ of Latter-day Saints.

Should you desire to become a member of the Church in the future, the local bishop or branch president in your area will be happy to help you."

Linda and I breathed a sigh of relief. It felt as if heavy and dishonest shackles had finally been removed from our lives. The sky appeared just a bit bluer. The wings of freedom lifted us to a higher level of happiness. A few weeks later, on Linda's birthday, a knock at the door interrupted our serenity. Linda answered. There she encountered two young and naive Mormon missionaries, armed with certainty and a message. They already knew our names. They arrived on our doorstep at the request of local Mormon leaders.

In <u>Philosophical Dictionaries,</u> Voltaire queried: *"How can you answer a man who tells you that he would rather obey God than men, and who is therefore sure to deserve heaven in cutting your throat?"* In like manner I ask, "How can you answer an institution that supports, and thrives on such pious and unremitting nonsense?"

I thought it best not to repeat the mistake made by my great grandfather, Michael, who neglected to fully educate his young children concerning the evil and deceptive practices of religious cults. I decided instead to channel my energy into a book entitled: Execution of the Penalty - A Letter to James Dean. I entrust our children with accurate information. Cultic religions prey on ignorance. Truly, they lie in wait to deceive.

A Crack in the Sky

Linda D. Flynn

CHAPTER 15

A Crack in the Sky

The sky cracked in 2006.
At 43, another world collided with mine.

Born and raised in southern California, I carry the heritage of Mormon polygamy. My great-great-great grandfather on my father's side, Thomas Ricks, founded Ricks College in Rexburg, Idaho. The name has now been changed to Brigham Young University-Idaho. Thomas Ricks followed the teachings of his prophet and became a polygamist. I descended from the first of five wives. Thomas married his third and fourth wives on the same day. The fourth wife was only sixteen years old. Thomas fathered 40 children. My mother's ancestors immigrated from Sweden, England and Denmark. Both sides have many pioneer stories of heroism and hardship. I grew up with great respect for my pioneer background. My mother's birthday is on July 24th, the most celebrated day in Mormonism, the day Brigham Young led the Mormon pioneers into the Salt Lake Valley.

I was raised with three brothers, one older and two younger. My two sisters came along when I entered high school. Being raised Mormon meant our family followed all their rules. We went to church every Sunday. We attended primary, mutual, early-morning seminary classes, youth dances, etc. We only dated Mormons and followed a list of other rules as well. Every Monday evening we held "Family Home Evenings." We grew a garden. Well, my mother grew the garden, a fantastic one. She grew all kinds of fruit trees, vegetables, melons and berries. We raised chickens, turkeys and rabbits as a food source. The Mormon Church commands its members to have a year supply of food stored at home. We maintained a two-year supply. They wanted us to be self-sufficient. We complied. We also stored unleaded, diesel and propane fuel tanks in our backyard.

For the most part, my memories of growing up with my family are wonderful. I played with cousins, spending weekends at each other's homes. We traveled to Hawaii and Mexico for family vacations. We planned yearly family reunions to southern California beaches. Most every summer we took a trip to Salt Lake City for the adults to work on genealogy. As a young teenager, my cousin and I sometimes tagged along to the genealogy library, copying documents of long searched for ancestors but mostly we went to ride the elevator up and down the 28-story church office building.

At age 14, I met the man who became my husband. His family and my family happened to be vacationing at the same Mormon mountain retreat in Utah. Brent was 18. Our teen group hung out and played games, while being closely monitored by young enthusiastic leaders. In the years that followed Brent went on a mission to Peru, and I grew up. We later reconnected at Brigham Young University. Adding courtship to our course load, we fell madly in love. Six days after my nineteenth birthday, we married in the Los Angeles temple. We have four wonderful children, Julie, Jason, Jessica and JD and we love the individual people they have become.

******

The year 2005 proved to be a big year for The Church of Jesus Christ of Latter-Day Saints, Mormons. This year celebrated the 200th year of the birth of Joseph Smith. All year long, the Church honored Smith. Musicals, talks and testimonies filled most of the meetings we attended. Church leaders shared awe-inspiring stories of the life of Joseph Smith. I joined in with all of the celebrating. I completed my second year serving as Relief Society President in our ward. I enjoyed being with the women. I liked most all of them. I could have gone without many of the extra meetings asked of me, but I put all my energy into my calling and did the best I could. I helped with ten funerals and their accompanying family luncheons. I made movies of loved ones who passed on and felt accomplishment serving others.

Toward the end of this year, Brent decided to study more about the Prophet Joseph Smith. He wanted to gain a stronger testimony of the Prophet. His search began online through the Church's website, familysearch.org. He pulled up Joseph Smith's name and to his surprise; a list of more than 30 women came up as being married to him. In all of Brent's 47 years in the Church, neither he, nor I, attended a meeting teaching anything about Joseph's wives except for his first wife, Emma Hale Smith. Yet, this information came directly from the Church. We accepted this information as reliable. Brent's curiosity piqued. He mentioned what he learned. I didn't know about Joseph Smith's wives. Polygamy in general didn't surprise me, because of my own family history. Brent's pedigree did not include polygamy.

A few months earlier I helped our daughter, Jessica, with a talk on Emma Hale. I ran into a story regarding a woman named Eliza R. Snow. After reading a few sentences, I noticed a sentence saying she had married Joseph Smith. It struck something inside my brain. I put it aside to read later, but never got around to it. Months later, I threw it away because I lost interest in the subject. Brent's interest, however, could not be held back. He wanted to understand Smith's polygamy. He began studying in December 2005, intentionally keeping out of "anti-Mormon" literature. He stuck to the Church's approved writings. Information started pouring in. Book orders arrived faster than they could be read. At times, there would be up to eight books laid out on the couch being cross-referenced, checked and double-checked, with Brent sitting in the middle of it all. Notes were carefully written down at every turn of the page. The book studying turned into 15-hour sessions each day.

Days extended into months. I watched in amazement at Brent's interest with Mormon Church history. My life buzzed by busily, not caring to join the investigation. But in the evenings, when the kids had gone to bed, I would sit and read with Brent and be given an update on what he learned throughout each day.

Some days I physically ached from the information. I cried and fought what we read. Why would our prophet marry a 14-year-old girl? Why did he marry other men's wives? Why did he marry married women that were pregnant with their husband's child? None of this made any sense to me. Why did he lie to his wife Emma, and to the entire congregation of his church? The wall of secrecy towered high around these marriages. Some of the women, married Smith in the woods, dressed in men's clothing. Several women received only a few hours to make up their minds about marrying Joseph. He told a few women an angel with a flaming sword appeared to him, and if they didn't marry him, the angel would kill him. This seemed like an evil form of emotional blackmail. What young woman, who adores her prophet, wants to be the person who gets him killed? A small number of parents acknowledged receiving a promise from Joseph Smith, guaranteeing them a place in heaven if they allowed Smith to wed their daughters.

The prophet approached one of these parents, Heber Kimball. Smith proposed to marry Heber's beloved wife. Agonizing for three days, Heber pondered his devotion to Smith and the Church. Orson Whitney, Heber's grandson, recorded, "Then with a broken and bleeding heart, but with soul self-mastered for sacrifice, he led his darling wife to the Prophet's house and presented her to Joseph." (In Sacred Loneliness by Todd Compton pages 495-497) Joseph smiled at the loyalty of Heber, standing with the love of his life at his door. Smith told Heber he passed the test. Smith then taught Heber about polygamy and required him to take a second wife. Joseph then assigned Heber the plural wife he must marry. The prophet further instructed Heber to keep the marriage secret from his wife, whom he loved so much.

After destroying Heber's personal boundaries, Joseph instructed Heber to commit adultery and lie about it. The path of destruction left by Smith warped Heber's moral compass.

One year later, Smith asked Heber to approach his fourteen-year-old daughter, Helen, concerning the subject of marrying the prophet. Helen's response was, "No, I wouldn't!...." Within twenty-four hours of her father approaching her on this matter, Joseph Smith himself, showed up and told her, *"If you take this step, it will ensure your eternal salvation and exaltation and that of your father's household and all your kindred."* (*In Sacred Loneliness*, Todd Compton pages 497-503) Helen sacrificed her youth to Smith to buy a place in heaven for her family. She became his 25th wife, one of four women married to Smith in May of 1843. Helen carried the title of "widow" one year later.

I began reading my own family history. I ran across this story in a collection of ancestral diaries a family member put together.

In 1887, a young 22-year-old English girl named Elizabeth Mercy Mills, came across the Atlantic from Liverpool, England to Logan, Utah. She wanted to "gather to Zion." She was introduced to my great-great grandfather, Hyrum Ricks Sr., son of Thomas Ricks. Elizabeth states, referring to their first meeting, "He later told me he had a feeling come to him that I was going to be his wife!"

Elizabeth was hired to work for Hyrum and help out Martha, the woman Hyrum was already married to. Desirous of observing the teachings of the Church regarding the Celestial Law of Marriage, Hyrum asked Elizabeth to become his second wife. Hyrum had a note delivered to Elizabeth asking her to be his wife. Hyrum arrived shortly after the note was delivered. He wanted to further explain his intentions, and ask Elizabeth to tear up the letter so others could not read it. She told him she had to think about his proposal. Elizabeth asked if Martha was willing. He said, "Yes, I told her before I married her that I was going to live the Celestial Law of Marriage and she agreed to it."

Years later, Martha told Marvin Ricks, my grandfather, that Hyrum told her, "If you don't agree to the Celestial law of Marriage, you will be disobeying the Lord and the sin will be upon your head."

November 16, 1887, in the dark of night, Hyrum and Elizabeth, later to be referred to as "Aunt Lizzie," wed in the Logan, Utah temple. She records: "There was a law against the practice of polygamy at this time, but the church still sanctioned it. I couldn't even tell my relatives. We couldn't go openly to get married. We had to go at night."

Although Martha had given her consent to the marriage, her heart ached with the idea of sharing her husband with another woman. Hyrum fathered 20 children. (*A Journal of Memories* : Hyrum Ricks Jr. and Alice Ovanda Cheney Ricks Histories and Allied Families Book II pages 32-33)

These stories made me sick to my stomach. How could this be? We would read quotes from these girls' diaries and even they had a hard time with the secret marriages. Some nights I would go to bed crying. A prophet of God is not supposed to lead us astray. Lying to his wife, committing numerous counts of adultery and deceiving his congregation didn't sound like acts a prophet should do. Especially the prophet God wanted to restore the Church of Jesus Christ of Latter-day Saints.

I prayed the books coming into our home were not being delivered by the devil himself, leading Brent astray. Taught all through our lives to be wary of Satan, these words echoed in my mind; "Stick with only Mormon approved books and information." I questioned Brent on these books and their sources. The books he focused on could be purchased through the Church-owned bookstore, Deseret Book. The list ran as follows: "The History of the Church" by B.H. Roberts, The original 1830 Book of Mormon, The 1833 Book of Commandments, The 1835 Doctrine and Covenants, "Rough Stone Rolling" by Richard L. Bushman, Lucy Mack Smith's

"Biographical Sketches" (The 1852 1st version, before it changed under the order of Brigham Young and almost all 1st version copies were collected and burned by the order of Young), "Lectures of Faith" by Joseph Smith and Joseph Smith's 1832 account of the First Vision.

As Brent expanded his reading, he found books Mormons considered "anti-Mormon," actually contained more factually correct information than the sanitized version of church history taught by current Mormon leaders. We branched out from there and added: "No Man Knows My History" by Fawn Brodie, "In Sacred Loneliness" by Todd Compton, "An Insider's View of Mormon Origins" by Grant Palmer, "View of the Hebrews" 1825 by Ethan Smith (no relation), "Mormon Enigma, Emma Hale Smith" by Linda Newell and Valeen Avery, and "The Keystone of Mormonism" by Azra Evans. He cross-referenced these books with credible primary source documentation. These books proved very accurate in keeping with actual documented Mormon history.

The list of books grew to over 100 titles. (See The Bibliography for a partial listing) We finally opened our eyes to all documentation and the fear to look at their integrity for historical truth disappeared. But at the time, it seemed frightening. We hid our reading from our children. We didn't speak to others about our findings. We knew they would never believe it. We could hardly believe it ourselves.

My turning point arrived around May 2006, while still actively engaged in my Relief Society Presidential duties. Throughout the day I tried to keep myself distanced from the information coming in, but at night I learned how our church took out historical facts over the years to hide corrupt practices. Our church constantly rewrote its own history all along the way. A careful study allowed us to see the changes as they occurred.

One evening, while reviewing more shocking polygamy stories, reading diaries and looking at the dates of the marriages, it suddenly hit me. Too scared to say what I silently thought, I twisted and turned in my chair. I knew if these words slipped from my lips God would strike me with a bolt of lightning. I wanted to say it so badly. With my head low I very cautiously said, "I think Joseph Smith was a sex addict." Relief filled me, finding myself still breathing. But the bolt of lightning had come in the form of realization. The Mormon Church was a concoction of Joseph Smith. It made him money and gave him power, which he abused to the fullest. Suddenly, all of Smith's actions made sense.

Comprehending the sexual addiction and fraudulent life of Joseph Smith and the evil fruits it bore helped me to freely question other Mormon beliefs. The white Mormon underwear or "garments" not only show you are "temple worthy" and in good standing with the Church, but they facilitate in determining what types of clothing you can wear, especially women. The garment bottoms go down just above the knee. The tops look similar to silky undershirts with capped sleeves. Mormon women's shirts always cover their backs, shoulders and bellies. Their shorts or skirts always drape to their knees or below. Mormon women know how to tell if someone they meet on the street is Mormon by the visible lines the garments make under their clothing. This helps them know if they are in good company or not.

I tried to obediently wear modest clothing as a young girl. The Church defines "modest" clothing as clothing long enough to hide garments. Even though I had never gone through the temple and was too young to wear the Church issued underwear, we were taught to follow this standard. Jealousy constantly haunted my mind when I saw girls who wore tank tops or shorts that didn't go to their knees. But I knew those girls had lower morals and standards than I had, their clothing said it all. The Church taught me their lack of modesty screamed out their immorality, and I believed it.

I wondered how Marie Osmond got away with wearing tank tops and short shorts on her TV show. She must have been given approval from the prophet to dress below our modesty code. I questioned this publicly. The answer came as a typical thought stopper. "She was engaged in missionary work." This answer rang the same for Donny Osmond, who did not go on a Mormon mission. He was doing missionary work through his show.

When I finally realized the Mormon Church was not true, I quit wearing their underwear. The feeling of nakedness overwhelmed me, even though my outer clothing did not change. I went to lunch with a friend and ran into two other women. A little corner of white garment peaked out of the corner of one lady's shirt. Immediately, I missed my garments. The garments represented purity. Could underwear really determine the goodness of a person? I decided I had to learn to feel good about myself because of what I did, not due to what underwear I wore.

I struggled trying to feel free in what I wore, even at home. If a neighbor came over, they would immediately know I was not wearing garments. I did not want gossip going around. I can't tell you how many circles of gossip I have heard about so-and-so seen not wearing their garments and look at what a bad person she turned out to be. I made a conscious effort to wear extra thick shirts. It seems so ridiculous to worry about what type of underwear someone is wearing, but to me, a Mormon, it was directly linked to personal morality and values.

The saying, lightning never strikes twice in the same place, is not true. The first day I wore a very modest tank top in public, in my mind, others walking by judged me. Another bolt struck my brain and I realized the mental mind control placed carefully by the Church had lost its grip. I was the one bring judgment to myself; it was all in my mind. I instantly saw with new eyes, beautiful carefree women walking around. They didn't care a bit about my wardrobe. In fact, their clothes looked quite similar to mine.

Pretty pajamas of all styles filled my closet. The first night I went to bed in a spaghetti strap nightgown with no garments underneath, the bolt struck again. Someone had been controlling what I wore in my own home, at night, in my room, with my door locked. The Church reached deep into my personal life even with the lights out and under my own blankets. I didn't realize it until we actively moved away from its grasp. They had me hooked for 43 years, but no longer. The next day I threw my garments away. I broke the spell. Freedom now knocked at my door.

******

Church members are constantly taught how miraculous it is that an uneducated farm boy could translate the Book of Mormon. A fair look at history takes the "miraculous" right out of the picture. First of all, Joseph showed skills of being a fantastic storyteller. People gathered for hours to listen to him recite stories he made up on the spot. His formal education came from home. Joseph's mother, a schoolteacher, taught him to read the bible. He read it religiously. The original 1830 Book of Mormon reflects his poor grammar. In letters he wrote to Emma in 1829, show that he was not the uneducated farm boy the Church makes him out to be. He was fully capable of writing, although he exercised a fair amount of poor grammar. He studied the Bible all his life. He read anything he could get his hands on. Many of his thoughts and ideas he copied came from writings of his time. These books were easily accessible where he lived. The entire premise of the Book of Mormon came from one such book called "View of the Hebrew" which sold out of two editions in Smith's immediate area.

The tremendous ego of Joseph Smith shows in his "King Follet's address" of 1844. While boasting, he placed himself above Jesus. Smith declared:

"I have more to boast of than ever any man had. I am the only man that has ever been able to keep a whole church together since the days of Adam. A large majority of the whole have stood by me. Neither Paul, John, Peter, nor Jesus ever did it. I boast that no man ever did such a work as I. The followers of Jesus ran away from Him; but the Latter-day Saints never ran

away from me yet. " (Pages 408-409 of Volume 6 of the Official History of the Church)

The Church edited away much of his overt arrogance but his incredible ego still bleeds through.

As my fear of freely speaking my thoughts privately with Brent subsided, my eyes opened. I saw hypocrisy being preached from the pulpit and through the actions of the Mormons around me. Mormons usually only have Mormon friends. They only get to know their non-Mormon neighbors if there is a missionary opportunity for conversion. As soon as the opportunity runs cold, their association trickles off to almost nothing.

I began to look at others around me differently. I saw people not as "non-members," but as equals. In church, many lessons revolved around informing me of how special I was, saved for these "latter-days." I had a message I needed to share with others ("every member a missionary" is the Church's slogan). Non-members needed my help to get to heaven. Baptism into the Mormon Church allowed them to take the first step to enter heaven. The other steps involved following all of the ordinances, rituals and paying ten-percent of their income to the Church.

From a Mormon's perspective, it doesn't matter if non-members love God already or live a life of charity. If they don't have the Mormon gospel, heaven is not an option and their families would not be eternal. Another Mormon trap is the teaching of eternal families. Members who follow all the rules, ordinances and rituals will be together forever. Unfortunately, if one member does not follow the guidelines, this individual's bond is broken and the family grieves for this person as if they had died. Being ostracized is common.

Before I opened my eyes, I went out with a friend for a bagel one morning. She was the only non-member friend with whom I associated. As she drank her coffee, she told me of an experience when she felt her prayers had been answered. I sat there listening to her and knew this could not happen. Drinking coffee and having her prays answered? She could never have her prayers answered because she was not Mormon. As time went on and my studies grew, I began to understand it didn't matter what faith people held, anyone could still have answers to their prayers. Mormons didn't have the corner on the prayer answering market.

I watched a mother walking down the street, pushing a stroller. I knew she didn't love her children as much as I loved mine because she had not bothered to join the Mormon Church. She probably wouldn't even cry much if a car hit her children and they died. Who thought this horrible scenario? I look back at the thoughts that rumbled through my brain and the monster I was becoming. My heart aches at the insensitivity. Since breaking away, I learned non-Mormon families love their children and want the best for them, as much as I do for my children. Husbands love their wives and wives love their husbands and everyone is not cheating on each other and wandering around drunk all the time.

The bolt struck my brain daily with new thoughts. I went to the grocery store and found the liquor isle not crowded with people hording alcohol. It was legal. They could have as much as they wanted. Why weren't people cleaning off the shelves? Aren't all non-Mormons complete raging alcoholics? Where were the bad people that can't make good choices without the Mormon Church? I rushed home to share my latest epiphany.

The natural kindness people engender represents my greatest epiphany. How can they be so kind? I don't remember any lesson teaching me this. The evil ones, the unenlightened, the lost souls turned out to be some of my best friends. These people were not out to tempt me to be evil. Most of the times, they don't try to offend others. They proved more tolerant than Mormons, although Mormons will quickly claim to be the most tolerant, yet their practices, habits, and doctrine are anything but tolerant. When you have a conversation with non-Mormons, it is about real life issues, not church callings or the latest ward gossip. Mythologies and ugly dogmas don't clog their brains.

They seem true to themselves and the world around them. They become your friend for no other reason than they like you.

******

As we studied the real history of Joseph Smith, questions continually came up. The "translation" of the golden plates somersaulted through my brain. At least four people documented how Joseph Smith put his face into a hat, in which he placed stones. Most of the time the supposed golden plates were hidden, kept out of sight from snooping eyes. Yet, all the Church publications show pictures of Smith dutifully holding and studying the golden plates. He claimed to read messages from God off the stones one word or phrase at a time. He claimed to have his scribes read God's words back to him so the Book of Mormon would be exactly, word for word, written by God. This is interesting, in light of all the nearly four thousand changes made to the Book of Mormon since its publication in 1830. It seems God not only exercised poor grammar, but also changed his mind as to the very nature and description of himself and Christ. After mentally leaving the Church, we allowed ourselves to see for the first time what the rest of the world already knew.

In 1826, Joseph was arrested for glass looking, tried and found guilty of fraud. Glass looking is a form of treasure hunting. Joseph claimed to know where treasures and gold lay hidden. He placed stones in a hat and sealed his face into the hat. This way he could see the buried treasure and let the people know where to dig. The treasures always seemed to elude them. Interestingly, the stones Joseph used for glass looking also helped him translate the Book of Mormon.

Hearing this for the first time, I did not know how to process the information. I told myself God must have wanted Joseph to be a glass looker to help prepare him in translating His sacred scriptures.

Mormons engage in bizarre mental gymnastics. When faced with information not fitting the perception or reality they want, members immediately conjuror up unsupported reasons to try and retain their desired view of reality. I was guilty of these same mental gyrations. Joseph Smith lied to people. He repeatedly told them he could find hidden treasures in the ground, which he never did. He charged people multiple times for this service. He was found guilty in a trial for his fraud. If all this is simply preparation to spiritually save our souls, I have to stop for a second and ask, "Who's fooling who?"

******

In February of 2006, still serving as the Relief Society President, I attended a ward conference. Our stake president came to speak to the women. He taught us how authority in the Church works. First, he drew on the chalkboard and explained how a democratic organization worked with information coming from the people up through their representatives and then to the leader or president.

He asked me if the Relief Society President represents the women of the ward. Yes, obviously, I had been representing them for years now. Feeling intimidated, I did not answer any questions out loud. Seeing none of the other women felt comfortable speaking up either, he answered his question for us. "No, the Relief Society President represents what the Lord wants for the women, only as directed through her bishop." His message shouted loud and clear. Women have no authority in the Church. They must ALWAYS stay subservient to their male priesthood leader.

He then proceeded to draw a diagram of how the authority of the Church works. All information comes from the Lord, through the prophet, to the apostles, to the stake president, to the bishop, and finally to the relief society president. No decisions could be resolved among the women, unless, first approved through the bishop; who might then need to ask consent from the stake president who may need to acquire authorization from the apostles who might need to appeal to the prophet who may need to inquire of the Lord what should be done for homemaking meeting that month. He told us, women choosing to make decisions and changes on their own, without the bishop's approval, had to end.

I couldn't believe what I heard. I had been doing things wrong all along. A change seemed in order. That day, I gave my all to the Lord and did everything by the book. As I stood and closed the meeting, I apologized to the stake president in front of my peers, who wondered what I had done to deserve this public humiliation. I told him I had been humbled and I would do things the way he taught. At this point, my emotions overcame me from his reprimand. I ran from the building sobbing. This moment marked the beginning of my panic attacks triggered through cognitive dissonance each time I stepped into the church building.

******

In April, I received a visit from my bishop, releasing me as Relief Society President. He then called me to teach Sunday school to the 14 year olds. The next Sunday, I attended Relief Society for the last time. The instructor droned on about "Kolob," the planet Mormons believe is next to the throne of God, and how wonderful it must be.

During the next few months, Brent and I continued to read together at night and discuss the things we learned, and our feelings about them. I still tried to side with the Church no matter how absurd the information looked. The excuses I gave our leaders for things they said and did became ridiculous. Reason and common sense did not enter my thoughts. I made up excuses so I could continue functioning at church.

The Sunday school lessons I taught came from the Old Testament. If I wasn't confused enough, I had to make sense of incest, child abuse, rape, adultery and murder on massive levels, all in the name of the Lord.

I taught about the prophet Elisha who took over for the

prophet Elijah. While he was out walking, forty-two children teased him and called him "bald head." Being a prophet, he used his special prophet powers and commanded two she bears to maul the children to death.   Excuse me? Who selects the materials and writes these lessons? The verses of the bears killing the children were in the chapters I was to prepare my lesson from, but not the scriptures I was assigned to read. Was reading the entire chapter wrong? The point of the lesson was to always obey the prophet or bad things might happen. The Church's lesson manuals cherry pick the scriptures and add Mormon based inferences that are not always supported, except through their own Mormon scriptures. Picking and choosing select scriptures does not help paint the full picture of the prophet Elisha. Picking and choosing small pieces of history about Joseph Smith does not thoroughly illustrate the life he lived. I could not teach these children the message of the lesson, "Follow the prophet in all he says" without giving them all the pieces to the puzzle.

As time went on, the lessons became more and more difficult. I presented the scriptures as stories. They were written hundreds of years after the fact, full of contradictions and errors. These scriptures/stories were then voted on to see which stories would be included in the creation of the Bible. It eventually became the ultimate storybook of all time. The kids and I discussed these stories together as a class, and how we felt about them. We discussed the decisions made, good or bad. Did the stories contain unbelievable situations? We would talk about allowing ourselves to think beyond the box, or book, in this case. I tried to teach them they had the right to use their reason, their God-given reason, to make up their own minds about things they heard and read.

One Sunday I asked the kids in my class, "How many of you know any non-Mormon neighbors?" One girl shouted, "I know a non-Mormon! She is the 'soccer-mom-lady'." This girl was the only one who slightly knew a neighbor, even though she had never spoken to her and didn't know her name. I gave my students an assignment to go to a non-Mormon neighbor and say "Hi."

One boy blurted out, "But what if they want to hurt me?" This was a strange response from a boy who received the title of being the biggest bully on my street. These kids were scared to meet their neighbors. I was shocked. I was more determined than ever to try to break down this wall of fear the Church had built.

It took me until the end of the week to build up my own nerve to meet the four non-Mormon families who lived behind our home. I took my three youngest children with me to teach them that it is good to get to know people who live near us, but are not Mormons. As we walked toward their homes, my children voiced their fears. We delivered eggs from our chickens and were greeted with excitement and kindness. We were invited to a Super Bowl party and told we should get together more often. Our experience was eye opening and pleasurable.

The next Sunday, as it turned out, I was the only one who had accomplished the assignment.

The summer came and went. The lessons became harder and harder for me to teach. I walked past the bishopric counselor in the hallway after class one Sunday, handed him my teaching manual and told him I would not be returning. I stopped going to church all together that day. Brent, who served as the Ward Membership Clerk for the past few years, asked to be released that summer as well.

Confusion about us completely overtook our local leaders. We had been extremely active our entire lives. We lived and served faithfully in our present ward for 10 years. We attended all our meetings and BAM! We just stopped going. We never gave any reasons; never let them enter our home for interviews. We politely stopped them at the door when they did show up unannounced.

We never answered questions about our sudden inactivity except to say, "we were taking a break." Callings continued to be extended to keep us involved and we kindly turned them down. A bishop's counselor insisted on coming over to our home one night to extend us a calling. He was shocked when we politely thanked him for having confidence in us, but we told him, "Thank you but, no thank you." He asked us to pray about it. We said, "No need. Our answer is no and it would not change." He said, "You can't say, NO!" We responded that we could and just did. He shot back, "Well, I want to take a break too!" We gave him permission to take a break, an option he apparently did not realized he had.

******

I married young. Six days before my 19th birthday, I went through the temple for the first time to take out my endowments. (A temple ritual in which one makes promises not to reveal secrets lest they be put to death, and one must wear Mormon underwear from that day on). Brent teased me, saying I had to walk naked down an aisle with people on both sides, watching. We laughed about this, but it made me nervous as to what really happens in the temple. I chose to go through the Salt Lake temple for my first temple experience. Salt Lake presented all live sessions, which meant actors, not a movie, acted out the endowment ceremony. The session took over 3 hours. We watched these old temple workers acting like Adam and Eve, God, Jesus and Satan. Satan kept falling asleep between his parts and someone would poke him just in time to say his lines. I got a kick out of watching him. Sweet Satan kept me awake through the mind-numbing ordeal.

Finally, able to enter a temple of God, I had achieved what all "good" Mormon girls dream of. Girls are taught from birth their greatest achievement is to get married in the temple to a return missionary and have babies. I had no idea what happened in the temple. (No one prepared me for the rituals I would participate in, or the covenants of secrecy I would promise to take, even unto my death.) I entered the temple innocent and uneducated. My parents, Brent and his parents attended with me. I was given a "new name" and told never to forget it or reveal it to anyone except to Brent, one time only in the temple. My head began to spin with thoughts. I reviewed my new name over in my mind trying to spell and respell it, as not to forget it. At the time of the resurrection, Brent would call out my new name to raise me from the dead. I wondered how I would ever remember it when they only showed it to me one time. Why didn't I get to know Brent's special new name or why did he even get one? Who used his secret name to raise him from the dead?

Eighteen years later, I forgot my special new name. Living in Arizona at the time, I went to the Arizona temple and asked to be reminded. The temple president asked me the date I took out my endowment and opened a book to a page with three names on it. They were using three different names that day for people attending the temple. Seeing the other two names on the page, I realized my special new name, chosen from a list, wasn't so special anymore. My name was Emmaline.

There is a funny story about temple names in a book titled, "Wife No. 19," by Eliza Ann Webb Young. One of Brigham Young's wives, Eliza believed she was the nineteenth wife, hence the title of her book. Later they discovered she was possibly his twenty-seventh wife. Brigham Young claimed 56+ wives by the time of his death. Eliza divorced him in 1873. In her book, she tells a story of speaking with women about their temple names. All the women's new secret names turned out to be the same, "Sarah." Eliza supposing the men, in those days, married so many women they didn't even know their wives' real names. "The day of the resurrection we'll hear a lot of men yelling, 'Sarah!'"

I didn't really care what happened in the temple when I went through for the first time. My mind focused on my marriage coming up in less then two weeks. I went through the motions and followed the leader showing me how I should take my life, if I ever told anyone about the promises I made in the temple. What! This didn't bother me? Looking back now, I can't believe I thought nothing of it. I do remember thinking, "Wow, if people tell, do they really die like this? Do their heads get cut off some how, maybe in freak car accidents or something? Or maybe their guts get cut out from a crazy fall." I would not die this way. I would never tell anyone. These suicide rituals, sacred, and directly from the Lord, showed my obedience and desire for attaining heaven. Why would I choose to risk my eternal salvation and glory? In 1990 the Church not only dropped the suicide rituals but they also dropped the covenant women took of complete obedience and subservience to their husbands. It would appear the Church changes to survive.

Once one is found worthy to enter the temple for the first time, the men and women are separated. New arrivals are "washed and anointed," given a new name and new underwear, garments, and told to wear the Church issued underwear both day and night for protection against evil and to remind oneself of the promises made in the temple. (I sat through many stories told in Sunday school of people in accidents where only their arms or legs below their garment lines were injured. Such overt nonsense is made up to support the belief that garments can actually physically protect people.) Once dressed in white temple clothing, one carries a pouch of additional items, i.e. a fabric fig leaf apron, robe, sash, and hat (or veil for the women). You are ushered into a room with men on one side of the isle and women on the other. Here, you are put under a covenant of secrecy not to reveal anything you learn or do to anyone outside the temple. If this is your first time through, you don't even know what promises you will make until after you have been sworn to secrecy. You watch a movie and temple workers help you learn secret handshakes and make sure you act out your oaths and covenants properly. The Book of Mormon is against secret societies with secret combinations and handshakes. Yet, I was doing them in a Mormon temple. These secret handshakes get you to different levels, working your way up to entering the Celestial Kingdom. According to Mormons, the Celestial Kingdom is the highest level of glory or Heaven. The Celestial

Kingdom is where God and Jesus live and only the holiest can live there, only Mormons. Once you have passed through the "veil," in the temple, you enter the final room, the Celestial room. You relax for a while contemplating what just happened, thinking about your life and how much more work you need to do to become perfect. You are encouraged to return to the temple often, at least once a month, to do the same rituals for the dead, so they will have a chance in the afterlife to accept Mormonism and live with God. According to the Church, no one can live with God unless his or her work has been done in the temple. This work includes being baptized into the Mormon Church.

******

I watched a movie with my children called "Luther." It portrayed Martin Luther and how he broke away from the Catholic Church. One of his eye opening experiences came when he went to Rome and watched people pay money, indulgences, for dead relatives, thereby saving their ancestors from purgatory. The priests wrote the name of the dead down, handing the person a paper declaring the ancestor saved. The faithful member doing the work would then crawl on their knees and ascend the church steps, offering a prayer at each step. Martin Luther realized that paying money for a piece of paper only made the Church richer, the people poorer and it did nothing for the dead. The Mormon Church repeats this ugly cycle.

Genealogy and temple work are Mormon indulgences. People spend hours of time researching, piecing together their ancestry. They pay tithing to be able to go to the temple and do the rituals believing they will save their dead relatives. This is making the Church richer and keeping the people busy, while fleecing them of their time, talents and money. The Mormon Church actively carries on this very old myth, that money and effort releases dead loved ones from hell and into heaven.

Learning history is wonderful. I have no problem with

genealogy, finding out a person's ancestral line, and learning about their lives. The problem is when money is paid (tithing, 10% of your income) to someone (the Church) and then a person spends hours and hours, years upon years doing temple ceremonies so these dead loved ones can supposedly be saved. The Church collects millions of names to have temple work done. The Native American and Jewish communities became greatly disturbed by these actions. They feel the Church has no right doing work for their dead. Baptizing holocaust victims and changing them from Jews to Mormons has brought lawsuits upon the Mormon Church. The Church also made sure it baptized celebrities and people of interest, including the Founding Fathers of the United States of America. They now are Mormons, qualified to enter heaven.

******

As time went on, the feelings of being lost and alone overwhelmed me. My husband and I could not speak openly with anyone except each other. We basically kept our information between us. Searching online, I tried to find support groups for people leaving or who had left the Church. To my surprise, many such websites existed. I read story after story about people who left. I realized I wasn't alone. Many others found out the false claims of the Church. What a relief. I wasn't crazy after all. I began listening to podcasts. Healing voices of people who left the Church simply because it is not what it claims to be filled my ears. One of the people I listen to was Bob McCue.

Quite a few years ago, before our investigation of the Church, Brent surfed the web and came upon a website by Bob McCue. This man served as Brent's zone leader while he labored on his mission in Peru. I read Bob's story of leaving the Church. Bob studied church history to help a young man from loosing his testimony. A bishop at the time, Bob's own son was on a mission. Through his research he discovered the truth of the

Church. He wrote and asked the leadership in Salt Lake to respond to the information he discovered. They told him not to share the information with anyone or they would excommunicate him. Bob promptly left the Church. With Brent's lack of background in Church history he felt so bad for Bob, he emailed him, hoping Bob might reconsider and return to church.

The Church tells its members that people leave the Church because of sin or they were offended. They minimize other reasons that should be given, such as doctrinal issues or deceit and lies on the part of the Church.

******

One of my sisters called me the end of August 2006, after a family reunion where topics such as tolerance, DNA, the Book of Mormon, and virtue for virtue's sake were discussed. These conversations left my sisters and mom wondering what evil thoughts spun in our heads. I knew the possibilities of the fallout my comments would create. I had not yet prepared myself for a phone call such as this. My sister asked a direct question and I answered it. I told her I no longer believed the truth of our Church and its claim of being, "the one and only true church on the face of the earth." I did not believe Joseph Smith could be a prophet of God. We spoke candidly and without tears until my sister made a three-way call patching my other sister and mother in on our phone conversation.

I went over the information again with them and then the emotions came. My mother broke down and said, "I always thought all my daughters would be by my side in heaven." In essence, everyone else in the family would be in heaven except for me. I had now secured a place to live eternally in hell. I assured my mother we would all be together.

They asked me about my temple covenants I was abandoning. I told them when I went through the temple, to get married, I covenanted to love my husband. I am still doing that and I will continue to be devoted to Brent because I truly love him. They told me God did not acknowledge my marriage to my husband or my eternal family any longer. I told them I couldn't stand behind Joseph Smith or Brigham Young for the things they had done. I couldn't stand behind the leaders of today because they continue the lies and deceptions.

The conversation ended with comments of always loving each other no matter what. I know I broke their hearts. They probably wished something else happened, like cancer, anything. My sister, who had begun this call, told me she felt I had not done my part to gain a testimony. I should have studied years ago, young like her, to be stronger and not gullible enough to believe the information I read. She didn't want me to become "one of those bitter ex-Mormons" who leave the Church. I told her it is really hard not to be angry when you find out you have been lied to all your life.

Word spread fast, after my conversation with my sisters and mother. I received an email from a brother saying, *"...I don't want to see you become like so many others that can't just walk away but have to turn and fight it. This church is a rock you will break yourselves against. If you want to leave and chose a different path then do that, but leave it alone. I've seen a lot of my friends leave the church and say that it's not for them and that they really never believed it and found every fault they could with it. At the base of every last one of them was the fact that rather than just apologize and repent of their sins or change their lifestyle to be in accordance with God's teachings they looked to justify themselves in finding fault in others."*

How can a person find this information out and not become bitter? How can an individual let an organization brainwash them into believing if others don't believe as you do, they are going to hell? How can I not be angry when I have to tell my 23-year-old daughter her parents are leaving the Church and if she decides to marry in the temple, we would not be allowed to go in and participate? Not out of any sin we have committed, unless studying church history and being honest with ourselves is a sin.

Temple sessions were arranged for the next day as well as a family fast. One of my cousins called to inform us that the weeping and wailing had begun. My family wanted God to convince me to go back to church. Instead of spending hours in the temple, why didn't they call and talk to me? Why did they have conversations about me and not with me about their concerns? My husband and I understood conversations would be difficult seeing we had forbidden information. Each side felt guarded in what to say, I knew they needed time to heal from this hurt. My sisters are among the most wonderful people on earth. It saddens me that church doctrine dictates they should feel hurt, or duty-bound to try and save us.

After receiving the email from my brother, I felt the time had come to clear the air and show them what we had discovered. I tired of others begging me to repent and turn away from whatever sin I had committed. I wrote an email to my brothers, sisters and parents explaining I had not committed a sin. I included information from our months of research to show them the inconsistencies were no small matter of human weakness, but entailed much larger and broader patterns of institutionalized lies. Joseph Smith was caught in so many lies, it baffles the mind. The letter went as follows:

Dear family,

Let me start out and tell you all how much I love you and desire the very best for you and your families. I know Brent's and my feelings about the Church have gone around. Our church teaches that when someone leaves the Church it is because they have been offended by someone, are too prideful, or have sinned. None of these is our reason. And anyone saying otherwise is completely wrong. What our Church does "not" teach is some people move away from the Church simply because they do not believe it is the one and only true church upon the face of the earth. To reach this conclusion, one does not need to sin. One simply needs to be open to honest research.

Being born in the Church, I never thought of researching my own religion. This last year brought up questions for us. With the 200th year celebration of Joseph Smith, our Church seemed to push getting a testimony of Joseph and the Book of Mormon. We didn't see anything wrong with looking into this man's life that restored the gospel and put himself up there next to Christ. My whole life has revolved around the Mormon Church. I don't think I should be afraid or feel it is wrong to understand it as much as I can. After all, isn't our God a God of Truth?

Our own prophets lay their claim to authority and the veracity of this church at the feet of Joseph Smith. Joseph Fielding Smith proclaimed the following:

"Mormonism must stand or fall on the story of Joseph Smith. He was either a <u>*Prophet of God, divinely called, properly appointed and commissioned or he was one of the biggest frauds this world has ever seen. There is no middle ground.*</u> *If Joseph was a deceiver, who willfully attempted to mislead people, then he should be exposed, his claims should be refuted, and his doctrines shown to be false."* (Doctrines of Salvation Vol. I pp.188-189)

The decision that Brent and I have made has not been easy. It has been the most difficult thing we have ever done. In leaving, we are only leaving behind the unearned guilt. We are taking with us the good, moral virtues that exist inside and outside of the Mormon religion. We are free to understand them in ways that are defined by us and not others. We are able to teach our children to be more accepting of others, no matter their religious preference.

In saying these things, I am sure I have offended some of you. This is not my intention. My only intention is to help you understand us, and where we are coming from, so judgments are not made without justification.

I will share some of the information we have found throughout our research so you can help us come back to the belief that Joseph Smith was a true prophet of God. Tell us how the following information is incorrect. We found it in well-documented, original source material. This is only a brief sketch of the wealth of information available regarding Joseph Smith's life.

The First Vision Story

There is no historical documentation anywhere in the entire world that states anything about the first vision (which supposedly happened in the spring of 1820) until Joseph Smith revealed it happened in his own handwritten account in 1832 (12 years later). In this account he asked for forgiveness of his sins and only Jesus showed up. He emphatically states that he already arrived at the conclusion that all the churches of the world were in sin, and he sought Jesus to have his sins forgiven. Jesus "alone" showed up and forgave him, and that was the end of it. In 1838 (18 years after the supposed "vision") he re-wrote his history and gave a completely different account of what supposed occurrence. The Pearl of Great Price contains the rewritten, 1838 account, of what supposedly happened in 1820. The 1838 account was not in Joseph Smith's own handwriting like the 1832 account. This historical 1832 document came to us via our own LDS Church, although most Mormons don't even know that it exists. If you would like to read it, "Google" it. And see the original document. While current LDS leadership may wish this document did not exist, they nevertheless own up to its veracity.

Altered and False Revelations

Joseph Smith retroactively changed his own "revelations" to make them sound credible. He also constantly added ideas of convenience to revelations that had already been given. There are differences between the 1833 "Book of Commandments" and the 1835 D&C [Doctrine and Covenants]. Clearly Joseph Smith added to previous revelations such things as the entire concept of the Aaronic and Melchizedek Priesthood. These concepts were added in 1834, 4 years after the Church was actually organized. In 1830 even Oliver Cowdery, according to his own account, did not know about the Aaronic and Melchizedek Priesthood. Which is strange considering he was suppose to have been with Joseph on May 15th, 1829 having John the Baptist conferring the Aaronic Priesthood on his head. Until 1834, Oliver, along with all founding members of the Church were taught that only a "desire to serve" God, such as it says in the 4th section of the D&C, was required to receive a calling from God. The Priesthood were retroactively added in 1834 and entered into the 1835 D&C. Make no mistake, this is exactly how our history reads, and if anyone looks, they will see it for themselves. Entire volumes have been written clearly showing original documents and later changes made to them to change their meanings. In addition, Joseph Smith made many prophecies that did not come to pass. There are too many to list here. Other prophecies made, in fact, had been later changed in order to make them appear that they did come true.

Polygamy

The only justifiable argument for polygamy is found in section 132 in today's D&C. So, if God says to do it the debate is over right? ...not so fast. History also shows that "God" was saying "not" to do it at the same time. What people don't know about section 132 is that this revelation was not added to our D&C until long after Joseph Smith's death. In 1876, Brigham Young added section 132 to the D&C and the original "Articles of Marriage" from the 1835 D&C (while Smith was alive) were taken out.

As stated earlier in the 1835 D&C, God did "not" support polygamy. The doctrine stated that polygamy was evil...don't listen to others who try to explain it away or minimize it, just read it yourself! It is as clear as any revelation ever was. If one looks to the preface of today's D&C sec. 132 one would see that the "revelation" was supposedly given to Joseph Smith on July 12, 1843. But when you look at today's accepted genealogical record of Joseph Smith's wives, you find that he married 16-year-old Fanny Alger in 1831! That is why there is a disclaimer proceeding sec. 132 of the D&C in the last sentence of the preface.... "It is evident from the historical record that the doctrines and principles involved in this revelation had been known by the Prophet since 1831."

So which is it? Was it evil in 1835 as the 1835 D&C suggests, or was he justified in hiding his actions until he was caught doing them in 1843? (In 1843 he gave this revelation to his brother Hyrum to try and convince Emma that what he had been doing in secret since 1831 was really all right. Needless to say, Emma was not convinced.)

What were some of those polygamist actions? Let me list a few that are from the same "historical record" that B.H. Roberts (LDS Apostle and Church historian) used to construct our "History of the Church."

Fact: He was married to 30 plus wives apart from Emma. These wives do not include the additional women who had themselves sealed to him after his death and did not know him in life.

Fact: He married 10+ women who were already married, to both members and non-members. These women continued to live with their husbands after their marriages to Joseph and continued to have children with their husbands. One was Orson Hyde's wife.

Fact: The women he married ranged in ages between 14 and 57

years of age. Ten girls were in their teens.

Fact: He denied to the members of the church and non-members alike that he engaged in polygamy and stated that it was against their beliefs. (History of the Church Vol. 6, p 411)

Fact: He was killed because of his attempt to hide his polygamous relationships from his own church members. He attempted to marry William Law's wife, Jane, but William and Jane would have nothing to do with it and threatened to expose him in their newspaper "The Nauvoo Expositor." Only one edition was published on June 7, 1844 (Google it and read it yourself, or order an exact photo static copy for yourself.) and Joseph had the town counsel destroy it as a "public nuisance." For having ordered the destruction of the press, Governor Ford was forced to have him imprisoned in Carthage.

Arguments against polygamy

1. He hid his marriages from the Church and from Emma.

2. He swore his brides to secrecy so that they did not know who else he was married too, other than Emma. The wives could not tell Emma either.

3. He married his brides in secret ceremonies.

4. He married some brides while their husbands were away on missions, and the husbands did not know about the marriages. He married others whose husbands did know and agreed to it.

5. He publicly preached against it.

6. God did not think it was "OK" in 1835. The 1835 D&C states that we believe in one man and one woman marriages and not in polygamy. This remained in force until 44 years after his death.

7. He "translated" the Book of Mormon, which is against polygamy. Jacob 1:15, 2:24, 2:27. (The Book of Mormon was produced in 1829, published in 1830, and he married his first polygamous wife in 1831.)

8. Section 132 was not given to the Church by way of revelation. It was dictated to his brother Hyrum, at his brother's request to try and convince Emma she should allow Joseph to practice polygamy.

9. Section 132:38-39 states that David and Solomon of old were justified before God to do it, which directly contradicts the Book of Mormon, Jacob 1:15, 2:24, 2:27.

10. Emma was against it when she found out. She threw several of the women out of her house.

11. When Emma was talked into it, she chose two sisters for him, not knowing he was already married to them. Several women he proposed to turned him down, Nancy Rigdon, Sara Pratt, Jane Law etc. In each case, after he was rebuffed, he claimed to have just been testing them to see if they were virtuous.

13. He made promises to families of girls he married that if he married their daughters then their families would be sealed in heaven with Joseph's family.

14. D&C section 3:4 states: *"For although a man may have many revelations, and have power to do many mighty works, yet if he boasts in his own strength, and sets at naught counsels of God and follows after the dictates of his own will and carnal desires, he must fall, and incur the vengeance of a just God upon him."* His own teaching preached against it.

15. He boasted that he was better than Jesus Christ (History of the Church Vol. 6 p. 409) *"I boast that no man ever did such a work as I. The followers of Jesus ran away from Him; but the Latter-day Saints never ran away from me yet."*

16. Sec. 132 says the purpose for polygamy is *"to multiply and replenish the earth,"* then why did he marry already-married women?

17. He believed polygamy was a righteous principle as early as 1831 as the History of the Church (HC) suggests, yet he allowed the 1835 D&C to be published and all his sermons preach against polygamy.

18. He excommunicated those who would not practice polygamy after having been taught about it in secret, i.e. William and Jane Law.

19. He excommunicated those who practiced it openly, such as John C. Bennett.

20. He excommunicated Oliver Cowdery for insinuating that Joseph was guilty of it, and at the time Joseph actually was guilty of it.

21. Sec. 132 says that Emma will be "destroyed" if she did not permit him to practice polygamy. Emma did not allow him to do it and, in fact, threw women out of her house who married him, and she took the manuscript of sec. 132 and threw it in a fire in front of him and made him promise never to practice it. Emma lived a long life; Joseph was the one who was destroyed.

22. Polygamy is like an embarrassing little secret in our church today and is all but ignored. Anyone practicing it today is excommunicated. It is completely ignored in the new Joseph

Smith film. [Shown at the temple visitor centers around the world]

23. His own words work against him. Sec. 121:37 states: ... *"but when we undertake to cover our sins, or to gratify our pride....Amen to the priesthood or the authority of that man."*

24. Polygamy was illegal in every state in which he practiced it.

What do you call a man who enters into secret marital relationships with multiple women, and according to diaries of these women he fully consummated these relationships, and hides them for over a decade from his wife, his friends, his extended family, the Church and the public?...and while he is doing all this, he is actively preaching against it!

In this day and age we would excommunicate him from the Church and call him an adulterer and a hypocrite. He would be on the FBI's 10 most wanted list. Polygamy was just as illegal in all the states the early saints lived in as it is today.

Problems with the Book of Mormon

1. There is no such thing as a "Lamanite." DNA genetic studies have proven that 99% of the American Indians came from Asia, not the Middle East. This evidence is not going to go away, it is just going to become stronger and more obvious in the future. (In November 2007, the Church officially changed the preface to the Book of Mormon to refer to Lamanites as "among" the inhabitants instead of "principally" the inhabitants. It seems the Church is continuing to change supposed revelations from God to Joseph Smith to concur with what science has exposed as a false teaching.)

2. There are a dozen different human skeletons found throughout America, which have been dated 9-13 thousand years old. (i.e. The Arlington Springs woman was recently reanalyzed by the

latest radiocarbon dating techniques and was found to be approximately 13,000 years old. The Gordon Creek Woman 9,700 years old, the Bulh woman 10,800 years old, the Grimes Point Girl 8-10 thousand years old, Kennewick man, 9,300, Pelican Rapids Woman, Spirit Cave man etc.) These dates not only predate the Jaredites, they predate Adam and Eve. This evidence will not just disappear. It is not "bad" science simply because it doesn't fit with LDS doctrine.

3. In 1823, the entire pretext for the Book of Mormon was written by "Ethan Smith" (unrelated to Joseph Smith). In fact, his book was so popular that in 1825 it was re-published and quickly sold out again. (Joseph Smith supposedly received the golden plates in 1827.) The book is called "View of the Hebrews." It seems more than a coincidence that this local book was later to have been found in Joseph Smith's Library in Nauvoo. In View of the Hebrews, Ethan Smith speculates that a lost tribe of Israel comes to America, breaks up into two factions, a wicked group that loses the ability to read and write and a righteous group that keeps holy records and retains its ability to read and write. The book also tells how the wicked group hunts wild animals, while the righteous group is a farming group. It also tells how the wicked group made war on the righteous group and wiped them out leaving only a book behind to tell their history. The leader of the wicked group ends up burying the book. View of the Hebrew also quotes the same chapters out of Isaiah that Joseph Smith quotes in Second Nephi. The amount of information Joseph Smith copied out of this book is too great to ignore, which is why B.H. Roberts did a detailed study of it in the book "Studies of the Book of Mormon."

4. The Book of Mormon states they used coins and even talks of the different sizes, yet to date not one single coin has ever been found in the entire archeology on the American continent.

5. Horses and chariots, pulled by horses, are all through the

book, yet horses did not exist on the Pre-Columbian American continent.

6. Steel swords, breastplates, helmets, etc. have never been found on the American continent. (Except those from the Spaniards)

7. Elephants did not exist. (Except prehistoric Mastodons) the Book of Mormon said they did. America also did not have wheat, barley, and figs until they were brought over by the post-Columbus Europeans.

8. Not one single city has ever been located that is mentioned within the Book of Mormon. There were cities in America prior to Columbus, but none has ever resembled or has been identified by the Church as one of the cities in the Book of Mormon. The reason is obvious that nothing matches and every attempt to do so has in time been proven wrong.

9. The Book of Mormon is supposed to contain the "fullness" of the Gospel and yet, it does not mention such basic Mormon things as the Aaronic and Melchizedek Priesthood or that God had a body of flesh and bones as tangible as man's. Indeed, when Joseph first wrote the Book of Mormon he believed in the trinity/spirit nature of God. The 1830 edition of the Book of Mormon clearly states this, and yet, as with so many other supposed revelations, these have been changed over the years. There have been some 4,000+- changes to the Book of Mormon since its first publication, and it is not just simple punctuation changes, but doctrinal changes. It says nothing about the pre-existence as we describe it today, or the importance of temples even though they supposedly built temples.

10. No ancient text in Hebrew or Egyptian has ever been found on the American continent.

11. Since its first publication in 1830, the Book of Mormon has

been edited by the Church. This process still continues. They recently changed it from the Lamanites becoming "white," which was offensive, to Lamanites becoming "pure." Why was it changed? To date, no Indian has ever turned white.

12. The Book of Mormon is full of anachronisms! To be an accurate book, this cannot happen.

13. The Book of Mormon has 3,100 direct and near direct quotes from the King James Version of the Bible. [The King James Version was written in the 1700's, thousands of years after the time the Book of Mormon was buried.]

14. Joseph Smith did not "translate" it like most people think. Most of the time the "golden plates" were not even present when he "translated" them.

15. Joseph used his own seer stones to translate the golden plates. These stones he had used to find buried treasure for people for money. He never found any treasure and was later sued for fraud.

16 The Mayan written language has now been cracked and can be read. It contains a history of kings, their reigns, and dates prior to Christ and continued through the same time the Book of Mormon events were suppose to be happening in America. The Mayan language does not resemble Egyptian or Hebrew. The written history given by the Mayans is distinctly different than the history of the Book of Mormon. In addition, its history does not mention anything about Christ coming to America nor anything about a white race of people. Furthermore, the Mayan written history extends on beyond the end of the supposed ending of the Book of Mormon, which states that the dark Lamanites were not capable of reading, writing or recording their own history. Someone forgot to tell the Mayans that not only were they not supposed to read and write for over 1,000 years,

but also they were suppose to stop reading and writing at the end of Smith's Book of Mormon.

Now, if one does not know the information above, one could possibly fall for the argument that no man could have written such a "perfect" book without God's help. It turns out it is not as perfect as it is made out to be. It is also obvious that Joseph Smith was not aware of true ancient American history or the nature of its inhabitants, their DNA, their culture, their mythologies, their languages, their customs, their food, their plants, their animals, their level of technology, their cities or locations.

Joseph Smith did not know where, when, or how indigenous natives came to America. Today, that information is common knowledge.

Again, tell us where any of this information is incorrect? Help us to understand how this Church can be true, when the Book of Mormon is so historically false, and is not what Smith, or the Church today, claims it to be?

The Book of Abraham.

Joseph Smith fooled all the people of his day into thinking he could translate ancient languages. He pretended to translate the papyrus that the Church purchased in 1835 from Michael Chandler. For many years, the original papyrus was considered lost. In 1966 the papyrus scrolls were found in the Metropolitan Museum of Art in New York. Based on this rediscovered source material of the Book of Abraham, Egyptologists have found that the illustrations (facsimiles) and the original text of the Book of Abraham were not what Joseph said they were. Indeed, they are nothing more than common funeral texts, the book of breaths describing events in the afterlife of deceased Egyptians. This is consistent with other historical and archaeological evidence. Our Church currently owns these, but they will never again see the light of day! Once the Church had them retranslated in 1967 and discovered the fraud Joseph Smith had imposed, they were embarrassed and into the vault they went. In trying to explain this whole episode away, Church apologist, Huge Nibley changed his explanation of Smith's fraud three different times. Even hard-core Church apologists remain baffled. Yet, the answer stares them in the face. Joseph lied.

But where did such a simple uneducated man come up with ideas such as "intelligences that progress," and "Kolob," and "the revolutions of the governing bodies and time," and the "throne of God," and "worlds without end," etc. Surely, he was inspired to come up with these things...or maybe he just stole it from a book that predates 1835 and coincidentally was also found in his Nauvoo library. The book, "Philosophies of a Future State" by Thomas Dick is that book. It contains all those far out ideas found in the Book of Abraham to a tee!

The more we study Joseph Smith and the literature of his day, the more we realized that nothing was really original with him. His real genius, it appears, was taking ideas from others and claiming credit for them.

<u>Glass Looking</u>

Joseph Smith was arrested and brought to trial on fraud charges. He defrauded investors by telling them he could find buried treasures in the area by looking through his seer stone, also called a peep stone, which he said he found while digging a well. He engaged in this activity between 1823-1826. The trial took place in 1826. For many years our Church denied all this and tried to minimize his money digging days and activities as Joseph Smith himself tried to minimize it in his second personal history of 1838. The truth, however, came out when the actual court documents were discovered and indeed, another embarrassing truth about Joseph Smith's life was revealed to all. The trial documents even show that he confessed to all of the above.

More deception

Truly there are so many frauds, lies and inconsistencies laced throughout the history of the Church, it would take days to go through them all. Examples, we have not touched included: the Kinderhook Plates, which exposed Smith's lies, Blood Atonement, Adam-God theory, the Kirtland Safety Society (his failed "anti"-bank), stolen temple rituals from the Masons, the secret organization of the Danites, the secret counsel of the fifty, Joseph's secret ordination as "King over all Israel and the world," and the list goes on and on. It is very hard not to see a pattern of deception that runs throughout Joseph's "real" life.

Now, if all these things were lies created by Satan to throw truth seekers astray, if all these things came from anti-Mormon literature, then we could easily discount them. But the simple truth is the above information is unequivocally substantiated by our own LDS historical documents. In fact, most LDS apologists, including the BYU Farms don't deny they happened, but rather their arguments seem to spin a tale that somehow all these things were justified back then or they try and minimize or rationalized the implications of those events. They have even gone so far as to misrepresent the original source facts only to knock down their own specious misrepresentations.

The fact the Church today will not honestly address its own history and, in fact, has excommunicated those who seek the truth of it, begs even more questions. How long can Church leaders actively engage in hiding the truth behind its sandy foundation?

Could it be the problem with Church history is...Church history? Could it be that the Joseph Smith our Church currently presents did not exist? If the information above is false, tell us how it is false? If it is not false, how then do we explain Joseph Smith's chronic pattern of deceit? Can I just ignore such information and convince my inner self I am still honest? Was I not given intelligence and reason to use it? Surely God's reasoning is higher than my reasoning, but that has nothing to do with the authentic history of our Church. Deception and evil was just as wrong in the days of Joseph Smith as they are in our day. It is beyond comprehension to simply believe Joseph Smith got a special pass from God to deceive, lie and commit whoredoms.

Warren Jeffs was arrested outside of Las Vegas. He was charged with having arranged and participated in marriages with young teenage girls. His defense was God told him to do it. Just because he said God told him to do it...does that mean I must believe him? Am I obliged to base my salvation on Warren Jeffs and his claims? And if I am going to base my salvation on Prophet Jeffs' words, should I, at the very least, investigate his life to see if maybe he's not just another fraud? What if Warren Jeffs' words are no more than a sandy foundation? I suppose if I had grown up in Colorado City I would be just like his followers today. They still believe in him, they are afraid of the outside world, and they have been taught they only need to have faith in him. They are led to believe that to investigate him would show a lack of faith and would be wrong. They are taught that he has the "power unto salvation." I suspect if Mr. Jeffs' followers don't get over their fear to investigate, and if they are never exposed to accurate information regarding Mr. Jeffs, then they will die resting their hopes of salvation upon his words.

It is not an easy thing to openly investigate ones' own church. But it is not a sin either.

Now there are a lot of sayings that instill fear into members of the Church. One is, *"In the last days many will be fooled by Satan, yea even the very elect."* We do not deny in anyway that there is evil in this world. We, in fact, believe life should be filled with a pursuit of knowledge. We should following moral virtue wherever it may be. Our goals in life are not to become bitter opponents to the LDS Church. We respect any moral principles found within the LDS Church. Good is good, no matter where it comes from. Good people are good people, no matter what religion they ascribe to. We seek nothing less than tolerance towards all people regardless of their faiths. We seek openness.

We debated on whether or not to even share some of this

information listed above. We appreciate your concern and love for us. But because our actions have been mischaracterized by some of you, we wanted to clear the record. It is the sandy foundation of Joseph Smith, not to mention Brigham Young, that scares us. How can we base our salvation on these men? We have no problem with all the love and virtues any church espouses. But, we ask that you be careful to not mischaracterize and falsely judge us.

For those of you who have engaged in such talk, please stop. For those of you who realized we carry the same moral values as we did last year, we thank you. We still love our children and will endeavor to teach them all the best values found both within the Church and without the Church. We still love and hope the best for all of our family. Our feelings of love and support for you has not changed. We just assume you will remain members of the Church. It is not our intention to say anything negative about the Church in front of your children. We don't plan on talking about the Church, unless the subject is brought up before us, in which case, we would be happy to discuss it. The fact we cannot openly discuss our own Church's history is telling unto itself.

I do not share this information with you out of bitterness towards the Church. I share it because it is at the heart of our actions. We have gone through several stages of grief, denial, anger and confusion in coming to terms with the implications of the information we have come across. We have felt betrayed by the Church. It is not open to the truth of its own history. Informed consent has to be based on accurate information. Half-truths, as Pres. Hinckley has said, are only lies. Yet, we are the ones who are looked down upon for wanting to know the whole truth.

Again, I am sorry for offending and hurting you. If I could go back in time and unlearn the things I have learned, I would not do it. There is nothing wrong with learning. I hope to become a better person with what I have learned.

I love you and always will,

Linda

Soon after sending my email, I received emails back that shocked me. There was overwhelming anger and false accusations expressed from people who supposedly loved me. One brother claimed he wouldn't read but a few paragraphs of my letter. Here is his response:

Linda,

I am returning your email after having read the first few paragraphs. I have no interest in reading the garbage you think is the truth. I know from my heart the truth. Apparently, you need to rely upon others to make your determination. Your newfound beliefs are based on nothing of lasting substance. Unfortunately, your children will be the ones that will suffer because of your failure to focus on the Gospel of Jesus Christ.

At 14, I truly wanted to know the truth of the Gospel. After serious study and intent prayer, I knew the Gospel of Jesus Christ [was] true. Nothing would persuade me from that knowledge and clear understanding. I did not need to read the works of men far more flawed and weak than our prophets. I did not need to turn to scientific evidence that has been wrong so many times. I did not need to turn my back on teachings that I knew could only make my life happier to know that the things I read were true.

You and Brent are wrong, plain and simple. You have been deceived by your own desire for ease and pleasure in life. Your e-mail says it all in the first few paragraphs. You say you believe in God and Christ, but in a way you want to believe in them. Either Christ is true, or he too was a supposed fraud. I [am] sorry, did you see either of them? How do you know they are there? I haven't seen any scientific facts to support their existence. The reason I know they are there is because I first believed in the words of a man who claimed to have seen them in the Sacred Grove. Thereafter, I asked for my personal confirmation and I received it.

I find it interesting that you claim to move away from your "unearned guilt". I feel no guilt in living my religion. Rather, I feel freedom. I know that when my children leave my home they will have been taught that there is a God, that he has expectations and that [He] stands ready to bless them with so much that it is incomprehensible. Linda, you and Brent have been blessed beyond measure, but those blessings are now your challenges. You claim that this decision is not motivated by pride, but it is. You believe you know more than the prophet of God. You believe you know the will of God, yet you don't. You believe that you can save yourselves in the hereafter without the saving ordinances of the Gospel, but you can't. I am deeply troubled by the blindness you have caused yourselves. You are not free but have trapped yourselves in your self-centered world. There can be no escape except through humility and the atonement of our Savior. I hope you realize that sooner rather than later.

I was heartbroken when I learned of your decision. However, I wonder how committed you are to this new found "truth". If the Church is not true, renounce your membership, cancel your covenants and do not burden the Church with your hypocrisy. Either you believe or you don't. Either it's true or it's not. I know its true and will firmly commit myself to its cause and the building up of the Kingdom of God on Earth. Good luck to you in building anything without the Gospel in your life. Your decision now will have a profound impact on your children. What happens when they choose to do things that are contrary to the teaching[s] you have received all your life? Are you going to tell Julie and Jessica, you're free to engage in sex, but just use a condom? Why not? Lots of good people engage in such conduct and there is nothing legally wrong with it.

Your decision not to allow Jessica to attend seminary is

already having an impact on her right to make her own decision. You will be responsible for what happens to her because of your decision. The same for JD. At least let them make that decision, not you. I would welcome them in my home to have a gospel based home if that is what it takes.

Joseph Smith never put himself up there with Christ. But he was the chosen prophet of God. He was not a perfect man, but he was a good man that brought forth Christ's church in these latter days. If perfection was the prerequisite then there would be no worthy person found on the Earth. Humility and obedience was necessary. Joseph Smith gave the Lord someone to work through to restore his church. The Book of Mormon is true. Its teachings have answered my needs in times of trouble. I have found great power and strength in the lessons shared in that book. I do not need science to prove it to me. Science has been wrong far to many times.

I know Christ lives. I have felt his atonement in my life. I could not raise my children without Him and his Gospel. You have chosen a life similar to a boat floating in the ocean, as long as you have not sunk you must be doing great. The Gospel gives me the sail and the rudder to get to a destination. I know that if I just float around, I will never arrive anywhere and will eventually sink or die, or both. I choose not to flounder.

The Holy Ghost is my Iron Rod. Not the whims of man. I pray for you constantly that you will have enough strength and humility to turn from this path that will lead to your downfall and the downfall of your children and grandchildren. Immerse yourself back in the study of the Holy Scriptures and fervent prayer with a real desire to obey the teachings of our Savior.

My home is open to your children if they choose not to follow your insane path. Turn around now I plead with you.

Love,

[Your Brother]

After receiving this email, I anguished in private, not

sharing my hurt with anyone except my husband and our oldest daughter, Julie. We understood they were simply repeating back to us the appropriate "church-programmed" response. But it hurt, deeply. My family could not see me beyond what the Church allowed. They did not understand my feelings, nor would they address any of my concerns directly. I had become an outcast. Not because of any immoral sin, but because I did not believe in the lies and legacy of Joseph Smith. We asked them to show us the inaccuracies of our information. Instead it was easier to just blame us. We never claimed to know some special truth, we just knew that truth did not come packed in lies. To follow Smith, as a prophet, required personal dishonesty. Neither Brent nor I could do that. Our families do not have to agree with us, but we could not very well leave the Church without telling them our reasons. Our invitation still stands. If any of them can show us Joseph Smith did not commit all these lies, cons, frauds, etc., we would like to hear about it. Sadly, the latest evidence is not leaning in the Church's favor.

To the credit of my younger brother who sent the first email, he has since apologized. He is a wonderful brother and I realize his initial accusations were simply Church inspired rhetoric.

******

A 40th birthday party, scheduled for my youngest brother, fell one week after we received these letters from my two other brothers. I called my youngest brother to see if he felt it a problem if I showed up to his celebration. He was the only one who didn't respond to my letter. He immediately said, "Live and let live." These words spoke so sweetly to my ears. Of course, I was to be there. He had no issues with my newfound understandings and chose not to let it get in the way of our relationship. He has never spoken to me about any information I have found and I suppose I won't bring it up unless he wishes.

I felt nervous going to California for this event. I had

thrown away all my garments days before. I packed carefully not to bring clothes that revealed I no longer wore the special underwear. Not a word crossed the lips of my family regarding our situation the entire two days Brent and I visited. It was as if nothing had ever happened. This is a great defense mode Mormons use, ignore the situation and in time, you will either forget about it or it just won't bother you anymore because you will be able to come up with some excuse to work around it.

I visited my sisters and mother shortly after my brother's birthday. Surprised to still feel like the 800-pound gorilla in the room, no one said a word about my recent discovery. For God's sake, I was going to hell! No one asked a question. Three days came and went. I knew they bubbled with questions and concerns. If any one of us obtained a new job or learned some new and interesting information, we would spend hours talking about it. As for my new discovery, not a word was spoken. I was now a threat. Now that I was different, they only knew to build a wall of silence where none existed before. I officially become invisible.

******

When I think about what happened to me, I view it as, "A crack in the sky." This is in reference to the movie "The Truman Show." Truman, played by Jim Carrey, lived in a city where everything was perfect. He had a great wife, a job, nice house, nice neighbors, but something felt amiss. His life needed more. Every time he would get close to finally leaving town to go on a vacation and explore the world, something would happen and get in the way.

One day, a large camera light fell from the sky, as he looked up he saw a crack in the sky. The crack quickly filled in. His mind began to wonder what just happened and what his life meant. Everyone encouraged him to ignore these thoughts and go back to his regular routine. Unknown to Truman, a movie company watched and filmed his every move. His life, broadcast on television, entranced millions. All the people in the city were actors and in on the scam, including his wife and best friend. One day, Truman decided to leave town no matter what. The movie company didn't want him to find out the truth. He came to the conclusion his life was not his own. Truman focused on changing this. The company made it so difficult for him to leave he almost died in the process. More determined then ever to find out the truth, Truman reached the outer wall of the set. He found a door and knew whatever lay beyond the door had to be better than the lies he lived. Though frightened as to what might be found on the other side, he walked through the door to begin his life, on his own terms.

When I saw the crack in my sky, it was as if the Church wanted me to ignore its history, but I couldn't. When I went to see what caused the crack, pieces of the sky came crashing down on me. Information and books fell from my sky. I could not unlearn these things to piece the sky back together in my perfect Mormon world. I came to the conclusion that I had to make the same choice as Truman. I walked through the door.

Walking through the door frightened me, but I knew I could no longer return to the Mormon fairy tale life of lies and deception and ever find happiness there again. My happiness lay beyond its boundaries, beyond its grasp and influence. I no longer give the Church control over my children. I am their parent. I will teach them. They will learn to understand the world around them with their eyes, hearts and minds open. We hope they will learn to gain and accept their own personal authority and take responsibility for their own actions.

******

As I think back upon events in my Mormon past, I remember when I attended a stake meeting. As typically happened, I had two overlapping meetings. One meeting occurred at the stake level and the other was a Cub Scout dinner for our ten-year-old son. The guilt was spread out thick to not miss the stake meeting.

I arrived at the meeting and planned on leaving early to attend my son's dinner. As I sat at a table in the High Council room, I realized the difficulty I would have in sneaking out. I watched the people around me give their full attention to the Stake President. They gave all the perfect pat answers, quickly finding the scriptures he referenced. I listened to the Stake President, hoping I would personally feel some kind of inspiration. I wanted to feel the "spirit," and be led back to the truth. As I listened and watched him pontificate in front of us, it dawned on me, "The emperor has no clothes!" I looked around the room to see if anyone else saw the huge light bulb over my head. But conformity proved strong that night and I guess nobody wanted to look like a fool. After spending 30 minutes in a meeting going nowhere fast, I decided to go support my son at his Blue and Gold Cub Scout banquet. The Stake President stopped talking and stared directly at me as I quietly stood up and dismissed myself from the meeting, never to look at him the same way again.

******

Sundays became our "Family Day." We took the phone off the hook late Saturday night until Monday morning. We turned the doorbell off and put our "Please Do Not Disturb" sign on our front door. On these days we did acts of charity, sometimes went to museums or just played games and laughed together. We had great conversations about life. We tried to open our children's eyes to the world around us, not just the Mormon world. Sometimes we had a "word of the day."

One day, we introduced the word INDOCTRINATION. We talked about what it means, how do people become indoctrinated and what can be done if you feel it's happening to you. We talked about if it is good or bad. We watched a movie called "The Village."

In this movie, a few couples met in a grief-counseling group. They decided not to experience any more grief in their lives. They created their own community, hidden from the rest of the world in the middle of an animal preserve. Protected from the world, they promised to never tell their children what lay on the other side of the wall except for the bad things that go on out there. The founding group, or the "Elders," dressed in wolves' costumes to frighten the people and keep them away from the forest and the surrounding wall.

While the world progressed outside this "Village," the people inside became stunted in their development and learning. Grief, hurt and pain still continued, in their protected community. When the Elders became older, they needed to find replacement Elders, people who would keep their secrets. A blind girl needed to cross the wall to get medicine. Chosen to travel because of her visual impairment, the Elders thought it would keep her from seeing the truth. A young man from the other side helped her with what she needed. Surprised of his kindness, for it didn't match what she had been taught.

A year later, my husband and I took our children over the wall and left our "Mormon village." We could not keep the dirty little Mormon history secrets or propagate them like Mormon leaders continue to do today. The world we found outside the wall was vastly different from what we had been taught within the walls of our village.

******

While on a family vacation in 2006, we told our oldest daughter, Julie, about our findings. We wanted her to know we loved her, but if she chose to get married in the temple, the Church would not allow us be there with her. She understood our feelings and started studying the information on her own.

We waited to tell our other children until a year later, just two months before our move to California. While living in Arizona, we did not speak openly with our children about our findings even though we stopped going to church. We tried to protect them from ward members who constantly wanted to "help" them. We tried to keep friendships intact until we moved. No one in our ward knew our reasons for not returning. We didn't want to give any fuel to the fire for a "Court of Love" to be arranged on our behalf or in other words, an excommunication and its subsequent stigma and demonization. We wanted to leave on our terms, not theirs.

Brent and I felt the time had come for our children to know why we had quit going to church. We sat with Jason and told him about the lies the Church tells about Joseph Smith and its history. We told him we couldn't be part of a lie like this. He responded, "Good, because I didn't like going anyways. It always got so boring and I never learned anything new." We laughed together. His world did not come crashing down. It felt like a load had been lifted from my shoulders. He asked if he could throw away his Book of Mormon. We told him, "Yes!" He wondered where people get married if they are not Mormon. We told him, "Anywhere they would like and everyone can come and celebrate the wonderful event."

I spoke with our youngest son, JD, that same afternoon. Butterflies turned in my stomach as I thought of when and how to start. I realized how wrong for me, the parent, to be nervous to talk to my own son about anything. So I just blurted out, "Do you know why Dad and I don't go to church anymore?" He said he didn't know. I told him about Joseph Smith and polygamy. I told him there was so much more. His best friend had told him his dad and I were bad parents for not taking him to church. I asked JD how his friend would feel if he shared this information with him. JD said he would stop being his friend and would never speak to him again. JD understood, to keep his friendship, the information should not to be shared. JD asked if the Church tried to brainwash people. I told him it was like the movie "The Village." Dad and I looked over the wall and realized things weren't as they claimed to be and we could no longer live this way.

One thing bothered JD. For one year he worked really hard to earn a hundred dollars. At tithing settlement he said the bishop talked him into giving twenty-five dollars away for tithing. He remembered how frustrated he felt giving it to him and now JD wanted his money back. I would love to get our money back too, seeing it had been obtained through fraudulent information.

The time finally came for us to speak with our, then 14-year-old daughter, Jessica. We had held off telling her for as long as possible. The year before, Jessica called us liars and hated us for not following the prophet. She took the information harder than the boys did. Her identity had become emotionally woven into it. But she did ask lots of questions and seemed extremely curious about things. What she couldn't understand was why the Church would build a new shopping mall across the street from the Salt Lake City temple and spend over 2 billion dollars in its construction.

After talking to her for over an hour and a half, she asked if she could still go to girls' camp that summer. We told her, "No." We had to end the indoctrination. Her last youth trip, she came home even more indoctrinated with stories regarding Joseph Smith we knew to be false. She understood our concerns, but it didn't mean she liked them.

A new relationship began developing between us, as parents, and our children. We spoke openly on every issue. We researched topics of our choosing for information. We worked together as a family and decided our own boundaries. We didn't need to look to anyone for guidance on how to love each other. We started becoming whole again.

******

The transition from the "Mormon mindset" to a "human mindset" has been difficult. Realizing my own church deceived its members for over 170 years about its history hurts. A church representing itself as the only way to salvation, back to God, and the only true church on the face of the earth had turned out to be a fraud. I felt something inside me dying. The "Mormon me," gradually dying, and I couldn't stop it. I began going through the stages of grief. First denial. How could this be happening? There must be some mistake. Why would the leaders of our church willfully deceive their followers? I tried to twist and turn my thoughts to keep the Church true until I could no longer fool myself.

Anger is a major stage in grief. I don't know how long this will last. I've heard it takes years. Another step is bargaining. I know I did this through the whole discovery process. Another stage is depression. This is hard. I had a tough time understanding who I was. My entire sense of identity had been destroyed. I had to create a new me. I didn't trust my thoughts. Intertwined with Mormon thinking, I didn't know how to think for myself. My confidence in my own reasoning skills had been stunted. I didn't need to use reason while an active Mormon. I just followed the crowd. Now, I questioned myself at every turn, wondering if I could make the right decision. It took me a while to realize there is not always one right decision. Sometimes any decision could be great.

The final stage of grief is acceptance. Accepting my life and I am in control of it. The world is not a scary place. And most of all, I need to be able to find tolerance for others and accept them in their decisions, including other Mormons. Even though I wanted to scream out at the top of my lungs the Mormon Church is a money-hungry, family-dividing, deceptive cult, I didn't. There are some people that will never see the Church this way or simply don't care. Whatever their choice is, it is their choice. It is just unfortunate children are deprived of a full view on life.

******

Time marches on; my children no longer go to church, mutual, primary activities, seminary, institute or ward parties.

We are hoping to dilute the Mormon influences out of their lives. We removed our names from the Church. We moved from our home in Arizona to a home near Los Angeles.

Moving to California proved to be one of the scariest things I have done. I left behind my entire identity. I asked my children to leave everything they knew, their friends, and their schools, for two of them, the city of their birth. I took my children to a place where I really didn't know what we would find. We researched the schools and determined them to be highly rated, the neighborhood to be exceptionally safe and our house overlooked the ocean. But I had been taught, all my life, not to trust people outside of the Church. Unclean, impure, dishonest, and unkind, "they will try to deceive you." What was I doing? How could I raise good children around people like this?

******

On June 13, 2007, at 117 degrees, my husband and I drove our first U-haul of belongings to California. Two hours into our seven-hour drive, Brent began to have major health problems. He quickly pulled into a rest stop and almost fell out of the truck. He needed help. He couldn't continue driving and couldn't stand up. He asked me to take him to a hospital. I helped him into my car and sped off towards Blythe, California, 50 miles away. I contacted 911 who told me to pull over and wait for an ambulance. Brent began to convulse and his limbs began to paralyze. As he gasped for breath, he asked me to call 911 again to send a helicopter; he would not make it. He was dying. I tried to stay calm, as directed by the 911 operator, but Brent kept saying, "I'm going to die before they get here." Sobbing on the side of the road, I tried to sound encouraging. Doing his best to stay alive for me, I could see the difficulty of each breath. He told me how much he loved me and if he had the chance to do it all over, he would marry me again. He asked me to make sure I told the kids how much he loved them. I tried to tell him to relax so his breathing could slow to normal. He told me if he did, he would die. Consciously making his body take a breath, he could feel his entire body paralyzing, piece by piece. If he relaxed, he worried his breathing would stop and he couldn't start again.

Praying felt odd; I quit praying months ago. I wanted to, but I concluded over the last few months God, Jesus (as a deity) and religions were man made. But just in case, I quietly said a prayer to myself. If God did exist, this proved to be the time I needed Him to step in and help. I wondered if I would hear any voice or feel a comforting hand, but all I felt was the heat of the desert and the panic and loneliness of possibly losing my husband at my side in a truck stop parking lot in the middle of nowhere.

I ran the options through my mind about being a widow at 44, of continuing my move with my children, of going through this drastic life change alone. I knew I wouldn't go back. I had come too far. I knew my family would say God was trying to tell us we were making the wrong decisions. A month after this incident my husband's brother-in-law said God wanted us to go back to church. My conviction about how wrong the Church was and how much damage it had done to my family relationships and to me was enough to seal the deal. I would never go back. If I had to go through the rest of this transition alone, I knew I could do it. I had to, for my children, for truth.

Time continues to heal both Brent and myself. The doctors diagnosed him with extreme heat dehydration. Family and old friends constantly ask me if I am really happy with our move. I can't explain to them the utter joy I feel for having done what I did. The freedom and the wonderful new experiences are absolutely exhilarating. They look at me and can't comprehend my happiness; their thought processes cannot allow us to find joy outside the Church. I truly feel more alive then ever. I feel I look at people and things with the excitement a little child has on Christmas morning. I have come home numerous times with fantastic experiences of meeting someone or being in a new situation I could never have experienced living in the sheltered life I left.

People are overwhelmingly kind. The things I had been told about people outside our religion are bald-faced lies to keep its members living in fear of leaving. The neighbors we have met are outstanding people. Most of them don't go to church and are not "religious," yet they are good, kind people. They have wonderful well-rounded children. They serve their community with the only goal of improving the area they live, not to convert or un-convert. They don't talk incessantly about religion. In fact, their conversations don't speak of religion at all. They speak about things that matter, life, family and love.

******

Our daughter Julie fell in love. She moved from Manhattan, New York, home with us in California. When I picked her up from the airport her left hand hid behind her back and I knew. She became engaged over the weekend. I felt happy and sad. Happy for her happiness, and sad because I knew I would be excluded from the marriage ceremony. I hoped she would not align her life with mythological beliefs to assist in making her choices. I put a happy face on for two days and then we had a heart to heart talk. I wanted to make sure she knew the Church would wedge itself between us, as a family. I spoke very openly with her about the covenants she would be asked to make in the temple. I told her about the rituals before the changes in 1990. I told her I would be replaced in the temple marriage ceremony and how badly that hurt. She felt trapped. She loved Simon and this was where he wanted to get married. She wanted to please her fiancé and her parents at the same time.

Julie and I enjoyed our days planning the wedding. We were determined to make this a wonderful wedding celebration. She decided not to invite any family members from either Brent's or my side to the temple marriage ceremony. She told them if her parents couldn't be there, then she didn't feel it right for other members of the family to be there. I appreciated her decision and I know how difficult it must have been for her. This ruffled a few feathers. The feelings of entitlement the Church engenders in its members are tough to overcome. My family could not understand why they couldn't go in the temple. After all, they demonstrated their worthiness; they had temple recommends. Our decision of leaving the Church should not make them miss out on attending the ceremony.

As the months moved quickly and the preparation became frantic, I felt I would run out of time to share with Julie all I could before she got married. I tried to have small learning moments to help keep her eyes open. I worried about her becoming intertwined in the Church to the point of no return. I also worried about her being made to feel "less than." She would always be on a list or be someone's project. I tried to warn her how the Church will wedge itself between spouses if they are not at the same level of activity. I warned her about the Church making the children feel if one parent is not as active as the other, then the less active one is not as good as the other. I wanted Julie to have as much information as I could give her, before my influence on her became limited.

Throughout the wedding planning, Julie and I called her reception the "wedding celebration." She wanted all the celebrating to happen in the evening after the temple wedding with all her family and friends present. She chose the Bel-Air Bay Club in Pacific Palisades, California for the location of this celebration. I arrived in the morning of the wedding day with my sister-in-law and her partner, who both left the church over 18 years ago. I knew they would not judge me if I broke down and cried thinking about Julie and the way the Church divides families in these situations.

Karen and Michelle approached me at 1:30pm with a bottle of champagne for a toast. They said it was 1:30. I was surprised how fast the time had passed and how much more we had to do to be ready for the evening's events. Then it hit me; my daughter was being married at that moment in the Los

Angeles Mormon temple without her mother as her escort and her father as her witness. I sobbed. The injustice this church does to families is unforgivable. The trap they put people in, thinking this is the only place to be married, and then being the filter of who can and can't attend is truly shameful.

Julie's wedding celebration was wonderful. She and Simon shared their vows with each other in front of one hundred and fifty friends and family. Brent spoke and took his last dance with our beautiful daughter. Jessica toasted Simon and Julie. Simon's parents and a brother spoke as well as myself. The tears flowed and special moments of love were shared throughout the evening. We are very proud of Simon and Julie. They are both wonderful people.

******

Our lives continue to be affected by Joseph Smith's actions. Having discovered his history, we understand how cults like the FLDS Church (The Fundamentalist Church of Jesus Christ of Latter-day Saints) function. The FLDS Texas raid was in the news. While reading, "Escape" by Carolyn Jessop who ran away from the FLDS with her eight children, my daughter, Jessica, asked me about it. This question opened an important conversation about polygamy and Joseph Smith. She asked me how long ago it had been since Carolyn had run away. It had only been five years. She couldn't believe this kind of thing happened nowadays in the United States. Later that night, Larry King interviewed a few of the wives from the FLDS group that had been raided. Jessica was shocked at the way they acted, dressed and spoke. She asked why they talked like robots, she said it sounded as if they were brainwashed. They were. She couldn't believe they believe in the Book of Mormon. I can't believe I once did as well.

Even though Carolyn escaped from the FLDS, it still grips her family. Her oldest daughter, who was twelve at the time of the escape, decided to return to the organization when she turned 18. Carolyn has not heard from her since. I told Jessica I would do everything in my power to keep this from happening to my children. Going back is not an option.

******

The blinking red light across the sky confirmed my certainty that Santa and Rudolph were hard at work and heading my way.

On a cold Christmas Eve in Kentucky, my parents whisked me off to bed so Santa could deliver my presents. As I looked out my bedroom window I watched Rudolph's nose blink as it moved through the sky. No one could convince me otherwise that night.

As time went by and I grew older, I also grew out of believing the myth of Santa. No one shed tears of my losing faith in Santa. No one called me a sinner or said I was going to hell. And yet, when my family learned I had grown out of believing the myths of Joseph Smith, the sky came crashing down. I was critiqued and criticized behind my back. My loss of belief was not addressed to my face.

I realized my life could move on even without believing these myths. I still found happiness, love, kindness and goodness without Smith's mythologies.

Having learned the blinking red light was an airplane, I can not go back to believing a story of a man riding in a sleigh being pulled by flying reindeer, sliding down chimneys and delivering gifts to all the good little boys and girls around the world. None of my children believe in Santa any longer, and yet, we still enjoy Christmas with anticipation and the thrill of a surprise. We enjoy the time together, the traditions we have begun and the memories we make.

Not having certainty does not scare me. I am not certain what happens after this life. I am not certain if there is a God that put this whole world in motion. I am all right with that. What I am certain of is that I love my husband and my children.

I look forward to each day we have together. The anticipation of a possible surprise and a new memory, fill my heart with joy.

******

The apple, red and delicious was too tempting to pass up. Eve, having been commanded not to taste of the forbidden fruit of the tree of knowledge of good and evil, bit hard and began to understand the difference between right and wrong.

After convincing Adam to do the same, God punished them by kicking them out and telling them their lives would be miserable from that day on. It seems strange a God would want people to stay ignorant and uneducated, commanding them to progress in life with no way of doing so without eating the fruit of knowledge.

When others, like us, have tasted the forbidden fruit of knowledge of our church history, they find themselves facing the wrath of the Church. They are quickly removed and told how miserable their lives will now be. For Brent and I, luckily the misery did not follow. But for some who find out the deceptions of the Church alone, their spouses just can't participate in tasting of the forbidden fruit. They choose to be blind to knowledge, feeling it is the right choice to make. Marriages break up. Families fall apart. Guilt and fear have been preached so many times of how horrible their lives will be without the Mormon Church. Some don't share their findings for the sake of their marriage and suffer through a life of quiet desperation. My heart goes out to people who struggle alone this way. I am lucky Brent loved me enough to share the forbidden fruit. I am even luckier I was open enough to accept the fruit and appreciate the knowledge in every sweet bite.

******

The crack in my sky brings a new experience each day. I stay busy meeting our children's needs. Julie is off and married, traveling the globe with her wonderful, loving husband and baby on board. Jessica has a pile of friends along with a pile of dreams. I love enlightening her by reading and discussing eye-opening material together. JD is learning to appreciate diversity. He recently attended a friend's Bar Mitzvah party on a yacht. I still do not know Jason's future. His heart is big. He attends a local community college, and has been accepted into a larger university with a program where he can meet peers facing similar challenges. We are like most people, which is comforting. We quietly work toward an ever-brighter future. My love for my husband is my own, not tied to temple visits or promises made to outside influences. We share peaceful walks during the end of the day. But with all the joy and happiness in my life, there is still a hole in my heart. I desperately want to mend my relationships with my sisters and mother. They are wonderful people. I have now stepped out of their belief system and they are not sure how to fit me back in their lives without sadness or judgment. To them I am a lost soul. But to me, the joy I feel with my new open mind is incomprehensible.

One day, I hope their sky will crack just enough to start their journey of exploration. It will have to come from their desire to know and understand a world they do not see. Until then, I will wait, hoping to be an example for them of what is out there. And if their sky does crack, I will lovingly hold their hands and show them what a wonderful world we live in.

Acknowledgments

Writing this book evoked feeling of sadness and joy. Linda and I consider our lives blessed and meaningful, despite, or perhaps due to, all the twists and turns. I could not have written my portion of this book without the support of my Mother and Father. Their knowledge, time and organizational skills breathed life into this story. They shared pictures and stories that enlightened me. I am also indebted to the positive feedback and support of my sister Karen and Michelle. They provided me with perspectives that have been most valuable. I am grateful to the friends and family members, who helped prepare this book, but wish to be anonymous. I am indebted to my ancestors. Regardless of their beliefs, they endured and made my life possible. I am very grateful to my family, past and present, who chose love of reality over love of beliefs. They buoyed me up in solidarity. We are grateful to discover that there is a normal world outside of Mormonism. We have met so many wonderful friends who have sympathized with us and strengthen us with their love and support. We would like to thank the authors and researchers who have courageously gone before us and shared their discoveries through the written word. I thank Nancy for her literary insight. As for Sarah, and her inane tirade of sailor colloquialisms, and all of Linda's new friends, I thank you for bringing laughter back into her life. Your manna nourishes our hearts. Your perspectives help us live again and view the world with clarity. Most of all I am in debt to my co-author, Linda, for her positive feedback, encouragement and support. Our love for one another has survived many traumas, including, reestablishing our own identities outside the seductive embrace of a cult.

Characteristics of a Cult

Members of cults commonly believe that their organization is unique, when in fact, it is similar to other cult groups. I have provided a list of books in the bibliography under the heading: "Psychology and Cults." These books identify mind-control techniques employed by cults leaders to manipulate their members. I reviewed and chose three books, which I highly recommend for basic cult-awareness education. They are well written, fully referenced and succinct. The following excerpts show their characterization of cults.

In <u>Combatting Cult Mind Control - Rescue, and Recovery from Destructive Cults</u>, author Steven Hassan masterfully describes the basic elements of mind control as they relate to "cognitive dissonance theory," which includes control over behavior, thoughts and emotions. Steven Hassan also adds control over information as a key component to mind control.

Additionally, he lists the following elements in the cult experience:

"The Doctrine Is Reality".... "Its power comes from its assertion that it is the one and only truth: that it encompasses everything".... "Since it is TRUTH, perfect and absolute, any flaw in it is viewed as only a reflection of the believer's own imperfection."

"Reality is Black and White, Good Versus Evil"... "There is no room for pluralism. The doctrine allows no outside group to be recognized as valid (good, godly, real) because that would threaten the cult's monopoly on truth."...

"Elitist Mentality"... "Cult members have a great sense not only of mission but of their special place in history" ... "Ironically, members of cults look down on anyone involved in any other cult groups. They are very quick to acknowledge that

"Those people are in a cult" or "They are the ones who are brainwashed." They are unable to step out of their own situations and look at themselves objectively."

"Group Will over Individual Will"... "In any group that qualifies as a destructive cult, thinking of oneself or for oneself is wrong. The group comes first. Absolute obedience to superiors is one of the most universal themes in cults."

"Strict Obedience: Modeling the Leader"... "everyone has similar odd mannerisms, clothing styles, and modes of speech. What the outsider is seeing is the personality of the leader passed down through several layers of modeling."

"Happiness through Good Performance"... "One of the most attractive qualities of cult life is the sense of community that it fosters. The love seems to be unconditional and unlimited at first, and new members are swept away by a honeymoon of praise and attention. But after a few months...the cult member learns that love is not unconditional but depends on good performance."... "Of course, when anyone does leave the group, the "love" formerly directed to him turns into anger, hatred, and ridicule."... "Relationships are usually superficial with these groups"...

"Manipulation through Fear and Guilt"... "Problems are always the fault of the member, and are due to his weak faith, his lack of understanding, "bad ancestors," evil spirits, and so forth. He perpetually feels guilty for not meeting standards. He comes to believe that "evil" is out to get him.

"Emotional Highs and Lows"... "A member swings between the extreme happiness of experiencing the "truth" with the insider elite, and the crushing weight of guilt, fear and shame."

"Changes in Time Orientation"... "A member's past is rewritten"... "A cult member's sense of the present is

manipulated, too. He feels a great sense of urgency about the tasks at hand."... "To a cult member, the future is a time when you will be rewarded...or it is a time when you will be punished." "In most groups the leader claims to control, or at least have unique knowledge of the future."

"No Way Out"... "In a destructive cult, there is never a legitimate reason for leaving. Unlike non-cult organizations that recognize a person's inherent right to choose to move on, mind control groups make it very clear that there is no legitimate way to leave. Members are told that the only reasons why people leave are weakness, insanity, temptation, brainwashing (by deprogrammers), pride, sin, and so on.

Members are thoroughly indoctrinated with the belief that if they ever do leave, terrible consequences will befall them, their family, and/or mankind. Although cult members will often say, "Show me a way that is better then mine and I will quit," they are not allowed the time or mental tools to prove that statement to themselves. They are locked in a psychological prison."

In Take Back Your Life - Recovering from Cults and Abusive Relationships, authors Janja Lalich and Madeleine Tobias go into great depth discussing the social structure, social-psychological, and interpersonal behavioral patterns commonly found in cultic environments. On page 327 of their book, Janja Lalich, Ph.D. and Michael D. Langone, Ph.D., provide the following cult checklist as an analytical tool.

"The group displays excessively zealous and unquestioning commitment to its leader, and (whether he is alive or dead) regards his belief system, ideology, and practices as the Truth, as law.

Questioning, doubt, and dissent are discouraged or even punished.

Mind-altering practices (such as meditation, chanting, speaking in tongues, etc.) are used in excess and serve to suppress doubts about the group and its leader(s).

The leadership dictates, sometimes in great detail, how members should think, act, and feel.

The group is elitist, claiming a special, exalted status for itself, its leader(s), and its members (e.g., ... or the group and/or the leader is on a special mission to save humanity).

The group has a polarized, us-versus-them mentality, which may cause conflict with the wider society.

The leader is not accountable to any authorities.

The group teaches or implies that its supposedly exalted ends justify whatever means it deems necessary.

The leadership induces feelings of shame and/or guilt in order to influence and control members. Often this is done through peer pressure and subtle forms of persuasion.

Subservience to the leader or group requires members to cut ties with family and friends, and radically alter the personal goals and activities they had before joining the group.

The group is preoccupied with bringing in new members.

The group is preoccupied with making money.

Members are encouraged or required to live and/or socialize only with other group members.

The most loyal members (the "true believers") feel there can be no life outside the context of the group. They believe there is not other way to be, and often fear reprisals to themselves or others if they leave - or ever consider leaving the group."

In <u>Blind Faith - Recognizing and Recovering from Dysfunctional Religious Groups</u>, author Kay Marie Porterfield, M.A., lists the following as characteristics of dysfunctional religious groups:

"A powerful charismatic leader who claims divinity or infallibility.

Authoritarian power structure.

Intrusion and blurred personal boundaries.

Monopoly on truth.

Total control over members' lives.

Rigid institutional boundaries.

Secrecy and deception, both inside and outside the group.

A mission or a cause."

Kay Marie Porterfield goes into detail describing these symptoms along with giving examples. She also illuminates the *"Pitfalls of Perfectionism."* She further lists some of the "Danger Signs of Dysfunctional Religious Groups" as:

The teachings are dogmatic and rigid.

The group seems preoccupied with recruitment and fund-raising.

When doing what the leader claims is God's will, the group believes the end justifies the means.

Group members talk about their leader as if he or she is God.

The group claims to hold exclusive rights to truth. Outsiders are considered spiritually ignorant or evil.

Group members are expected to give up family or friends.

Members are manipulated by being either shamed or rewarded.

The group controls information and social contacts.

The group is rigidly hierarchical.

Women are not treated as equals with men.

Sexual coercion is practiced.

Critical thinking and questioning are forbidden.

The group makes great demands on its members and uses guilt to punish those who do not comply.

The group provides a sense of instant intimacy.

Questions are ignored or given simplistic answers based on circular logic.

Members are required to make long-term commitments and prove their allegiance by quitting jobs, renouncing family, or giving money to the group.

Members use pressure, charm, and manipulation to persuade others to join."

Amazingly, these cult psychology books describe the inner workings and methodology of the Mormon Church to a tee, even though the authors gained much of their knowledge and experiences from other cults.

Steven Hassan draws much of his brilliant insights into cult psychology from the time he spent as a member of the Unification Church, a religious cult also known as the "Moonies." Author Janja Lilich belonged to a radical cult for 11 years, and Madeleine Tobias is a former member of the cult group "Transcendental Meditation." These authors not only share their personal experiences, but expose abusive physical and psychological techniques used by religious cults such as: David Koresh and the Branch Davidians, Heaven's Gate, Krishna, Jim Jones and the People's Temple, the Church of Scientology, Church Universal and Triumphant, The Way International, Rajneesh, Jehovah's Witnesses, etc.

There are literally thousands of religious/spiritual cults, which have sprung up from the Bible, Koran, Talmud, Cabala as well as from other books and eastern mysticism. Interestingly, despite the diversity in cult origins and names, they universally share similar destructive mind control techniques.

Regardless of your belief, lack of belief, or religious persuasion, I highly recommend these books to everyone. Recognizing and understanding the psychology behind destructive cults and abusive relationships should be considered part of a mainstream education. It may very well be the key to having your children and loved ones avoid cults and abusive relationships altogether.

References/Notes

Chapter One - For God, Queen and Country

1. Florence Nightingale's most famous contribution came during the Crimean, which became her central focus when reports began to filter back to Britain about the horrific conditions for the wounded. On 21 October 1854/1854, she and a staff of 38 women volunteer nurses; trained by Nightingale and including her aunt Mai Smith, were sent (under the authorization of Sidney Herbert) to Turkey, some 545 km across the Black Sea from Balaklava in the Crimea, where the main British camp was based. Nightingale arrived early in November 1854 at Selimiye B in Scutari in Istanbul. She and her nurses found wounded soldiers being badly cared for by overworked medical staff in the face of official indifference. A sanitary commission had to be sent out by the British government to Scutari in March 1855, almost six months after Florence Nightingale had arrived, which flushed out the sewers and improved ventilation. Death rates were sharply reduced. Nightingale continued believing the death rates were due to poor nutrition and supplies and overworking of the soldiers. It was not until after she returned to Britain and began collecting evidence before the Royal Commission on the Health of the Army, that she came to believe that most of the soldiers at the hospital were killed by poor living conditions. This experience would influence her later career, when she advocated sanitary living conditions as of great importance. Consequently, she reduced deaths in the Army during peacetime and turned attention to the sanitary design of hospitals.

2. *Penicillium sp.* were first described in France by Ernest Duchesne in 1897. Britain following the re-discovery of by Alexander F were yet to be discovered, victims fell pray to the notorious "*hospital gangrene.*" Their wounds would become inflamed and swollen and fill the air with a stench which almost a trade mark of the awful business taking place inside.

3. Banks, John, *UNTO YOU WHO ONCE KNEW THE TRUTH, THE LIGHT TO YOUR JUSTIFICATION; BUT BEING TURNED FROM IT INTO THE UNCLEAN WORLD, IT IS NOW YOUR CONDEMNATION.* The Journal of John Banks. In: Evans, William and

Evans, Thomas, eds. *Friends' Library,* Vol. II. Philadelphia: Printed by Joseph Rakestraw, 1838, pages 48-50.
4. Fitzpatrick, H., Penal Laws, Which Aggrieve The Catholics of Ireland: With Commentaries. Part I. Dublin, 1812, page 26
5. Fitzpatrick, H., Penal Laws, Which Aggrieve The Catholics of Ireland: With Commentaries. Part I. Dublin, 1812, page 26-27

Chapter Two - Down Under

1. Smith, Joseph Jr., *Joseph Smith History,* Pearl of Great Price 1:19
2. Smith, Joseph Jr., *History of the Church of Jesus Christ of Latter-day Saints.* Vol. 4, p. 461, An Introduction and Notes by B. H. Roberts, Deseret Book Company, 1980
3-5 While these quotes can be found elsewhere, I recommend: Buerger, David John, *The Mysteries of Godliness: A History of Mormon Temple Worship* (2nd ed.), Salt Lake City: Signature Books 2002

To read the excerpts from the temple session, refer to Chapter Seven, reference #23.

For brevity I only reference the sections highlighting "The Execution of the Penalty," the penalties and some of the secrets. The following script was read aloud in Mormon Temples prior to 1990. Underlined portions in are the blood oaths Reuben and I were subjected too...cutting open your throat, chest and guts.

Secret Blood Oath #1; slitting your throat.
Narrator: "We will now give unto you the First Token of the Aaronic Priesthood with its accompanying name, and sign, and penalty. Before doing this, however, we desire to impress upon your minds the sacred character of the First Token of the Aaronic Priesthood, with its accompanying name and sign, and penalty, as well as that of all the other tokens of the Holy Priesthood, with their names, and signs, and penalties, which you will receive in the temple this day. They are most sacred, and are guarded by solemn covenants and **obligations of secrecy** to the effect that made in the presence of God, Angels and these witnesses to hold them sacred and under no condition, even **at the peril of your life,** will you ever divulge them, except at a certain place in the temple that will be shown you hereafter. The representation of **the execution of the penalties indicates different ways in which life**

may be taken. The execution of the penalty is represented by placing the thumb under the left ear, the palm of the hand down, and by drawing the thumb quickly across the throat to the right ear, and dropping the hand to the side. I will now explain the covenant and **obligation of secrecy** which are associated with this token, its name, and sign and penalty, and which you will be required to take upon yourselves...after making the sign at the same time representing **the execution of the penalty:** I will never reveal the First Token of the Aaronic Priesthood, with its accompanying name, and sign, and penalty. **Rather than do so, I would suffer my life to be taken.** *(The Officiator demonstrates the execution of the penalty... Thumb of right hand drawn across the throat).*

Secret Blood Oath #2; cutting open your chest.

Second Token of the Aaronic Priesthood with its accompanying name, and sign, and penalty. *(The officiator demonstrates.)* **The Execution of the Penalty is represented by placing the right hand on the left breast, drawing the hand quickly across the body, and dropping the hands to the sides.** I will now explain the covenant and obligation of **secrecy**, which are associated with this token, its name, and sign, and penalty, and which you will be required to take upon yourselves. If I were receiving my own endowment today,... repeat in my mind those words, after making the sign, at the same time representing **the Execution of the Penalty:**...I will never reveal the Second Token of the Aaronic priesthood, with is accompanying name, and sign, and penalty. **Rather than do so I would suffer my life to be taken**. All arise. *(All Patrons stand.)* ...Now, repeat in your mind after me the words of the covenant, at the same time representing **the Executing of the Penalty.** I...solemnly covenant, before God, angels, and these witnesses that I will never reveal the second Token of the Aaronic Priesthood, with its accompanying name, and sign, and penalty. **Rather than do so, I would suffer my life to be taken**. *(All patrons sit down.)*

Secret Blood Oath #3; cutting open your guts.

We will now give unto you the First Token of the Melchizedek Priesthood, or the sign of the Nail, with its accompanying name, **and** sign, and penalty. The sign is made by bringing the left hand in front of you with the hand in cupping shape, the left arm forming a square; the right hand is also brought forward, the palm down, the fingers close together **with** the thumb extended, and the thumb is placed over the left hip. This is the sign. **The penalty is represented by drawing the thumb quickly across the body and dropping the hands to the sides.** I will now explain the covenant and obligation of **secrecy,** which are associated with this token, its name, **and sign and penalty,** and which you will be required to take upon yourselves. If I were receiving the Endowment today, either for myself or for the dead, I would repeat in my mind these words, after making the sign, at the same to representing **the Execution of the Penalty:** I solemnly covenant before God, angels and these witnesses in the name of the Son that I will never reveal the First Token of the Melchizedek Priesthood or Sign of the Nail, with its accompanying name, and sign and penalty. **Rather than do so, I would suffer my life to be taken.** *(Patrons perform the action as the Officiator guides them.) (All patrons sit down.)*

"THE PRAYER CIRCLE" repeats The Execution of the Penalties all over again.

(Patrons make each sign as they are mentioned by the Narrator.)

We will begin by making the Sign of the First Token of the Aaronic Priesthood... **The Execution of the Penalty is represented by placing the thumb under the left ear, the palm of the hand down, and by drawing the thumb quickly across the throat to the right ear, and dropping the hand to the side.**

We will now make the Sign of the Second Token of the Aaronic Priesthood... **The Execution of the penalty is represented by placing the right hand on the left breast, drawing the hand quickly across the body, and dropping the hands to the sides.**

We will now make the sign of the First Token of the Melchizedek Priesthood or Sign of the Nail... **The Execution of the penalty is represented by drawing the thumb quickly across the body, and dropping the hands to the sides.**

Chapter Three - Detroit Meets Hope

1. Interview Questions for Recommends to Enter a Mormon Temple

1. Do you believe in God, the Eternal Father, in his Son, Jesus Christ, and in the Holy Ghost; and do you have a firm testimony of the restored gospel?

2. Do you sustain the President of The Church of Jesus Christ of Latter-day Saints as the prophet, seer, and revelator; and do you recognize him as the only person on the earth authorized to exercise all priesthood keys?

3. Do you sustain the other General Authorities and the local authorities of the Church?

4. Do you live the law of chastity?

5. Is there anything in your conduct relating to members of your family that is not in harmony with the teachings of the Church?

6. **Do you affiliate with any group or individual** whose teachings or practices are contrary to or oppose those accepted by The Church of Jesus Christ of Latter-day Saints, or do you sympathize with the precepts of any such group or individual?

7. Do you earnestly strive to do your duty in the Church; to attend your sacrament, priesthood, and other meetings; and to obey the rules, laws, and commandments of the gospel?

8. Are you honest in your dealings with your fellowmen?

9. Are you a full-tithe payer? (if not, a temple recommend will not be given)

10. Do you keep the Word of Wisdom?

11. Have you ever been divorced or are you now separated from your spouse under order of a civil court?

12. If you have received your temple endowment -- (a) Do you keep all the covenants that you made in the temple? (b) Do you wear the authorized garments both day and night? (this refers to "Mormon Underwear")

13. Has there been any sin or misdeed in your life that should have been resolved with priesthood authorities but has not?

14. Do you consider yourself worthy in every way to enter the temple and participate in temple ordinances?

Chapter Four - I Hope They Call Me on a Mission

1. *I Hope They Call Me on a Mission*, LDS Primary, Children's Songbook

2. *The Missionary Handbook* (commonly known as the "White Bible"). It is a little booklet that the missionaries carry in their shirt pocket. It contains 167 strict rules missionaries must obey. In addition, there are many rules the missionary is subjected to that are not in the White Bible.

3. Smith, Joseph Jr., Book of Mormon, 2 Nephi 5:21

4. Kimball, Spencer W., General Conference, 1960

5. Kimball, Spencer W., *"Of Royal Blood,"* Ensign, "A Special Lamanite Issue," July 1971, p.7

6. Packer, Boyd K., *"For the Blessing of the Lamanites,"* (In reference to a youth conference where 200 Indian Placement students gathered for a special conference.)

7. Lell JT, Brown MD, Schurr TG, Sukernik RI, Starikovskaya YB, Torroni A, Moore LG, Troup GM, Wallace DC. 1997. Y chromosome polymorphisms in Native American and Siberian populations: identification of Native American Y chromosome haplotypes. Hum.

Genet. 100:536-543.
8. Lell JT, Sukernik RI, Starikovskaya YB, Su B, Jin L, Schurr TG, Underhill PA, Wallace DC. 2002. The dual origin and Siberian affinities of Native American Y chromosomes. Am. J. Hum. Genet. 2002 70:192-206.
9. Zegura SL, Karafet TM, Zhivotovsky LA, Hammer MF. 2004. High-resolution SNPs and microsatellite haplotypes point to a single, recent entry of Native American Y chromosomes into the Americas. Mol. Biol. Evol. 21:164-175.
10. Bortolini, M., et al. 2003. Y-Chromosome Evidence for Differing Ancient Demographic Histories in the Americas. Am. J. Hum. Genet. 73: 524-539.
11. Bianchi, N.O., C. I. Catanesi, G. Bailliet, V. L. Martinez-Marignac, C. M. Bravi, L. B. Vidal-Rioja, R. J. Herrera, and J. S. Lopez-Camelo. 1998. Characterization of Ancestral and Derived Y-Chromosome Haplotypes of New World Native Populations. Am. J. Hum. Genet. 63:1862-1871.
12. Santos FR, A Pandya, C Tyler-Smith, SDJ Pena, M Schanfield, WR Leonard, L Osipova, MH Crawford, and RJ Mitchell. 1999. The Central Siberian Origin for Native American Y Chromosomes. Am. J. Hum. Genet. 64:619-628.
13. Ancestral Asian Source(s) of New World Y-Chromosome Founder Haplotypes. Am. J. Hum. Genet. 64:817-831.
14. Bortolini MC, Salzano FM, Bau CH, Layrisse Z, Petzl-Erler ML, Tsuneto LT, Hill K, Hurtado AM, Castro-De-Guerra D, Bedoya G, Ruiz-Linares A. 2002. Y-chromosome biallelic polymorphisms and Native American population structure. Ann. Hum. Genet. 66:255259.
Merriwether DA, Rothhammer F, Ferrell RE. 1995. Distribution of the four founding lineage haplotypes in Native Americans suggests a single wave of migration for the New World. Am. J. Phys. Anthropol. 98:411-430.
15. Malhi, R. S., et al. 2002. The Structure of Diversity within New World Mitochondrial DNA Haplogroups: Implications for the Prehistory of North America. Am. J. Hum. Genet. 70: 905-919.
16. Merriwether DA, Hall WW, Vahlne A, Ferrell RE. 1996. mtDNA variation indicates Mongolia may have been the source for the founding population for the New World. Am. J. Hum. Genet. 59:204-212.
17. Derenko MV, Malyarchuk BA, Dambueva IK, Shaikhaev GO, Dorzhu CM, Nimaev DD, Zakharov IA. 2000. Mitochondrial DNA

variation in two South Siberian Aboriginal populations: implications for the genetic history of North Asia. Hum. Biol. 72:945-973.
18. SL Bonatto and FM Salzano. 1997. Diversity and Age of the Four Major mtDNA Haplogroups, and Their Implications for the Peopling of the New World. Am. J.
12. Santos FR, A Pandya, C Tyler-Smith, SDJ Pena, M Schanfield, WR Leonard, L Osipova, MH Crawford, and RJ Mitchell. 1999. The Central Siberian Origin for Native American Y Chromosomes. Am. J. Hum. Genet. 64:619-628.
13. Ancestral Asian Source(s) of New World Y-Chromosome Founder Haplotypes. Am. J. Hum. Genet. 64:817-831.
14. Bortolini MC, Salzano FM, Bau CH, Layrisse Z, Petzl-Erler ML, Tsuneto LT, Hill K, Hurtado AM, Castro-De-Guerra D, Bedoya G, Ruiz-Linares A. 2002. Y-chromosome biallelic polymorphisms and Native American population structure. Ann. Hum. Genet. 66:255-259. Merriwether DA, Rothhammer F, Ferrell RE. 1995. Distribution of the four founding lineage haplotypes in Native Americans suggests a single wave of migration for the New World. Am. J. Phys. Anthropol. 98:411-430.
15. Malhi, R. S., et al. 2002. The Structure of Diversity within New World Mitochondrial DNA Haplogroups: Implications for the Prehistory of North America. Am. J. Hum. Genet. 70: 905ñ919.
16. Merriwether DA, Hall WW, Vahlne A, Ferrell RE. 1996. mtDNA variation indicates Mongolia may have been the source for the founding population for the New World. Am. J. Hum. Genet. 59:204-212.
17. Derenko MV, Malyarchuk BA, Dambueva IK, Shaikhaev GO, Dorzhu CM, Nimaev DD, Zakharov IA. 2000. Mitochondrial DNA variation in two South Siberian Aboriginal populations: implications for the genetic history of North Asia. Hum. Biol. 72:945-973.
18. SL Bonatto and FM Salzano. 1997. Diversity and Age of the Four Major mtDNA Haplogroups, and Their Implications for the Peopling of the New World. Am. J. Hum. Genet. 61:1413-1423.
19. YB Starikovskaya, RI Sukernik, TG Schurr, AM Kogelnik, and DC Wallace. 1998. mtDNA Diversity in Chukchi and Siberian Eskimos: Implications for the Genetic History of Ancient Beringia and the Peopling of the New World. Am. J. Hum. Genet. 63:1473-1491.
20. Stone AC, and M Stoneking. 1998. mtDNA Analysis of a Prehistoric Oneota Population: Implications for the Peopling of the New World. Am. J. Hum. Genet. 62:1153-1170.

21. Starikovskaya EB, Sukernik RI, Derbeneva OA, Volodko NV, Ruiz-Pesini E, Torroni A, Brown MD, Lott MT, Hosseini SH, Huoponen K, Wallace DC. 2005. Mitochondrial DNA diversity in indigenous populations of the southern extent of Siberia, and the origins of Native American haplogroups. Ann. Hum. Genet. 69:67-89.
22. Fix AG. 2005. Rapid deployment of the five founding Amerind mtDNA haplogroups via coastal and riverine colonization. Am. J. Phys. Anthropol. 128:430-436.
23. Lalueza-Fox C, Gilbert MT, Martinez-Fuentes AJ, Calafell F, Bertranpetit J. 2003. Mitochondrial DNA from pre-Columbian Ciboneys from Cuba and the prehistoric colonization of the Caribbean. Am. J. Phys. Anthropol. 121:97-108.
24. Dalton, R. 2005. Caveman DNA hints at map of migration. Nature 436:162.
25. Fagundes, N.J.R., et al. 2008. Mitochondrial Population Genomics Supports a Single Pre-Clovis Origin with a Coastal Route for the Peopling of the Americas American Journal of Human Genetics 82: 583-592.
26. Novick GE, Novick CC, Yunis J, Yunis E, Antunez de Mayolo P, Scheer WD, Deininger PL, Stoneking M, York DS, Batzer MA, Herrera RJ. 1998. Polymorphic Alu insertions and the Asian origin of Native American populations. Hum. Biol.70:23-39.
27. Corbin, Andrew, A senior editor at Doubleday, said that LDS leaders instructed his company to make the change so that it "*would be in accordance with future editions the church is printing.*"

Chapter Five - Life in the Fast Lane

1. Smith, Joseph, Jr., *"Behold, now it is called today until the coming of the Son of Man, and verily it is a day of sacrifice, and a day for the tithing of my people; for he that is tithed shall not be burned at his coming."* Doctrine and Covenants, 63:23

Chapter Six - An Awakening

1. Smith, George A., Journal of Discourses, Vol. 14, Chapter 4, page 217
2. Smith, Joseph Jr., *History of the Church of Jesus Christ of Latter-day Saints*. Volumes I-VII, An Introduction and Notes by B. H. Roberts,

Deseret Book Company, 1980

3. Compton, Todd, *In Sacred Loneliness*. Signature Books, 2005

4. Tanner, N. Eldon, Ensign Magazine. August 1979

5. Tanner, Jerald, Mormonism - Shadow or Reality? page 531

6. Painesville Republican, February 22, 1838, as quoted in Conflict at Kirtland, page 297 : Wilford Woodruff, who remained true to the Church and became the fourth President, confirmed the fact that Joseph Smith claimed to have a revelation concerning the bank. Under the date of January 6, 1837, he recorded the following in his journal: "I also herd [sic] President Joseph Smith, Jr., declare in the presence of F. Williams, D. Whitmer, S. Smith, W. Parrish, and others in the Deposit office that HE HAD RECEIVED THAT MORNING THE WORD OF THE LORD UPON THE SUBJECT OF THE KIRTLAND SAFETY SOCIETY. He was alone in a room by himself and he had not only [heard] the voice of the Spirit upon the Subject but even an AUDIBLE VOICE. He did not tell us at that time what the Lord said upon the subject but remarked that if we would give heed to the commandments the Lord had given this morning all would be well." ("Wilford Woodruff's Journal," January 6, 1837, as quoted in Conflict at Kirtland, page 296)

7. Avery, V. & Newell, L., Mormon Enigma: Emma Hale Smith, pp. 62, April, 1837

8. Marquardt, Michael, The Joseph Smith Revelations Text & Commentary

9. Packer, Boyd K., "*The Mantle is Far, Far Greater Than the Intellect*", 1981, BYU Studies. Vol. 21, No. 3, pp. 259-271.

10. Marquardt, Michael, The Joseph Smith Revelations Text & Commentary.

11. Hinckley, Gordon B., "Loyalty," April Conference, 2003

12. Descartes, Rene, *Cogito Ero Sum: "I Think Therefore I am."* Meditations. 1641

13. Bednar, David A., "And Nothing Shall Offend Them." October conference, 2006

14. Smith, Joseph, Jr., Doctrines and Covenants, Section 133, Verses 71-73

15. Festinger, Leon, *When Prophecy Fails*, 1957, Cognitive dissonance is a psychological state that describes the uncomfortable feeling when a person begins to understand that something the person believes to be true is, in fact, not true. Similar to ambivalence, the term cognitive dissonance describes conflicting thoughts or beliefs (cognitions) that

occur at the same time, or when engaged in behaviors that conflict with one's beliefs. In academic literature, the term refers to attempts to reduce the discomfort of conflicting thoughts, by performing actions that are opposite to one's beliefs. In simple terms, it can be the filtering of information that conflicts with what one already believes, in an effort to ignore that information and reinforce one's beliefs. In detailed terms, it is the perception of incompatibility between two cognitions, where "cognition" is defined as any element of knowledge, including attitude, emotion, belief, or behavior. The theory of cognitive dissonance states that contradicting cognitions serve as a driving force that compels the mind to acquire or invent new thoughts or beliefs, or to modify existing beliefs, so as to reduce the amount of dissonance (conflict) between cognitions. Experiments have attempted to quantify this hypothetical drive. Some of these have examined how beliefs often change to match behavior when beliefs and behavior are in conflict.

16. Compton, Todd, *In Sacred Loneliness.* p. 230-231. Signature Books, 200

Chapter Seven - A Bountiful Harvest

1. Packer, Boyd K., *"The Mantle is Far, Far Greater Than the Intellect"*, 1981, BYU Studies, Vol. 21, No. 3, pp. 259-271.
2. Oaks, Dallin H., *"The Mormons,"* PBS Special, Broadcast 2007; (Also seen on youtube.com)
3. Improvent Era, June 194
4. Hinckley, Gordon B., Ensign Magazine, November 1999; (Also seen on youtube.com)
5. Hinckley, Gordon B., interviewed by Mike Wallace, *"60 Minutes,"* CBS. April 1996; (Also seen on youtube.com)
6. Young, Brigham, Journal of Discourses. Vol. 3, page 266.
7. Grant, Jedediah M., Journal of Discourses. Vol. 4, page 49,1856.
8. Young, Brigham, Journal of Discourses. Vol. 4, page 220,1857.
9. Young, Brigham, Journal of Discourses. Vol. 4, page 53,1856.
10. Grant, Jedediah M., Journal of Discourses. Vol. 4, page 50,1856.
11. Young, Brigham, Journal of Discourses. Vol. 4, page 53,1856.
12. Young, Brigham, Journal of Discourses. Vol. 4, page 220,1857.
13. Kimball, Heber C., *The Twenty Seventh Wife*, Irving Wallace, p. 101.
14. Kimball, Heber C., *The Lion of the Lord*, New York, 1969, pp.129-30.

15. Hinckley, Gordon B., LDS General Conference, April 2007
16. Emma Hale Smith died April 30, 1879. Brigham Young died August 29, 1877
17. Young, Brigham, *"Adam, Our Father and God,"* Millennial Star, Vol. 15, p.769, 1853.
18. Young, Brigham, Journal of Discourses, 13:271
19. Young, Brigham, Journal of Discourses Vol. 10, p.206
20. Bennett, John C., *The History of the Saints*, p. 265-266
21. Hickman, B. (1904). *Brigham's Destroying Angel: Being the Life, Confession, and Startling Disclosures of the Notorious Bill Hickman, the Danite Chief of Utah*. Boston: Shepard Publishing Co..
22. & 23. My recommendations for further reading: Buerger, David John, *The Mysteries of Godliness: A History of Mormon Temple Worship* (2nd ed.), Salt Lake City: Signature Books, 2002
Prior to 1927, the temple Ceremonies included:

"The Law of Vengeance"

"You and each of you do covenant and promise that you will pray and never cease to pray to Almighty God to <u>avenge the blood of the prophets</u> upon this nation, and that you will teach the same to your children and to your children's children unto the third and fourth generation. All bow your heads and say yes." **In addition, the following blood oaths were removed:** *"We agree that our <u>throats be cut from ear to ear and our tongues torn out by the roots.</u>" "We agree to have <u>our breasts cut open and our hearts and vitals torn from our bodies and given to the birds of the air and beasts of the field.</u>" "Should we do so, we agree that<u> our bodies be cut asunder in the midst and all our bowels gush out</u>*

24. Nelson, Russell M., *"Truth and More,"* Ensign, Jan. 1986, page 6
25. Young, Brigham, Journal of Discourses, Vol. 1, p. 188, 1853.
26. Smith, Joseph Jr., Doctrine and Covenants, Section 132
27. Winkler, Albert, "The Circleville Massacre: A Brutal Incident in Utah's Black Hawk War," *Utah Historical Quarterly* 55 (1987); Carlton Culmsee, *Utah's Black Hawk War* (Logan: Utah State University Press, 1973), 90-91.
28. Hickman, B. (1904). *Brigham's Destroying Angel: Being the Life, Confession, and Startling Disclosures of the Notorious Bill Hickman, the Danite Chief of Utah*. Boston: Shepard Publishing Co..
29. The September Six were six noted intellectuals and feminists expelled from the Mormon Church, in September 1993. They included:

Lynne Kanavel Whitesides, a feminist; Avraham Gileadi, a Hebrew scholar and literary analyst: Paul Toscano, a Salt Lake City attorney who co-authored, *Strangers in Paradox: Explorations in Mormon Theology*; Maxine Hanks, a feminist theologian who compiled and edited the book *Women and Authority: Re-emerging Mormon Feminism*; Lavina Fielding Anderson , a feminist writer who edited the books *Sisters in Spirit: Mormon Women in Historical and Cultural Perspective*; and D. Michael Quinn, a Mormon historian.

30. Young, Brigham, Journal of Discourses, 10:110, March 8, 1863
31. In June of 1978, the LDS-owned Deseret News newspaper printed an announcement by the LDS First Presidency stating that God, by revelation, would now allow all worthy male members in the LDS Church to receive the priesthood as well as "blessings of the temple." (Deseret News, 6/9/78, 1A). This "revelation," known as Official Declaration 2, can be found in printed form at the end of the Doctrine and Covenants.
32. Hewlett, Lorraine, "The Second Great Accommodation," board, 17 June 2004
33. Oaks, Robert, Ensign, July 2005

Chapter Eight - The Forer Effect

1. Forer B.R., *"The Fallacy of Personal Validation: A classroom Demonstration of Gullibility,"* Journal of Abnormal Psychology, 44, 118-121. 1949
2. Dickson, D.H. and I.W. Kelly. *"The 'Barnum Effect' in Personality Assessment: A Review of the Literature,"* Psychological Reports, 1985, 57, 367-382.
3. Hyman, Ray, "'Cold Reading': How to Convince Strangers That You Know All About Them," *The Skeptical Inquirer* Spring/Summer 1977.
4. Randi, James, *Flim-Flam!* Buffalo, New York: Prometheus Books, 1982
5. Randi, James, Video. NOVA. "Secrets of the Psychics."
6. Steiner, Robert A. *Don't Get Taken! - Bunco and Bunkum Exposed - How to Protect Yourself* , Wide-Awake Books. 1989
7. Thiriart, P., "Acceptance of personality test results," *Skeptical Inquirer*, 15,116-165. 1991
8. Rowland, Ian, *The Full Facts Book of Cold Reading,* 3rd. ed (2000).

9. Kimball, Spencer W., BYU Devotional, 1980. Ostling, Richard. Mormon America: The Power and the Promise. New York: Harpercollins Publishers,U.S., 2000.
10. Talyor, John, Times and Seasons, Vol. 6, No. 1, p.811

Chapter Nine - Walk Toward the Light

1. Oaks, Dallin H., *"Reading Church History,"* CES Doctrine and Covenants Symposium, Brigham Young University, 16 Aug. 1985, page 25.
2. Oaks, Dallin H., *"Elder Decries Criticism of LDS Leaders,"* quoted in The Salt Lake Tribune, Sunday August 18, 1985, p. 2b
3. Oaks, Dallin H., *"Criticism,"* Ensign. Feb. 1987, page 68

Chapter Ten - A Land of Milk and Honey

1. Packer, Boyd K., May 1993
2. Ingersoll, Robert, *What's God got to do with it?* On Free Thought, Honest Talk and the Separation of Church and State. Hanover: Steerforth, 2005.

Chapter Eleven - Saving Jessica

1. Kinkead, Lucinda Dillon and Romboy, Dennis, *Deadly taboo: Youth suicide an epidemic that many in Utah prefer to ignore.* Deseret Morning News. Published: Monday, April 24, 2006, and, Utah Department of Health, Youth Suicide Study. Utah's consistently high youth suicide rate prompted the development of the Utah Youth Suicide Study, with the goal of identifying opportunities for prevention among adolescents. Gray et al., 2001
2. Packer, Boyd K., *For Young Men Only.*, This talk quickly became famous because the Church made it into a pamphlet called "For Young Men Only" and give it to all twelve-year-old boys. 1976-2007.
3. Kimball, Spencer W., *The Miracle of Forgiveness*, page 65
4. Vavere, Arturs, Men's Sexual Health Institute. "Developing inferiority complexes, man, especially young men who masturbate, thanks to ruling dogmas, starts to consider himself worse than others.

Usually after ejaculation guilt feeling rises – "why am I doing this?" -
He hides it from everyone putting himself to shame. Guilt feeling
grows into inferiority syndrome. Man stops taking himself as a man
psychologically and starts to be afraid of other kind of relationships.
Because of this problems may start in man's sexual life. "Medicine and
psychiatry recognize masturbation as a healthy developmental stage
toward maturity that young men experience in order to prepare for
healthy bonding with their wife and future family. It is rightly called by
some professionals "marriage preparation" or "marriage rehearsal
play." The term masturbation is popular but is an old one that predates
developmental psychology. Today, contemporary history of
masturbation is known. It is no wonder it has suffered such a bad
reputation in the past. Prior to 1900, Western medicine believed that
loss of semen damaged the nervous system and caused insanity. Many
diseases such as tuberculosis and STD's were falsely attributed to
masturbation. By the 1940's, we had scientific data that proved all
these ideas false. This data showed that almost 100% of males report
masturbation during puberty. This demonstrates that it does not lead to
a change of sexual orientation, or disease, or anything negative, but that
it is developmentally appropriate and leads primarily to a healthy
marriage bond in the majority of cases. Mormon Church Leaders only
began talking about it in the very late 1800's when they told the youth
the same false medical information that was popular at the time - that it
caused insanity. A few decades later, when that was obviously not the
case anymore, and everyone knew the masturbation insanity and
disease story was false, church leaders adopted the new popular
socially conservative American moral view (the "worldly" view). The
church has a continual history of mimicking popular conservative
public opinion when it comes to masturbation. This behavior should
make it pretty obvious that the Lord has not revealed the truth of the
matter through the church leaders, otherwise they would have not fallen
for any of the false tales of "the world" and would have revealed the
truth. Not only have LDS youth not received the truth about
masturbation, they have suffered from extremely damaged self-worth."
5. Kimball, Spencer W., Church News, October 9, 1983.
6. Kimball, Spencer W., The Miracle of Forgiveness
7. Goldman, Russell, *Two Studies Find Depression Widespread in
Utah, Study Calling Utah Most Depressed*, Renews Debate on Root
Causes, ABC News, March 2008, also, Sanjay Gupta, *Home States and
Depression*, CNN, November 28, 2007

8. Kimball, Spencer W., *Miracle of Forgiveness*, p.209,

9. Kimball, Spencer W., *Miracle of Forgiveness*, p.210,

10. Kimball, Spencer W., *Miracle of Forgiveness*, p.325

11. Anderton, Dave "Utah stays No. 1 in Bankruptcies," Deseret News, Salt Lake City, Utah June 21, 2004

12. The 13th Mormon Article of Faith includes "We believe all things," which is essential to all doctrines based on illusions. It may also be the reason Utahans fall victim to scams, white-collar crime, than any other state.

13. Hassan, Steven (1990). *Combatting Cult Mind Control*, Great Britian: Aquarian Press.

14. Interview Questions for Recommends to Enter a Mormon Temple; 6. <u>Do you affiliate with any group or individual</u> whose teachings or practices are contrary to or oppose those accepted by The Church of Jesus Christ of Latter-day Saints, or <u>do you sympathize with the precepts of any such group or individual?</u>

15. Oaks, Dallin H., *"The Mormons,"* PBS Special, Broadcast 2007

16. Packer, Boyd K., "The Unwritten Order of Things," a devotional address delivered at Brigham Young University on 15 October 1996.

17. According to definitions of a "Cult," by several leading Cult awareness professionals, The Mormon Church, The Church of Jesus Christ of Latter-Day Saints, <u>is a cult</u>. Experts in cult dynamics include: Shirley Harrison, *Cults - the battle for God*; Steve Eichel, *Building Resistance to Manipulation*; James R. Lewis, *Cults in America;* Isaac Bonewits, *Advanced Bonewits Cult Danger Evaluation Frame"*; Anthony Storr, *Feet of Clay - A Study of Gurus;* Robert J. Lifton, *Thought Reform and the Psychology of Totalism;* Steven Hassan, *Combatting Cult Mind Control* and *Releasing The Bonds: Empowering People to Think for Themselves*.

Chapter Twelve - The "D" Word

1. Packer, Boyd K., *Children of God,* This address was given at the BYU Women's Conference, May 5, 2006.

Chapter Thirteen– A Legacy of Love

1. Stewart, Mathew, *The Courtier and the Heretic, Leibniz, Spinoza,*

and the Fate of God in the Mordern World, pages 33-34
2. Shirley, S. (1982), *BARUCH SPINOZA. The Ethics and Selected Letters*. Indianapolis: Hackett.
3. Hassan, Steven (1990). *Combatting Cult Mind Control*, Great Britian: Aquarian Press.
4. Buerger, David John (2002). *The Mysteries of Godliness: A History of Mormon Temple Worship* (2nd ed.), Salt Lake City: Signature Books
5. Smith, Joseph, Jr., Doctrines and Covenants, Section 132, Verses 1-4
6. Official LDS Website, LDS.org, states: "When we accept the new and everlasting covenant, we agree to repent, be baptized, receive the Holy Ghost, receive our endowments, receive the covenant of marriage in the temple, and follow and obey Christ to the end of our lives."
7. Buerger, David John (2002). *The Mysteries of Godliness: A History of Mormon Temple Worship* (2nd ed.), Salt Lake City: Signature Books
8. Buerger, David John (2002). *The Mysteries of Godliness: A History of Mormon Temple Worship* (2nd ed.), Salt Lake City: Signature Books
9. Smith, Joseph, Jr., Doctrines and Covenants, Section 76, Verses 33-44
10. Smith, Joseph, Jr., Doctrines and Covenants, Section 76, Verses 104-106
11. Smith, Joseph, Jr., Doctrines and Covenants, Section 101, Verses 90-91
12. Smith, Joseph, Jr., Doctrines and Covenants, Section 133, Verses 71-73
13. Smith, Joseph, Jr., Doctrines and Covenants, Section 29, Verses 15-21

Chapter Fourteen - A Letter to James Dean

1. Smith, Joseph, Jr., Pearl of Great Price, *Joseph Smith History* 1:19
2. Smith, Joseph, Jr., Church History Vol. I Aug-Sept 1830 Newel Knight autobiography
3. Smith, Joseph, Jr., Church History Vol. I Sep 1830
4. Smith, Joseph, Jr., Church History Vol. I Sep 1830
5. Smith, Joseph, Jr., Church History Vol. I 1831, The Ohio Experience and Joseph Smith and the Restoration & Journal of Discourses
6. Smith, Joseph, Jr., Church History Vol. I Feb. 1831, and Book of John Whitmer

7. Jessee, Dean, The Personal Writings of Joseph Smith, Deseret Book, 2002, pp. 11 and 17

8. Jensen, Andrew, Historical Record, Vol. 6, p.234 1887

9. Compton, Todd, In Sacred Loneliness by Todd Compton, pp. 476-477

10. Smith, Joseph, History of the Church, Vol. 6 page 411, May, 1844

11. Jensen, Andrew, Historical Record, Vol. 6, p.234 1887

12. Smith, Joseph, Jr., History of the Church, VI (1912), pp. 430-432. The council met on June 8 and June 10 to discuss the matter.

13. Paine, Thomas, Age of reason, Part 1 Vienna: Nuvision Publications. 2008

Bibliography

Original Source Mormon Documentation

Smith, J. (1970). *Book of Mormon: 1830 Replica Edition.* Independence, MI: Herald Publishing House.

Dick, T. (1831). *Philosophy of Religion.* New York: S. King

Smith, J. (1833). *A Book of Commandments for the government of the Church of Christ,.* Jackson County, Missouri, W. W. Phelps & Co.

Smith, J. (1971). *Doctrine and Covenants: 1835 Replica Edition.* Independence, MI: Herald Publishing House.

Smith, J. (1976). *History of the Church Volumes 1-7.* Salt Lake City, UT: Deseret Book Company.

Smith, J. (1981). *The Book of Mormon: Another Testament of Jesus Christ (Official Edition).* Salt lake City, Utah, U.S.A: Church Of Jesus Christ Of Lds.

Smith, J. (1981). *Book of Mormon Doctrine and Covenants Pearl of Great Price (Triple Combination).* Salt Lake City: Church Of Jesus Christ Of Lds.

Law, W. (1844). *Nauvoo Expositor, July 7, 1844.* Nauvoo, IL: Nauvoo Expositor.

Whitmer, D. (2006). *An Address To All Believers In Christ: By A Witness To The Divine Authenticity Of The Book Of Mormon.* New York: Kessinger Publishing, Llc.

Smith, J.F. (1905). *Blood Atonement and the Origin of Plural Marriage.* Salt Lake City, UT: The Deseret News Press.

LDS Church (1880). *A String of Pearls Second Book of the Faith-Promoting Series.* Salt Lake City, UT: Juvenile Instructor Office.

LDS Church (1884). *Heroines of "Mormondom" The Second Book of the Nobel Women's Lives Series.* Salt Lake City, UT: Juvenile Instructor Office.

LDS Church (1882). *Early Scenes in Church History Eighth Book of the Faith-Promoting Series.* Salt Lake City, UT: Juvenile Instructor Office.

General Superintendency and Board of the Deseret Sunday School Union (1896). *Latter-day Saints' Sunday School Treatise.* Salt Lake City, UT: J. H. Parry, Printer.

Young, J. (1878). *History of the Organization of the Seventies.* Salt Lake City, UT: Deseret News Steam Printing Establishment.

Jenson, A. (1882). *The historical record,: A monthly periodical devoted exclusively to historical, biographical, chronological and statistical matters.* Salt Lake City, Utah: A. Jenson.

Ballard, M. (1922). *Three Degrees of Glory: a Discourse.* Salt Lake City, Utah: Deseret Book Company.

Latimer, D. (1932). *Opening of the seven seals and the half hour of silence,: Which gives a birds-eye-view of history from the fall of Adam to the end of the world, explaining ... and Magog, the new heaven and the new earth.* Salt Lake City, Utah: Pyramid Specialties Corp.

Talmage, J. (1915). *The philosophical basis of "Mormonism": An address delivered by invitation before the Congress of Religious Philosophies held in connection with the Panama-Pacific International Exposition ... San Francisco, California.* Independence, Missouri: Press of Zion's Printing and Publishing Company.

Walters, W. (1981). *Use of the Old Testament in the Book of Mormon.* Salt Lake City UT: Utah Lighthouse Ministry.

Widtsoe, J. (1975). *DISCOURSES OF BRIGHAM YOUNG - Second President of the Church of Jesus Christ of Latter-Day Saints.* Salt Lake City, UT: Deseret Book Company.

Madsen, B., & Mcmurrin, S. (1992). *Studies of the Book of Mormon.* Salt Lake City, Utah: Signature Books.

Smith, E. (2002). *View of the Hebrews 1825.* Colfax, Wisconsin: Hayriver Press.

Tanner, J. & Tanner, S. (1996). *3,913 Changes in the Book of Mormon.* Salt Lake City, UT: Utah Lighthouse Ministry.

Dick, T. (2003). *Complete Works of Thomas Dick, Part 1.* New York: Kessinger Publishing, Llc.

Dick, T. (2003). *Complete Works of Thomas Dick, Part 2.* New York: Kessinger Publishing, Llc.

Larson, C. (1992). *By His Own Hand Upon Papyrus: A New Look at the Joseph Smith Papyri.* Grand Rapids, MI: Inst For Religious Research.

Walters, W.P. (1974). *Joseph Smith's Bainbridge, N.Y., Court Trials.* Westminster Theological Journal 36 (Winter): 139-40.

Young, A. (2007). *Wife No. 19.* New York: Digireads.Com.

Carroll, L. (1994). *The Complete Works of Lewis Carroll.* New York: Barnes & Noble.

Hedengren, P. (1985). *In Defense of Faith: Assessing Arguments Against Latter-day Saint Belief.* Provo, UT: Bradford and Wilson.

Madsen G. (1990). *Joseph Smith's 1826 Trial: The Legal Setting.* Provo, UT: Brigham Young University Studies 30 (Spring): 91-108.

Zechariah Tarble (1826). Bill of Costs, Clerk of the Board of Supervisors, Chenango County Office Building, Norwich, New York; Levi Bigelow Bill of Costs, 1826, Clerk of the Board of Supervisors, Chenango County Office Building, Norwich, NY; and James Humphrey Bill of Costs, 1826, Chenango County Historical Society, Norwich, NY.

Albert Neely (1826). Bill of Costs. Chenango County Office Building, Norwich, NY: Clerk of the Board of Supervisors

Hogan, M. (1986). *The Mormon Temple and the Masonic Lodge.* Harvard, MA: M.B. Hogan.

Bennett, J. (2000). *The History of the Saints : Or, an Expose of Joe Smith and Mormonism.* Urbana: University of Illinois Press.

Marquardt, H., & Smith, J. (1999). *The Joseph Smith Revelations: Text and Commentary.* Salt Lake City, Utah: Signature Books.

Ingleton, R.V. (2005). *History of Joseph Smith by His Mother Lucy Mack Smith: The Unabridged Original Version.* Arlington, Virginia: Stratford Books.

Howe, E. (1987). *Mormonism Unveiled: Or, a Faithful Account of That Singular Imposition and Delusion from Its Rise to the Present Time (Communal Societies in America).* New York: Ams Pr Inc.

(1981). *Bible, King James Version.* Salt Lake City: Church Of Jesus Christ Of Lds.

Office, J. (1882). *EARLY SCENES IN CHURCH HISTORY. EIGHTH BOOK OF THE FAITH-PROMOTING SERIES.* Salt Lake City, Utah: Juvenile Instructor Office.

Tanner, J. & Tanner, S. (1970). *Mormon Scriptures and the Bible: Papyrus Bodmer II- About 200 A.D..* UT.: Utah Lighthouse Ministry.

Tanner, J. & Tanner, S. (1970). *Mormon Scriptures & the Bible.* Salt Lake City, Utah: Modern Microfilm Company.

Tanner, J. & Tanner, S. (1988). *Mormonism, Magic and Masonry.* Salt Lake City, Utah: Utah Lighthouse Ministry.

Tanner, J. & Tanner, S. (1998). *Changes in Joseph Smith's History.* Salt Lake City, Utah: Utah Lighthouse Ministry.

Tanner, J. & Tanner, S. (1988). *Joseph Smith's Plagiarism of the Bible.* Salt Lake City, Utah: Utah Lighthouse Ministry.

Witte, B. (1975). *Where Does it Say That.* Grand rapids, MI: Gospel Truths

Hickman, B. (1904). *Brigham's Destroying Angel: Being the Life, Confession, and Startling Disclosures of the Notorious Bill Hickman, the Danite Chief of Utah.* Boston: Shepard Publishing Co.

Contemporary Mormon Sources

Evans, A. (2003). *The Keystone of Mormonism.* St. George, UT: Keystone Books Inc.

Palmer, G. (2002). *An Insider's View of Mormon Origins.* Salt Lake City, UT: Signature Books.

Compton, T. (1997). *In Sacred Loneliness: The Plural Wives of Joseph Smith.* Salt Lake City, UT: Signature Books.

Avery, V., & Newell, L. (1994). *Mormon Enigma: Emma Hale Smith.* Urbana: University of Illinois Press.

Brodie, F. (1995). *No Man Knows My History: The Life of Joseph Smith.* New York: Vintage.

Marquardt, H., & Walters, W. (1998). *Inventing Mormonism: Tradition and the Historical Record*. Salt Lake City, Utah: Signature Books.

Quinn, D. (1994). *The Mormon Hierarchy: Origins of Power (Mormon Hierarchy)*. Salt Lake City, Utah: Signature Books.

Quinn, D. (1997). *The Mormon Hierarchy: Extensions of Power (Mormon Hierarchy)*. Salt Lake City, Utah: Signature Books.

Wagoner, R. (1992). *Mormon Polygamy: A History*. Salt Lake City, Utah: Signature Books.

Ostling, R. (2000). *Mormon America: The Power and the Promise*. New York: Harpercollins Publishers, U.S..

Johnson, E., & Mckeever, B. (2000). *Mormonism 101: Examining the Religion of the Latter-day Saints*. Grand Rapids, Michigan: Baker Books.

Robert., & Bryant, E. (2004). *Mormonism 101; The Mormon Church And Their Web Of Deception*. Oak Ridge, TN: Holy Fire Publishing.

Mckeever, B. (1991). *Answering Mormons' Questions*. Tulsa, OK : Bethany House.

Larson, S. (1997). *Quest for the Gold Plates*. Salt Lake City, UT: Freethinker Pr.

Crouch, W. (1968). *The Myth of Mormon inspiration*. Grand rapids: Lambert's Book House.

Krakauer, J. (2004). *Under the Banner of Heaven: A Story of Violent Faith*. New York: Anchor.

Shipps, J. (1987). *Mormonism: The Story of a New Religious Tradition*. Urbana: University of Illinois Press.

Petersen, L. (2000). *The Creation of the Book of Mormon : A Historical Inquiry*. Salt Lake City, UT: Freethinker Pr.

Tanner, J. (1979). *The Changing World of Mormonism*. Chicago: Moody Pr.

Wood, C. (2004). *The Mormon Conspiracy*. Chula Vista, CA: Black Forest Press.

Naifeh, S., & Smith, G. (2005). *The Mormon Murders*. New York: St. Martin's Paperbacks.

Anderson, R. (1999). *Inside the Mind of Joseph Smith: Psychobiography and the Book of Mormon*. Salt Lake City, Utah: Signature Books.

Brooke, J. (1996). *The Refiner's Fire: The Making of Mormon Cosmology, 1644-1844*. New York: Cambridge University Press.

Anderson, D. (2003). *Farewell to Eden: Coming to terms with Mormonism and Science*. Boston: 1st Books Library.

Wagoner, R. (2005). *Sidney Rigdon: A Portrait of Religious Excess*. Salt Lake City, Utah: Signature Books.

Bushman, R. (2007). *Joseph Smith: Rough Stone Rolling*. New York: Vintage.

Morgan, D. (1986). *Dale Morgan on Early Mormonism: Correspondence and a New History*. Salt Lake City, Utah: Signature Books.

Buerger, David John (2002), *The Mysteries of Godliness: A History of Mormon Temple Worship* (2nd ed.), Salt Lake City: Signature Books.

Leaving Religion

Beck, M. (2006). *Leaving the Saints: How I Lost the Mormons and Found My Faith*. New York: Three Rivers Press.

Robertson, J. (2001). *Out of Mormonism: A Womans True Story*. Tulsa : Bethany House.

Braithwaite, T. (2003). *A Mormon Odyssey: Journey to the Center of My Soul*. New York: Xlibris Corporation.

Spencer, J. (1984). *Beyond Mormonism : An Elder's Story*. Old Tappan, NJ: Chosen Books Pub Co.

Morin, B., & Morin, C. (2004). *Suddenly Strangers*. San Diego, CA: Aventine Press.

Ali, A. (2007). *Infidel: My Life*. New York City: Free Press.

Belief in General

Armstrong, K. (1994). *A History of God: The 4,000-Year Quest of Judaism, Christianity and Islam*. Chicago: Ballantine Books.

Harris, S. (2005). *The End of Faith: Religion, Terror, and the Future of Reason*. New York: W. W. Norton.

Dawkins, R. (2007). *The God Delusion*. New York: Mariner Books.

Littleton, C. (2004). *Mythology*. London: Duncan Baird Publishers.

Ingersoll, R. (2005). *What's God Got to Do with It? Robert Ingersoll on Free Thought, Honest Talk and the Separation of Church and State*. Hanover: Steerforth.

Russell, B. (1957). *BERTRAND RUSSELL: WHY I AM NOT A CHRISTIAN*. New York: Simon and Schuster.

Hitchens, C. (2007). *God Is Not Great: How Religion Poisons Everything*. New York: Twelve.

Psychology and Cults

Freud, Sigmund, and James Strachey. (1961). *The Future of an Illusion*. New York: W. W. Norton & Company.

Hassan, S. (1990). *Combating Cult Mind Control*. Great Britian: Aquarian Press.

Hassan, S. (2000). *Releasing The Bonds: Empowering People to Think for Themselves*. Danbury, CT: Aitan Publishing Company.

Lalich, J. (2004). *Bounded Choice: True Believers and Charismatic Cults*. Berkeley: University of California Press.

Lalich, J. (2006). *Take Back Your Life: Recovering from Cults and Abusive Relationships*. Berkeley, California: Bay Tree Publishing.

Stricker, M. (2000). *The Pattern of The Double-Bind in Mormonism*. USA: Universal Publishers.

Porterfield, K. (1993). *Blind Faith: Recognizing and Recovering from Dysfunctional Religious Groups*. Minneapolis: Compcare Publications.

Winn, D. (2000). *The Manipulated Mind: Brainwashing, Conditioning and Indoctrination*. New York: Malor Books.

Martin, W. (2003). *Kingdom of the Cults, The*. Tulsa, OK : Bethany House.

Davis, K. (2005). *Don't Know Much about Mythology*. New York, NY: HarperCollins.

Shermer, M. (2002). *Why People Believe Weird Things: Pseudoscience, Superstition, and Other Confusions of Our Time*. New York: Owl Books.

Gilovich, T. (1993). *How We Know What Isn't So: The Fallibility of Human Reason in Everyday Life*. New York, NY: Free Press.

Dennett, D. (2007). *Breaking the Spell: Religion as a Natural Phenomenon*. Boston: Penguin (Non-Classics).

Philosophy

Shirley, S. (1982). *BARUCH SPINOZA. The Ethics and Selected Letters*. Indianapolis: Hackett.

Feldman, S., Shirley, S., & Spinoza, B. (2001). *Theological-Political Treatise: Gebhardt Edition*. Indianapolis, IN: Hackett Publishing Company.

Stewart, M. (2007). *The Courtier and the Heretic: Leibniz, Spinoza, and the Fate of God in the Modern World*. New York: W. W. Norton.

Hobbes, T. (1997). *Leviathan*. New York: Touchstone.

Machiavelli, N. (1984). *The Prince (Bantam Classics)*. New York: Bantam Classics.

Jacoby, S. (2005). *Freethinkers: A History of American Secularism*. New York: Holt Paperbacks.

Jacoby, S. (2008). *The Age of American Unreason*. New York: Pantheon.

Russell, B. (2007). *A History of Western Philosophy*. New York: Simon Shuster.

Voltaire, F. (1984). *Philosophical Dictionary (Penguin Classics)*. London: Penguin Classics.

Redman, B., Voltaire., & Voltaire, F. (1977). *The Portable Voltaire (The Viking Portable Library)*. Boston: Penguin (Non-Classics).

Paine, T. (1995). *Thomas Paine : Collected Writings : Common Sense / The Crisis / Rights of Man / The Age of Reason / Pamphlets, Articles, and Letters*. New York: Library of America.

James, W. (2005). *Pragmatism and The Meaning of Truth (The Works of William James)*. Cambridge: Harvard University Press.

Fowler, J. (1995). *Stages of Faith: The Psychology of Human Development*. New York: Harperone.

Strathern, P. (1997). *Socrates in 90 Minutes (Philosophers in 90 Minutes)*. Chicago: Ivan R. Dee, Publisher.

Strathern, P. (1996). *Plato in 90 Minutes (Philosophers in 90 Minutes)*. Chicago: Ivan R. Dee, Publisher.

Strathern, P. (1996). *Aristotle in 90 Minutes (Philosophers in 90 Minutes)*. Chicago: Ivan R. Dee, Publisher.

Strathern, P. (1999). *Confucius in 90 Minutes (Philosophers in 90 Minutes)*. Chicago: Ivan R. Dee, Publisher.

Strathern, P. (1997). *St. Augustine in 90 Minutes (Philosophers in 90 Minutes)*. Chicago: Ivan R. Dee, Publisher.

Strathern, P. (1998). *Thomas Aquinas in 90 Minutes (Philosophers in 90 Minutes)*. Chicago: Ivan R. Dee, Publisher.

Strathern, P. (1998). *Machiavelli in 90 Minutes (Philosophers in 90 Minutes)*. Chicago: Ivan R. Dee, Publisher.

Strathern, P. (2005). *Nabokov in 90 Minutes (Great Writers in 90 Minutes)*. Chicago: Ivan R. Dee, Publisher.

Strathern, P. (2006). *Tolstoy in 90 Minutes (Great Writers in 90 Minutes)*. Chicago: Ivan R. Dee, Publisher.

Strathern, P. (2004). *Dostoevsky in 90 Minutes (Great Writers in 90 Minutes)*. Chicago: Ivan R. Dee, Publisher.

Strathern, P. (1996). *Descartes in 90 Minutes (Philosophers in 90 Minutes)*. Chicago: Ivan R. Dee, Publisher.

Strathern, P. (1998). *Spinoza in 90 Minutes (Philosophers in 90 Minutes)*. Chicago: Ivan R. Dee, Publisher.

Strathern, P. (2000). *Leibniz in 90 Minutes (Philosophers in 90 Minutes)*. Chicago: Ivan R. Dee, Publisher.

Strathern, P. (1999). *Locke in 90 Minutes (Philosophers in 90 Minutes)*. Chicago: Ivan R. Dee, Publisher.

Strathern, P. (2007). *Hume in 90 Minutes (Philosophers in 90 Minutes)*. Chicago: Ivan R. Dee, Publisher.

Strathern, P. (1996). *Kant in 90 Minutes (Philosophers in 90 Minutes)*. Chicago: Ivan R. Dee, Publisher.

Strathern, P. (2004). *Kafka in 90 Minutes (Great Writers in 90 Minutes)*. Chicago: Ivan R. Dee, Publisher.

Strathern, P. (2001). *Kierkegaard in 90 Minutes (Philosophers in 90 Minutes)*. Chicago: Ivan R. Dee, Publisher.

Strathern, P. (1996). *Nietzsche in 90 Minutes (Philosophers in 90 Minutes)*. Chicago: Ivan R. Dee, Publisher.

Strathern, P. (2001). *Marx in 90 Minutes (Philosophers in 90 Minutes)*. Chicago: Ivan R. Dee, Publisher.

Strathern, P. (1996). *Wittgenstein in 90 Minutes (Philosophers in 90 Minutes)*. Chicago: Ivan R. Dee, Publisher.

Strathern, P. (2002). *Heidegger in 90 Minutes (Philosophers in 90 Minutes)*. Chicago: Ivan R. Dee, Publisher.

Strathern, P. (1998). *Sartre in 90 Minutes (Philosophers in 90 Minutes)*. Chicago: Ivan R. Dee, Publisher.

Strathern, P. (2006). *Borges in 90 Minutes (Philosophers in 90 Minutes)*. Chicago: Ivan R. Dee, Publisher.

Strathern, P. (1997). *Hegel in 90 Minutes (Philosophers in 90 Minutes)*. Chicago: Ivan R. Dee, Publisher.

Strathern, P. (2000). *Foucault in 90 Minutes (Philosophers in 90 Minutes)*. Chicago: Ivan R. Dee, Publisher.

General Science

Southerton, S. (2004). *Losing a Lost Tribe: Native Americans, DNA, and the Mormon Church*. Salt Lake Ciry, Utah: Signature Books.

Dawkins, R. (2006). *The Selfish Gene: 30th Anniversary Edition--with a new Introduction by the Author*. New York: Oxford University Press, USA.

Diamond, J. (2005). *Guns, Germs, and Steel: The Fates of Human Societies, New Edition*. New York: W. W. Norton.

Diamond, J. (2005). *Collapse - How Societies Choose To Fail Or Succeed*. New York: Viking.

Diamond, J. (2006). *The Third Chimpanzee: The Evolution and Future of the Human Animal (P.S.)*. New York: Harper Perennial.

Cook, A., Lurie, R., Macneish, R., Nelken-Terner, A., & Vierra, R. (1983). *Prehistory of the Ayacucho Basin, Peru: Volume IV: The Preceramic Way of Life*. Ann Arbor: University of Michigan Press.

Edgar, B., & Johanson, D. (2006). *From Lucy to Language: Revised, Updated, and Expanded*. New York, NY: Simon & Schuster.

Darwin, C. (2006). *On the Origin of Species: By Means of Natural Selection (Thrift Edition)*. New York: Dover Publications.

Browne, J. (2007). *Darwin's Origin of Species: A Biography (Books That Changed the World)*. New York: Atlantic Monthly Press.

Sagan, C. (1997). *The Demon-Haunted World: Science As A Candle In The Dark*. New York: Random House.

Greene, B. (2003). *The Elegant Universe: Superstrings, Hidden Dimensions, and the Quest for the Ultimate Theory*. New York: W. W. Norton & Company.

Greene, B. (2005). *The Fabric of the Cosmos: Space, Time, and the Texture of Reality*. New York: Vintage.

Index

A

A Crack in the Sky, 62, 163, 165
abomination, other churches 14, 139, 144
aborigines, 15
Adam-is-God theory, 76
AIDS awareness, 134
Aikin party, 80
Altered and False Revelations, 53, 195
American Indians, who accepted the gospel, were indeed turning white.
  According to Kimball, 32
ancient inhabitants of America, 15
anti-Mormon, 50, 167, 171, 206
apologists, 50, 114, 205, 206
Atheist Jew, 156

B

Battle of Alma, 6
Bertram Forer, 87,
Bishop of St. Asaph, 10
Blood Atonement, 72, 76, 206
blood oaths, 18, 56, 62, 73, 78
bloody honor killing, 18
Book of Abraham, 123, 204, 205
Book of Mormon, 15, 19, 28, 31, 32, 33, 34, 37, 86, 92, 117, 119, 123, 126,
  136, 137, 139, 144, 150, 174, 178, 181, 190, 191, 198, 200, 201
boundaries, 58, 59, 60, 65, 113, 119, 173, 215, 219
Bountiful, 26, 36, 65, 67, 81, 107, 108, 114, 239
Box B, 41, 94
Boyd K. Packer, 33, 34, 67, 121
Brigham Young, 24, 41, 56, 69, 70, 71, 73, 75, 76, 77, 79, 80, 94, 102, 141,
  144, 145, 152, 161, 165, 166, 170, 182, 187, 192, 208
Brigham's Destroying Angel, 77
British Army, 5, 11, 29, 149
Bruce R. McConkie, 33
buried treasure, 24, 203
BYU Farms, 50, 206

C

D

E

F

W

Z

Authors

Brent and Linda Flynn married in 1982 and currently reside near Los Angeles, California with their children. Brent graduated with honors from Brigham Young University receiving a Bachelor of Science Degree. He then graduated summa cum laude from the University of Nebraska receiving a Doctorate Degree. In addition, he received a Master's degree from Indiana University. Linda is the mother of their four wonderful children. She enjoys photography, and does volunteer work with the homeless in the Los Angeles area. Although their life journey has been filled with unique challenges, they are fortunate to have traveled it together. They embrace life hoping their journey of discovery never ends.

Printed in the United States
217231BV00001B/2/P

9 780615 274430